PEARSON BACCALAUREATE

HISTORY PAPER 3

European states
in the inter-war years (1918–1939)

KEELY ROGERS • JO THOMAS

Supporting every learner across the IB continuum

Published by Pearson Education Limited, 80 Strand, London, WC2R 0RL.

www.pearsonglobalschools.com

Text © Pearson Education Limited 2017

Edited by Sarah Nisbet

Proofread by Sarah Wright

Typeset by Phoenix Photosetting

The rights of Keely Rogers and Jo Thomas to be identified as authors of this work have been asserted by them in accordance with the Copyright, Designs and Patents Act 1988.

First published 2017

20 19 18 17
IMP 10 9 8 7 6 5 4 3 2 1

British Library Cataloguing in Publication Data
A catalogue record for this book is available from the British Library

ISBN 9780435183158
eBook only ISBN 9780435183141

Printed in Slovakia by Neografia

Acknowledgements
The authors and publisher would like to thank Tom Buchanan for his invaluable help with and feedback on this title.

The publisher would like to thank the following for their kind permission to reproduce their photographs:

(Key: b-bottom; c-centre; l-left; r-right; t-top)

akg-images Ltd: Fototeca Gilardi 83bl; **Alamy Stock Photo:** age fotostock 72c, CBW 52bc, Chronicle 64bc, 92c, Everett Collection Historical 115t, GL Archive 202cl, Granger Historical Picture Archive 5cr, 101tl, 126bl, Heritage Image Partnership Ltd / Rodchenko & Stepanova Archive, DACS, RAO 2017 / © DACS 196br, 209tl, 217tr, 223tl, Hi-Story 117b, Peter Horree 48bl, 49br, INTERFOTO 24bl, 30, 59b, 71tr, 90br, 179tc, 202bl, ITAR-TASS Photo Agency 197br, Lordprice Collection 54bc, Hilary Morgan 4bl, Pictorial Press Ltd 100cr, 132cl, 169tl, 221bc, SPUTNIK 193bl, 203cr (b), World History Archive 19tr, 19b, 22bl, 139br, 141br, 147bl, 152, 154br, 169br, 203tr (a), 230c; **Bridgeman Art Library Ltd:** 226tr, De Agostini Picture Library / G. Dagli Orti / Bridgeman Images 186c, Institut d'Etudes Slaves, Paris, France / Archives Charmet / Bridgeman Images 215bc, Private Collection / De Agostini Picture Library / A. Dagli Orti 114b; **British Cartoon Archive, University of Kent www. cartoons.ac.uk:** David Low / David Low / Solo Syndication / Associated Newspapers Ltd 164c, / David Low / Solo Syndication / Associated Newspapers Ltd 166br; **Deutsches Historisches Museum, Berlin:** A. Psille 57bl, 159br; **Fotolia.com:** ug 78c, 98, 99, 100tl, 102bl; **Getty Images:** Luigi Betti / Alinari Archives, Florence / Alinari 87bl, Bettmann 109tr, 155tr, 162tl, 208, Corbis 36, Hulton Archive 82, 96, 203br (d), Hulton-Deutsch Collection / CORBIS 163bl, Mansell / The LIFE Picture Collection 77cr, George Rinhart / Corbis 188cr, Willi Ruge / ullstein bild 2, TASS 176, ullstein bild 113b, 203cr (c), Universal History Archive / UIG 7t, 168tl; **The Heartfield Community of Heirs/VG Bild-Kunst, Bonn:** / The Heartfield Community of Heirs / VG Bild-Kunst, Bonn / © DACS 43c, / The Heartfield Community of Heirs / VG Bild-Kunst, Bonn / © DACS 50tc; **Mary Evans Picture Library:** Iberfoto 124, M.C.Esteban / Iberfoto 138bl; **TopFoto:** Granger, NYC 228bc, Topham Picturepoint 90tr, World History Archive 66

Cover images: *Front:* **123RF.com:** Jose Angel Astor

All other images © Pearson Education

We are grateful to the following for permission to reproduce copyright material:

Figures
Figure on page 190 from *Flagship History, Russia 1855 - 1964* by Derrick Murphy & Terry Morris, Collins Educational, 2008, copyright © Derrick Murphy & Terry Morris, 2008. Reproduced by permission of HarperCollins Publishers Ltd.

Maps
Map on page 3 adapted from "The unification of Germany by Prussia brought most of north-central Europe into one Kingdom", http://kids.britannica.com. Adapted with permission from Encyclopædia Britannica, copyright © 2002 by Encyclopædia Britannica, Inc.

Tables
2 Tables on page 213 from *An Economic History of the USSR 1917-1991*, 3rd edition by Alec Nove, Allen Lane, The Penguin Press 1969, copyright © Alec Nove, 1969, 1972, 1976, 1982, 1989, 1992. Reproduced by permission of Penguin Books Ltd.

Text
Extracts on pages 3, 10, 31, 49 from *A History of Germany, 1918–2008: The Divided Nation*, 3rd edition by Mary Fulbrook, Wiley-Blackwell, 2008, pp.15, 25, 44, 71, copyright © Mary Fulbrook, 2009. Reproduced with permission of John Wiley & Sons, Inc.; Extracts on pages 10, 41, 44 after *Nazi Germany: A New History* by Klaus P. Fischer, Constable, 1995, pp.56-59, 280, 286, copyright © Klaus P. Fischer, 1995. Reproduced by permission of Little, Brown Book Group Limited and Bloomsbury Publishing Inc.; Extracts on pages 10, 46, 229 after *Modern Europe 1870-1945* by Christopher Culpin and Ruth Henig, Longman, 1997, pp.217, 265, 289. Reproduced with permission of Pearson Education Ltd; Extract on page 11 from *The Weimar Republic*, 2nd edition by Stephen J. Lee, Routledge, 1998, p.48, copyright © Stephen J. Lee, 1998, 2010. Reproduced by permission of Taylor & Francis Group; Extract on page 15 from *The Harold Nicolson Diaries: 1907-1964* ed. Nigel Nicolson MBE, Weidenfeld & Nicholson, 2005, p.23 (8 June 1919), copyright © the estate of Harold Nicolson, 2004. Reproduced by permission of The Orion Publishing Group, London; Extracts on pages 33, 37, 42, 44, 60 after *Profiles in Power: Hitler* by Ian Kershaw, Routledge, 2000, pp.55, 71, 73, 118, 151, copyright © Taylor & Francis, 1991, and Extracts on pages 34, 42, 206 after *The European Dictatorships 1918-1945*, 3rd edition, by Stephen J. Lee, Routledge, 2008, pp.44-45, 148, 150, 160, copyright © Stephen J. Lee, 1987, 2000, 2008. Reproduced by permission of Taylor & Francis Group; Extract on page 34 from *The German Empire 1871-1918* by Hans Ulrich Wehler, Berg Publishers, 1985, p.246, copyright © Hans Ulrich Wehler, 1985. Reproduced by permission of Bloomsbury Publishing Plc; Extracts on pages 44-45 after *The Dark Charisma of Adolf Hitler - Leading Millions into the Abyss* by Laurence Rees, Ebdury Press, 2012, pp.126-127, copyright © Laurence Rees, 2012. Reproduced by permission of The Random House Group and Andrew Nurnberg Associates; Extract on page 51 from *Resistance and Conformity in the Third Reich* by Martyn Housden, Routledge, 1996, p.64, copyright © Martyn Housden, 1997. Reproduced by permission of Taylor & Francis Books; Extracts on pages 53, 54 after *The Nazi Dictatorship* by Ian Kershaw, Bloomsbury Academic, 2015, pp.88, 205-207, copyright © Ian Kershaw, 2015. Reproduced by permission of Bloomsbury Publishing Plc; Extract on page 55 after *The Limits of Hitler's Power* by Edward N. Peterson, Princeton University Press, 2015, pp.432, 446, copyright © Princeton University Press, 1969. Reproduced with permission of Princeton University Press via Copyright Clearance Center; Extract on page 56 after *Germany 1866-1945* by Gordon A. Craig, Oxford University Press, 1980, p.601, copyright © Oxford University Press, Inc., 1978, and Extract on page 57 from *The "Hitler Myth": Image and Reality in the Third Reich* by Ian Kershaw, Oxford University Press Inc., 2001, p.1, copyright © Ian Kershaw, 1987. Reproduced by permission of Oxford University Press, www. oup.com; Extract on page 63 after *The Nazi Economic Recovery 1932-1938*, 1st edition by Richard Overy, The Macmillan Press Ltd, 1982, p.63, copyright © Cambridge University Press, 1982. Reproduced with permission; Extract on page 67 from *The Monopoly of Violence* by Professor James Sheehan, Faber & Faber Ltd, 2007, p.98. Reproduced with permission of Faber and Faber Ltd and Houghton Mifflin Harcourt; Extract on page 68 from *Dictating Demography: The Problem of Population in Fascist Italy* by Carl Ipsen, Cambridge University Press, 1996, p.12, copyright © Cambridge University Press 1996, and Extract on page 73 after *Italian Industrialists from Liberalism to Fascism: The Political Development of the Industrial Bourgeoisie, 1906–1934* by Franklin Hugh Adler, Cambridge University Press, 2002, p.22, copyright © Cambridge University Press 1995. Reproduced with permission; Extracts on pages 74, 78, 84 from *Mussolini and Fascism* by Patricia Knight, Routledge, 2003, pp.8, 11, 22, copyright © Patricia Knight, 2003, and Extracts on pages 74, 119, 123 after *Mussolini and Fascist Italy*, 3rd edition by Martin Blinkhorn, Methuen & Co. Ltd, 2006, pp.12-13, 52, 55, copyright ©

Martin Blinkhorn, 1984, 1994, 2006. Reproduced by permission of Taylor & Francis Group; Extract on page 74 after *The Cult of the Duce: Mussolini and the Italians* by Christopher Duggan, eds. Stephen Gundle, Christopher Duggan and Giuliana Pieri, Manchester University Press, 2013, p.24, copyright © Manchester University Press, 2013. Reproduced with permission; Extract on page 75 from *Access to History: Italy - Liberalism and Fascism 1870-1945* by Mark Robson, Hodder Education, 1992, p.34-35. Reproduced by permission of Hodder Education; Extracts on pages 75, 84 from *The Fascist Experience in Italy* by John Pollard, Routledge, 1998, pp.17, 22, copyright © John Pollard, 1998, and Extracts on pages 75, 84 after *Modern Italy, 1871 to the Present* by Martin Clark, Routledge, 2008, pp.177, 200, copyright © Taylor & Francis, 1984. Reproduced by permission of Taylor & Francis Group; Extract on page 77 from *Italy: A Modern History* by Denis Mack Smith, University of Michigan Press, 1959, p.313, copyright © 1959. Reproduced by permission of University of Michigan Press; Extract on page 82 after 'Sleeping Car to Power, Mussolini's Italy 1922–43' a lecture given at Oxford University in 1990 by Denis Mack Smith. Reproduced by kind permission of the author; Extract on page 87 after *Modern Italy – A Political History* by Denis Mack Smith, Yale University Press, 1997, pp.292–293. Reproduced by permission of Yale University Press and The University of Michigan Press; Extract on page 102 after *Fascism in Italy, Its Development and Influence* by Elizabeth Wiskemann, Macmillan, 1969, p.16. Reproduced with permission of Macmillan Higher Education; Extract on page 103 from *Italian Fascism: Its Origins and Development* by Alexander De Grand, University of Nebraska Press, 1982, p.42, copyright © The University of Nebraska Press, 1982, 2000. Reproduced with permission; Extract on page 108 from *Access to History: Italy - The Rise of Fascism 1896-1946*, 4th edition by Mark Robson, Hodder Education, 2015, p.87, copyright © Mark Robson, 2015. Reproduced by permission of Hodder Education; Extract on page 110 from *Mussolini* by Denis Mack Smith, Phoenix Press, 2001, p.142, copyright © Denis Mack Smith, 1981. Reproduced by kind permission of the author; Extracts on pages 112, 115 from *Fascist Italy* by John Hite and Chris Hinton, Hodder Education, 1998, pp.75, 153. Reproduced by permission of Hodder Education; Extract on page 116 from *Historical Dictionary of Fascist Italy* by Philip V. Cannistraro, Greenwood Press, 1982, p.572. Reproduced with permission of Greenwood Press via Copyright Clearance Center; Extract on page 119 after *The Times*, 31/10/1923, copyright © News UK & Ireland Limited, 1923; Extract on page 122 from *Fascism in Western Europe 1900-1945* by Harry R. Kedward, New York University Press, 1971, p.43. Reproduced with permission; Extracts on pages 123, 140 after *A History of Fascism 1914-45* by Stanley Payne, Routledge, 1995, pp.116-117, copyright © The Board of Regents of the University of Wisconsin System, 1995. Reproduced by permission of Taylor & Francis Group; Extracts on pages 125, 148, 171 from *The Spanish Civil War: Origins, Course and Outcomes* by Francisco J. Romero Salvadó, Palgrave Macmillan, 2005, pp.ix, 59, 179, copyright © Francisco J. Romero Salvadó, 2005. Reproduced with permission of Macmillan Higher Education; Extracts on pages 125, 130, 136, 141-143 from *The Spanish Civil War: Reaction, Revolution and Revenge* by Paul Preston, William Collins, 2016, pp.17, 34, 36, 62, 63, 83, copyright © Paul Preston, 1986, 1996, 2006. Reproduced by permission of HarperCollins Publishers Ltd; Extracts on pages 127, 138 from *Modern History Review* by Paul Preston, 1991, p.12. Reproduced by permission of Philip Allan (for Hodder Education); Extracts on pages 128, 168, 172 from *The Spanish Civil War* by Hugh Thomas, Penguin Random House, 1990, pp.906, 911, 912, copyright © Hugh Thomas, 1989. Reproduced with permission of The Wylie Agency (UK) Limited; Extracts on pages 128, 129, 132, 134 after *The Spanish Cockpit* by Franz Borkenau, Weidenfeld & Nicolson, 2000, pp.20, 40, 45, copyright © Franz Borkenau, 1937. Reproduced by permission of The Orion Publishing Group, London; Extracts on pages 129, 133 after *Spain, 1808-1975*, 2nd edition by Raymond Carr, Clarendon Press, 1982, pp.562, 566, copyright © Oxford University Press, 1966, 1982. Reproduced by permission of Oxford University Press; Extracts on pages 132, 139, 144, 147, 159, 161 from *The Spanish Civil War* by Andrew Forrest, Routledge pp.3, 22-23, 73, 98 copyright © Andrew Forrest, 2000. Reproduced by

permission of Taylor & Francis Group; Extract on page 136 after *Let the record speak* by Dorothy Thompson, Houghton Mifflin Co, 1939, p.4, copyright © Dorothy Thompson Lewis, 1939 © renewed Michael Lewis, 1967. Used by permission of Houghton Mifflin Co. All rights reserved; Extract on page 136 from *The Politics of Modern Spain* by Frank E. Manuel, McGraw-Hill Education, 1938, p.56, copyright © McGraw-Hill Book Company, Inc., 1938. Reproduced by permission of McGraw-Hill Education; Extract on page 145 after *Descent into Barbarism: A History of the 20th Century, 1933-1951* by Martin Gilbert, HarperCollins UK, 1999, pp.91-92, copyright © Martin Gilbert, 1999. Reproduced by permission of HarperCollins Publishers Ltd and United Agents on behalf of Sir Martin Gilbert; Extracts on pages 148, 170-171 after *The Battle for Spain: The Spanish Civil War 1936-1939* by Antony Beevor, Weidenfeld & Nicholson, 2006, p.332, copyright © Ocito Ltd, 2006. Reproduced by permission of The Orion Publishing Group, London; Extract on page 162 after "The Spanish Civil War: The International Dimension" by Francisco J Romero Salvadó in *Modern History Review*, February 1995. Reproduced by permission of Philip Allan (for Hodder Education); Extract on page 164 by Paul Preston, quoted from 'In Our Time: the Spanish Civil War' from BBC Radio 4's 'In Our Time' programme, 3 April 2003, http://www.bbc.co.uk/programmes/p00548wn. Reproduced with permission from The BBC and Professor Paul Preston; Extract on page 171 after *The Spanish Holocaust: Inquisition and Extermination in Twentieth-Century Spain* by Paul Preston, HarperPress, 2012, p.468, copyright © Paul Preston, 2012. Reproduced by permission of HarperCollins Publishers Ltd; Extract on page 172 from "Why the Republic lost" by Paul Heywood, *History Today*, March 1989. Reproduced by permission of History Today; Extracts on pages 177, 187, 206 after *The Soviet Union 1917–1991*, 2nd edition by Martin McCauley, Longman, 1993, pp.12, 25, 75-76, copyright © Taylor & Francis, 1981, 1993. Reproduced by permission of Taylor & Francis Group; Extract on page 196 from *Heinemann Advanced History: Lenin and the Russian Revolution* by Steve Philips, Heinemann, 2000, p.137 copyright © Heinemann Educational Publishers, 2000. Reproduced with permission of Pearson Education Ltd; Extract on page 206 from *Access to History: Stalin and Khrushchev: The USSR, 1924–64*, 2nd edition by Michael Lynch, Hodder Education, 2001, pp.21-22. Reproduced by permission of Hodder Education; Extract on page 213 after *The Harvest of Sorrow* by Robert Conquest, Oxford University Press Inc., 1986, p.233, copyright © Robert Conquest, 1986. Reproduced by permission of Curtis Brown Group Ltd, London on behalf of The Beneficiaries of the Estate of Robert Conquest and Oxford University Press, www.oup.com; Extracts on pages 217, 224 from *Hitler and Stalin: Parallel Lives* by Alan Bullock, HarperCollins Publishers, 1991, pp.295-296, 570-571 copyright © Alan Bullock, 1992. Reproduced by permission of HarperCollins Publishers Ltd and Curtis Brown Group Ltd, London on behalf of The Beneficiaries of the Estate of Alan Bullock; Extract on page 222 from "The Great Terror Reassessed" by Melanie J. Ilic in *20th Century History Review*, Vol 1 (3), 2006, pp.7-11. Reproduced by permission of Philip Allan (for Hodder Education); Extract on page 223 after "Hitler vs. Stalin: Who Killed More?" by Timothy Snyder, *New York Review of Books Daily*, 10/03/2011, http://www.nybooks.com/daily/2011/01/27/hitler-vs-stalin-who-was-worse/, copyright © 2011 Timothy Snyder. Reproduced with permission; Extract on page 224 from *The Road to Terror: Stalin and the Self-destruction of the Bolsheviks, 1932-1939* by J. Arch Getty and Oleg Naumov, Yale University Press, 1999, copyright © Yale University, 1999. Reproduced by permission of Yale University Press; and Extract on page 229 from *The Russian Revolution* by Shelia Fitzpatrick, Oxford University Press Inc., 2001, p.151, copyright © Shelia Fitzpatrick, 1994. Reproduced by permission of Oxford University Press, www.oup.com.

Text extracts relating to the IB syllabus and assessment have been reproduced from IBO documents. Our thanks go to the International Baccalaureate for permission to reproduce its intellectual copyright.

Contents

Introduction

Coverage of Paper 3 content and skills

This book is designed to be your guide to success in your International Baccalaureate examination in History. It covers the Paper 3 European region, Topic 14, European states in the inter-war years (1918–1939), and it follows the outline of content as prescribed by the IB for this topic. Thus the domestic policies of Germany, Italy and Spain for this period are covered in depth. For the additional case study we have chosen to cover the Soviet Union, as policies and events within this country are key to the dynamics of Europe in the inter-war period.

As well as covering the content for this topic, this resource aims to equip you with the knowledge and skills that you will need to effectively answer the essay questions in this section of the exam. Later in this section you will find some general tips on essay writing. In addition, within each chapter you will find:

- in-depth coverage and analysis of the key events
- a summary of, or reference to, historiography
- guidelines on how to answer Paper 3 essay questions effectively
- timelines to help you put events into context
- review and research activities to help you develop your understanding of the key issues and concepts.

Focus on History concepts

Throughout the book we also focus on and develop the six key concepts that have particular prominence in the Diploma History course: **change**, **continuity**, **causation**, **consequence**, **significance**, and **perspectives**. Each chapter will identify the key concepts covered within it.

Focus on History assessment objectives

This resource covers the four IB assessment objectives that are relevant to both the core externally examined papers and to the internally assessed paper. So, although this book is essentially designed as a textbook to accompany Paper 3, Topic 14, it addresses all of the assessment objectives required for the History course. In other words, as you work through this book, you will be learning and practising the skills that are necessary for each of the core papers.

Nevertheless, the main focus will be the assessment objectives assessed in Paper 3. Specifically these assessment objectives are:

Assessment Objective 1: Knowledge and understanding

- Demonstrate detailed, relevant and accurate historical knowledge.
- Demonstrate understanding of historical concepts and context.

Assessment Objective 2: Application and analysis

- Formulate clear and coherent arguments.
- Use relevant historical knowledge to effectively support analysis.

Assessment Objective 3: Synthesis and evaluation

- Integrate evidence and analysis to produce a coherent response.
- Evaluate different perspectives on historical issues and events, and integrate this evaluation effectively into a response.

Assessment Objective 4: Use and application of appropriate skills

- Structure and develop focused essays that respond effectively to the demands of the question.

The following objectives are linked to Paper 1 and IA and are also practised throughout.

Assessment Objective 1: Knowledge and understanding

- Demonstrate understanding of historical sources (IA and Paper 1).

Assessment Objective 2: Application and analysis

- Analyse and interpret a variety of sources (IA and Paper 1).

Assessment Objective 3: Synthesis and evaluation

- Evaluate sources as historical evidence, recognizing their value and limitations (IA and Paper 1).
- Synthesize information from a selection of relevant sources (IA and Paper 1).

Assessment Objective 4: Use and application of appropriate skills

- Reflect on the methods used by, and challenges facing, the historian (IA).
- Formulate an appropriate, focused question to guide a historical inquiry (IA).
- Demonstrate evidence of research skills, organization, referencing and selection of appropriate sources (IA).

Use of mark schemes

For the externally assessed components – Paper 1, Paper 2 and Paper 3 – there are two different assessment methods used:

- Markbands.
- Detailed specific markschemes for each examination paper.

For the internally assessed / moderated IA – there are set assessment criteria.

We will use and refer to the Paper 3 markbands extensively throughout the book. (See end of this section for the Paper 3 markbands.)

Links to IB programme as a whole

The regular use of command terms, inquiry based research tasks, the source based activities and reflection will not only prepare you fully for the Paper 3 essay questions, it will also help to prepare you for the requirements of your Paper 1 exam and your Internal Assessments.

'The Soviet Union 1918–1929' chapter is also relevant to Topic 12 of the Paper 3 syllabus.

ATL

Approaches to teaching and learning (ATL) reflect the IB learner profile attributes, and are designed to enhance your learning and assist preparation for IAs and examinations.

ATL run throughout the IB Middle Years Programme (MYP) and Diploma Programme (DP). They cover thinking, social, communication, self-management and research skills. These skills encompass the key values that underpin an IB education.

ATL skills are addressed in the activity boxes throughout the book, and each Historians' perspectives feature addresses ATL thinking skills.

Extended Essay section

At the end of this book you will find a section on the Extended Essay. History is one of the most popular choices for Extended Essays. Students that choose to write their EE in History benefit from gaining a better understanding of this subject. The skills are also transferable to their other diploma subjects and are excellent preparation for tertiary level studies.

How this book works

As well as the main text, there are a number of coloured boxes in every chapter, each with their own distinctive icon. These boxes provide different information and stimulus:

Essay questions

The essay questions that are at the start of each chapter will offer Paper 3 style questions for you to think about while working through the chapter. At the end of the chapter we will look at how you could approach these questions in the exam.

Information boxes

These boxes contain information which will deepen and widen your knowledge, but which do not fit within the main body of the text.

Pact of San Sebastián

An agreement by Republican parties to move towards the establishment of a Republic in Spain. A *'revolutionary committee'* was set up to prepare for the overthrow of the monarchy.

Historians' perspectives

This feature was requested by teachers and offers students an insight into different historians' opinions and sometimes opposing contemporary opinion on a historical event, action or period in time. Students will often be asked to identify evidence to support different perspectives, to consider the reasons why sometimes contemporaries and historians have drawn different conclusions and to reflect on the similarities and differences between historians' views and their own perspectives.

 Historians' perspectives

In pairs, discuss the following views of historians and decide whose views you mostly agree with. You should be able to support your viewpoint with evidence from this chapter.

Why did Primo de Rivera's regime fall?

- British historian, Hugh Thomas: Economic factors were the main problem for Primo de Rivera. The juxtaposition between people's high expectations in the new age of consumerism with the onset of the economic slump in the 1920s led to his demise.
- Tangiers-born Israeli historian, Shlomo Ben Ami (considered a leading authority on Primo de Rivera): Political factors were the main issue for Primo de Rivera. These political issues were caused by economic migration from the countryside to towns and cities, as people were drawn by potential employment in public works and expanded industries. This migrant population was more open to radical politics as they were now free of the *caciquismo*.
- The Spanish academic, A Ramos Oliveira: Primo de Rivera's regime was *'strangled'* by opposition from the groups whose interests it had damaged.

Significant individuals

This feature provides background information on key figures, enhancing understanding of events.

Significant individual: Manuel Azaña Díaz

Manuel Azaña was minister of war in the first Left government of the Spanish Second Republic. When Prime Minister Alcala-Zamor resigned in October, Azaña became prime minister of a coalition government of left wing parties. Azaña implemented a major series of reforms, although he was a liberal Republican and not a socialist.

Challenge yourself

These boxes invite you to carry out additional research on an aspect discussed in the chapter.

CHALLENGE YOURSELF

 ATL Social, research, communication, and thinking skills

Research more into the life of Rosa Luxemburg and her role in left-wing politics during this period. Also see if you can find out about other women who took an active part in politics during the Weimar era.

Hints for success

These boxes can be found alongside questions, exercises, and worked examples. They provide insight into how to answer a question in order to achieve the highest marks in an examination. They also identify common pitfalls when answering such questions and suggest approaches that examiners like to see.

For top markbands for Paper 3 essays:

Introduction and main body paragraphs

Responses are clearly focused.

The question is fully addressed and implications are considered.

The essay is well structured and the material effectively organized.

Supporting knowledge is detailed, accurate, relevant to the question and used to support arguments.

Arguments are clear, well developed and consistently supported with evidence.

There is evaluation of different perspectives.

Conclusion

The conclusion is clearly stated and it is consistent with the evidence presented.

	Structure	Focus on demands of the question	Knowledge
0	No structure.	No clear understanding of the set question.	No relevant knowledge.
1–3	Limited attempt to structure response.	Little understanding of the set question.	Knowledge is limited, inaccurate and/or lacks relevance.
4–6	Some attempt to structure. Some paragraphing. Lacks clarity.	Some understanding of the question.	Some knowledge, however tends to be inaccurate and/or lacks relevance.
7–9	The answer has structure but is not always coherently focused on set question.	There is understanding of the set question. Question is only partially addressed.	Knowledge is usually accurate. Lacks depth and detail.
10–12	Sound structure throughout and focuses on set question. Sometimes lacks clarity.	Whole question is understood and addressed.	Knowledge is consistently accurate and relevant. Evidence and examples used to support arguments.
13–15	Consistently well structured and clearly focused on set question.	Demonstrates a thorough understanding of the question and its implications.	Knowledge is consistently detailed, accurate and relevant to the question. Evidence and examples are effectively used to support all arguments.

Writing Paper 3 essays

Your Paper 3 essays will be assessed using the set markbands and the markschemes specific to each examination paper. The key difference between your Paper 2 and Paper 3 essays is that for Paper 3 you need to demonstrate a depth of knowledge and understanding of the topics covered, give very detailed supporting evidence and examples, and fully develop your critical analysis of the set question.

When planning and writing your Paper 3 essays you could use the grid below to check where your response meets the markband descriptors.

Context and concepts	Critical Analysis	Perspectives
No understanding of context and relevant concepts.	No analysis.	None.
Limited understanding of context of question and lacks development of relevant concepts.	Mainly description rather than analysis.	None.
Some basic understanding of context of question. Lacks or has limited development of relevant concepts.	Some limited analysis, however usually descriptive.	None.
The context of the question is established. Lacks development of relevant concepts.	Some analysis. Tends towards description.	None.
The context of the question is fully established, and there is clear understanding of historical concepts.	Analysis is clear and coherent. Arguments are well developed and supported with detailed examples. The conclusion is consistent with the analysis and evidence.	There is an awareness of different perspectives.
The context of the question is fully established, and there is thorough understanding of historical concepts.	There is consistent critical analysis and all arguments are fully developed. All points are supported with detailed evidence and the conclusion is well reasoned and consistent.	There is evaluation of different perspectives and this is synthesized into analysis.

Command terms

In order to write a focused and well-structured essay that addresses the demands of the set question you need to understand the **Command terms**.

Analyse

You need to break down the topic or theme of the question in order to establish key relevant elements. To avoid a descriptive approach you should attempt to find relevant analytical or thematic points. For example, for the question, 'Analyse the reasons for the outbreak of civil war in Spain' you could look at long-term and short-term political, ideological, economic and social causes.

Compare

You need to identify and develop an analysis of the similarities between two or more case studies, events or developments. You must refer to both or all throughout your response. For example, compare economic and social developments in Italy and Germany in the 1920s and 1930s.

Contrast

You need to identify and develop an analysis of the differences between two or more case studies, events or developments. You must refer to both or all throughout your response. For example, contrast economic and social developments in Italy and Germany in the 1920s and 1930s.

Compare and contrast

You need to identify and develop an analysis of the similarities and differences between two or more case studies, events or developments. You must refer to both or all throughout your response. For example, compare and contrast economic and social developments in Italy and Germany in the 1930s.

Discuss

You must offer a 'balanced' analysis. Usually this would involve identifying the successes or failures of, for example, a policy or the benefits and disadvantages of an inter-war economic or social development.

Evaluate

You need to identify and develop the strengths and limitations, or the successes and failures, of an assertion made in the question or, for example, a policy or development in the inter-war period.

Examine

You need to develop the concept or theme of the set question through different 'lenses'. For example, if you were asked to 'Examine the economic developments in Spain in the 1930s' you would begin by analysing the economic developments, then consider how these impacted social and political developments.

To what extent

You need to set up arguments supporting and challenging the factor or concept of the question. You would have a 'for' and 'against' approach. For example, for the question 'Nationalist strengths led to the defeat of the Republicans in the Spanish Civil War' you would develop arguments supporting the statement, i.e. Nationalist military, political and economic strengths led to victory, and then challenge the assumption in the question by developing the role of Republican weaknesses.

Structuring your essay

Use the tips below to help you structure your essay; this will help you to meet the descriptors in the markbands on page viii.

How do I write a History essay?

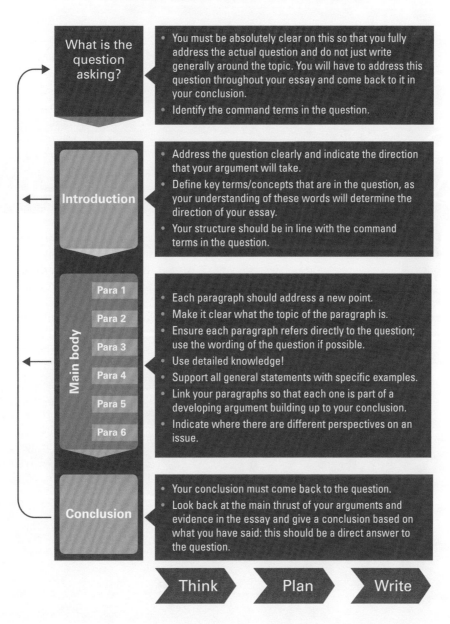

What is the question asking?
- You must be absolutely clear on this so that you fully address the actual question and do not just write generally around the topic. You will have to address this question throughout your essay and come back to it in your conclusion.
- Identify the command terms in the question.

Introduction
- Address the question clearly and indicate the direction that your argument will take.
- Define key terms/concepts that are in the question, as your understanding of these words will determine the direction of your essay.
- Your structure should be in line with the command terms in the question.

Main body
Para 1
Para 2
Para 3
Para 4
Para 5
Para 6
- Each paragraph should address a new point.
- Make it clear what the topic of the paragraph is.
- Ensure each paragraph refers directly to the question; use the wording of the question if possible.
- Use detailed knowledge!
- Support all general statements with specific examples.
- Link your paragraphs so that each one is part of a developing argument building up to your conclusion.
- Indicate where there are different perspectives on an issue.

Conclusion
- Your conclusion must come back to the question.
- Look back at the main thrust of your arguments and evidence in the essay and give a conclusion based on what you have said: this should be a direct answer to the question.

Think ▸ Plan ▸ Write

01

Weimar Germany: 1918–1933

> *Born in 1918 of military defeat and domestic revolution, it was riddled with compromises and burdened with difficulties.*
>
> **Mary Fulbrook (2008). *A History of Germany, 1918–2008*. Wiley-Blackwell, p. 15.**

Essay questions:

- To what extent was the Treaty of Versailles responsible for the difficulties faced by the Weimar Republic between 1919 and 1923?
- Examine the reasons for the collapse of the Weimar Republic by 1932.
- To what extent were the years 1924–29 a 'golden age' for the Weimar Republic?
- Discuss the reasons for Hitler's rise to power, 1929 to 1933.

Because the failure of democracy in Weimar Germany was followed by a ruthless dictatorship that had devastating effects, not just for Germany but for the whole of Europe and indeed the world, the events of 1919 to 1932 within Germany have been the subject of much analysis and debate by historians. As Ian Kershaw writes, '*The Weimar Republic… has been overshadowed by its end and what followed*'.

Germany after 1870

Key

1	Anhalt	6	Mecklenburg–Strelitz
2	Brunswick	7	Oldenburg
3	Grand Duchy of Hesse	8	Palatinate (to Bavaria)
4	Lippe–Detmold	9	Schaumburg–Lippe
5	Mecklenburg–Schwerin	10	Waldeck

Kingdom of Prussia 1866

German Empire 1871–1918

Key concept: *Causation*

In order to understand the Weimar Republic and the issues that it faced, it is necessary to look back at the key characteristics of Germany before the First World War. In fact, Germany had only been a unified country since 1870; before that time it had been collection of 39 states. Otto von Bismarck, the Chancellor of the largest German state, Prussia, had used the economic and military might of Prussia to expel the influence of both Austria and France and to bring all the states into a united Germany. Von Bismarck had proclaimed the Second German Reich at the Hall of Mirrors in the Palace of Versailles, outside Paris.

The new German Reich was ruled over by the Prussian Kaiser. There was also an assembly, the Reichstag, which was elected by universal male **suffrage**; however, this lacked real power. The leading minister, known as the Chancellor, and the other ministers were appointed by the Kaiser and could not be removed or replaced by the Reichstag. Political tension grew in the years 1871 to 1914 as opposition parties developed to challenge the rule of the Kaiser.

Economically, the new Germany was one of the most powerful states in Europe. The rapid industrialization that took place after 1870 increased social and political problems. The leading industrialists and aristocratic landowners known as the *Junkers* wanted political stability and so supported the existing **authoritarian** regime of the Kaiser and opposed any reform. However, many of the workers in the towns supported the Socialist Party, the SPD, which wanted political reform and social change. They also joined trade unions to campaign for improved wages and working conditions.

These divisions within German society and politics were becoming acute by 1914. Indeed, the ambitious foreign policy pursued by Kaiser Wilhelm II in the years before the First World War had the aim of winning working-class support and thus avoiding the threat of a socialist revolution.

Significant individual: Wilhelm II

Wilhelm II acted very much as an autocratic monarch. He was a keen advocate of all things military and loved wearing his numerous uniforms and having himself photographed while dressed in them. He also surrounded himself with the elite of Germany's military society. He was a strong opponent of socialism and he vigorously believed in *Weltpolitik* – increasing the strength of Germany through building up the German navy and expansion overseas. This policy was to bring Germany into conflict with other European powers, such as Britain.

What was the impact of the First World War on Germany, 1914–18?

Key concept: *Consequence*

The outbreak of war in 1914 temporarily united Germany. There was a wave of patriotism as all parties, including the SPD, united in favour of the war effort. However, the speedy victory that was expected in 1914 did not happen and Germany became tied into a war of attrition, fighting on two fronts. By the winter of 1916–17, support for the war was fast ebbing away as a result of severe food shortages and rapidly rising food prices. The British blockade of Germany exacerbated this situation.

The economic and military crisis faced by Germany increased when the US entered the war in 1917. In a last attempt to secure victory before US troops arrived in Europe, the German General Ludendorff gambled on a huge offensive on the Western Front. With German troops transferred from the Eastern Front after Russia withdrew from the war, Ludendorff launched his attack in March 1918. However, although the German attack nearly broke though the Allied lines, it faltered due to lack of supplies and high casualties, enabling the **Allies** to counter-attack and halt the advance with the help of the newly arrived American troops. By August 1918, the German army was in retreat along the Western Front. It was clear that defeat was only a matter of time; Germany's allies had sued for peace and within Germany there was growing unrest fuelled by the economic crisis.

What was the political impact of the war in 1918–19?

Timeline of events – 1918		
1918	**1 Oct**	Ludendorff asks Reichstag to sue for peace
	3 Oct	Prince Max of Baden appointed Chancellor; asks for peace based on Wilson's Fourteen Points
	3 Nov	German Grand Fleet mutinies at Kiel. Workers' and sailors' councils established
	9 Nov	General strike in Berlin. Kaiser flees to Holland. Ebert becomes Chancellor
		Republic declared
	11 Nov	Armistice signed
	30 Dec	German Communist Party (KPD) established

Revolution from above

With Germany facing defeat and the threat of invasion, General Ludendorff decided that Germany's best hope lay in asking the Allies for an **armistice**, which he hoped would be based on American President Wilson's Fourteen Points (see Significant individual box). However, realizing that Germany's autocratic system was an obstacle to negotiation, he persuaded the Kaiser to transform the Second Reich into a constitutional monarchy by handing over political power to a civilian government. Not only would this be likely to gain better peace terms from the Allies, but he hoped that it would also prevent the outbreak of political revolutionary demands from below and save the Kaiser's rule. In addition, he wanted to switch the blame for the military defeat of Germany onto a new civilian government. (This would help lay the

The impact of war on Germany

German soldiers killed in war: 2 million.

Wounded in war: 6.3 million.

War widows: 600,000.

Cost of war: £8,394 million.

Between 1913 and 1918 the German mark lost 75 per cent of its value.

Industrial production: two-fifths of wartime levels.

Grain production: about half of the pre-war level.

Civilian deaths from starvation and hypothermia: 293,000 in 1918.

Significant individual: President Wilson

President Wilson of the US believed that any future peace needed to be based on certain key principles if it was to be durable. He thus came up with a list of 'Fourteen Points', which included reduction of armaments, self-determination for nationalities in Europe and the establishment of a peacekeeping body, the League of Nations. Wilson also believed that Germany would need to be treated moderately; this, however, was in contrast to Clemenceau of France, who wanted to see Germany punished.

Key political terms

Left wing and **right wing:** left wing refers to those wanting social and political change as opposed to right-wing people, who want to maintain the existing situation. The term comes from the French Revolution in the Estates General; those sitting on the left of the King wanted radical change and those who supported the King and the status quo sat on the right of the King.

Socialist republic: this is a system of government without a monarchy that aims to bring in social and economic changes such as welfare improvements and nationalization of industry that will benefit everyone.

Soviet republic: this is a system of government without a monarchy that aims to introduce a communist state such as that established in Russia following the 1917 Revolution. It would be organized by workers' councils and supported nationalization and workers' control of major industries.

Conservatism: this is linked to 'right wing'. Conservatives tend not to like change and they tend to support the traditional aspects of society and forces of law and order.

Authoritarian government: this is when there is an emphasis on strict obedience to the law at the expense of individual freedoms.

foundations of the '*stab in the back*' myth, which would play a key part in the history of the Weimar Republic, see page 12).

Thus, in October 1918, Prince Max of Baden was appointed Chancellor and in the following month a series of constitutional reforms took place:

- The Chancellor and his government were made accountable to the Reichstag, instead of the Kaiser. Prince Max of Baden set up a new government based on the majority parties in the Reichstag.
- The armed forces were put under the control of the civil government.

At the same time, negotiations were opened with the Allies to agree on an armistice. The news that the new government was asking for peace terms was a shock to the German population, who had expected a great victory; they now became aware for the first time that their country was no longer in a position to keep fighting. In this situation, they were no longer prepared to put up with their suffering. Opinion hardened and by early November it was clear that a revolutionary situation was developing.

Revolution from below

The first serious trouble began in late October when sailors at the naval bases of Kiel and Wilhelmshaven refused to obey orders. The mutiny soon spread to other ports and cities, with the establishment of workers' and soldiers' councils, or soviets. On 8 November, the Bavarian monarchy was deposed and a republic was proclaimed.

With the SPD now refusing to support the new government if the Kaiser did not abdicate, Prince Max made the desperate move of announcing that the Kaiser would renounce the throne. He then handed over the Chancellorship to Friedrich Ebert, who was the leader of the SPD. At the same time one of the provisional government's leaders, Philipp Scheidemann, appeared on the balcony of the Reichstag building and proclaimed Germany a republic. In fact it was only later that day that the Kaiser abdicated. His position was no longer tenable. Wilson was refusing to negotiate with Germany while the Kaiser was still in position, and his generals told him that they would no longer fight for him. He thus had no choice but to sign the abdication, after which he fled to Holland.

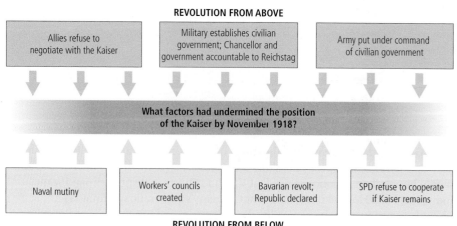

REVOLUTION FROM ABOVE

| Allies refuse to negotiate with the Kaiser | Military establishes civilian government; Chancellor and government accountable to Reichstag | Army put under command of civilian government |

What factors had undermined the position of the Kaiser by November 1918?

| Naval mutiny | Workers' councils created | Bavarian revolt; Republic declared | SPD refuse to cooperate if Kaiser remains |

REVOLUTION FROM BELOW

Ebert's coalition government

In order to the give the new government legitimacy, Ebert was determined to establish a new constitution and to hold elections as soon as possible. On 9 November 1918, Ebert created a provisional coalition government. It was to be provisional until a national election was held to vote for a National Constituent Assembly, and it was a coalition of the SPD and the German Independent Social Democratic Party (USPD) (see table showing the socialist parties, page 18). Two days later, on 11 November, Ebert signed the Armistice to end the war.

Ebert was a moderate who wanted to maintain law and order and to prevent the country falling into a civil war. His main concern was that the extreme left wing in Germany would try to take power; they were already using the newly established workers' and soldiers' councils to challenge the new government. He was also worried about the large numbers of soldiers who would be returning to Germany with the end of the war. Thus in the following months he made a key agreement with the army known as the Ebert-Groener Pact. By this agreement, General Wilhelm Groener, Ludendorff's successor, agreed to support the new government and to use troops to maintain the stability and security of the new republic. In return, Ebert promised to resist the demands of the soldiers' councils to democratize the army, and to resist any moves towards a communist-style revolution.

Friedrich Ebert

Activity 2   ATL Thinking skills

1. Why would the Ebert-Groener Pact be seen as a 'betrayal' by the left?
2. What justification would Ebert have given for signing this pact?

Ebert was criticized by the left for being too moderate and for compromising with the forces of conservatism. In December 1918, the USPD left the government. In January 1919, the Spartacists attempted a revolution (see next section).

Activity 1

ATL   Social and thinking skills

In pairs, brainstorm the problems that Ebert would have faced in 1919.

Divide the problems up under the following themes: political, economic, social and military.

What political challenges did the Weimar Republic face, 1919–23?

Key concepts: *Change, continuity and consequence*

Timeline of events – 1919–23		
1919	8 Feb	National Constituent Assembly meets at Weimar
	11 Feb	Ebert becomes president of new Republic
	29 June	Signing of Treaty of Versailles
1920	March	Kapp Putsch
1922	June	Rathenau assassinated
1923	Jan	Invasion of Ruhr by French and Italian troops
	Aug	Stresemann becomes Chancellor
	Sept	Hyperinflation
	Nov	Attempted putsch by Hitler in Munich

The Weimar Republic faced several political challenges after 1919: creating a new constitution, signing a peace settlement with the Allies, threats from political extremism and the instability created by weak coalitions.

1. The writing of a new constitution

Overnight we have become the most radical democracy in Europe.
Ernst Troeltsch, 29 December 1918.

Now we have a Republic; the problem is that we have no Republicans.
Walther Rathenau, 1919.

The government, which was elected in January 1919 against a backdrop of street-fighting, strikes and demonstrations, met in the town of Weimar rather than Berlin in order to keep away from the ongoing turmoil. The SPD had secured the largest share of the vote and had the largest number of seats. Under the voting system of proportional representation, however, it did not have an overall majority and so it had to form a coalition with the Catholic Centre Party and the liberal German Democratic Party (DDP). Ebert was elected as president of the Republic with Philipp Scheidemann leading the new government as head of the coalition cabinet.

One of the first challenges faced by this new government was writing a new constitution. There was a general consensus that this should be a break from the previous autocratic constitution, which had been drawn up in 1871, and that it should enshrine and guarantee the rights and powers of the people. However, as the Weimar Republic was only to last for 14 years, the constitution itself has been the focus of much scrutiny regarding its role in undermining the Republic and allowing Hitler to come to power. The focus has fallen particularly on:

- the role of the voting system, proportional representation, in creating weak governments;
- the relationship between the president and the Reichstag, particularly the role of Article 48;
- the continued existence of traditional institutions which helped maintain traditional, conservative values.

The following boxes show the main features of the new constitution:

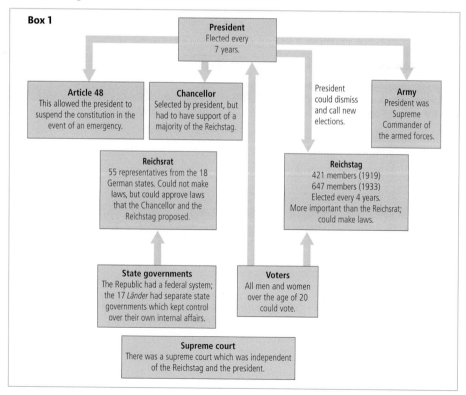

Box 1

President
Elected every 7 years.

Article 48
This allowed the president to suspend the constitution in the event of an emergency.

Chancellor
Selected by president, but had to have support of a majority of the Reichstag.

President could dismiss and call new elections.

Army
President was Supreme Commander of the armed forces.

Reichsrat
55 representatives from the 18 German states. Could not make laws, but could approve laws that the Chancellor and the Reichstag proposed.

Reichstag
421 members (1919)
647 members (1933)
Elected every 4 years.
More important than the Reichsrat; could make laws.

State governments
The Republic had a federal system; the 17 *Länder* had separate state governments which kept control over their own internal affairs.

Voters
All men and women over the age of 20 could vote.

Supreme court
There was a supreme court which was independent of the Reichstag and the president.

Box 2

Key articles of the constitution

- Article 1: The German Reich is a republic. Political authority derives from the people.
- Article 22: The Reichstag delegates are elected by universal, equal, direct and secret suffrage by all men and women over 20 years of age, in accordance with the principles of proportional representation.
- Article 23: The Reichstag is elected for four years.
- Article 41: The President is chosen by the whole German people.
- Article 47: The National President has supreme command over all the armed forces of the Federation.
- Article 48: If public safety and order in the Federation is disturbed or endangered, the National President may take the necessary measures to restore public safety and order.
- Article 53: The National Chancellor and the National Ministers are appointed and dismissed by the National President.
- Article 54: The National Chancellor and Ministers require for the administration of their offices the confidence of the Reichstag. They must resign if the Reichstag withdraws its confidence.

Box 3

Part Two: Fundamental Rights and Duties of Germans

- Article 109: All Germans are equal before the law.
- Article 114: Personal liberty is inviolable (cannot be taken away).
- Article 117: Every German has the right, within the limit of general laws, to express his opinions freely, by word, printed matter or picture, or in any other matter... Censorship is forbidden.
- Article 124: All Germans have the right to form unions and societies.
- Article 135: All inhabitants of the Reich enjoy full religious freedom and freedom of conscience.
- Article 153: The right of property is guaranteed by the Constitution.
- Article 156: The Federation may... [with compensation] ... transfer to public ownership private business enterprises adapted to socialization.
- Article 161: The Reich shall organize a comprehensive system of [social] insurance.
- Article 163: Every German has the moral obligation... to exercise his mental and physical powers in a manner required by the welfare of all. Every German shall be given the opportunity to earn his living through productive work. If no suitable opportunity can be found, the means necessary for his livelihood will be provided.
- Article 165: Workers and employees are called upon to cooperate, on an equal footing, with employers in the regulation of wages and of the conditions of labour.

Box 4

Proportional representation: how it worked

With this voting system, the number of deputies that a party could send to the Reichstag was directly linked to the percentage of votes that they received. For every 60,000 votes in a district, a party would be able to choose one deputy from its list of candidates to send to the Reichstag. This system enabled the smaller as well as the large parties to gain seats in the Reichstag. It also meant that it was hard for one party to have an overall majority and so it was necessary for parties to create coalitions in order to rule; for example, this involved the largest party negotiating with several smaller parties until it had enough deputies to create a majority government.

Task One

Study the information in Boxes 1–4 (on pages 8–9) carefully and then discuss the following questions in pairs:

1. Which features of the Weimar constitution would you consider to be the most democratic?
2. Which features could be considered undemocratic?
3. Which of the rights in Part Two of the constitution (Box 3) would appeal to workers and socialists?
4. Which rights would appeal to the more conservative groups in society such as the industrialists?

Task Two

Read the following verdicts on the constitution made by historians. What weaknesses in the constitution are highlighted by each historian? Add these points to your answers for questions 1 and 2 in Task One.

Source A

 In the event, the nature of the party system in the Weimar Republic, and what might be called the 'political culture' of a number of Weimar parties, rendered post-election bargaining over possible governmental coalitions much more difficult than it has proved to be in other democracies where proportional representation prevails; thus, as we shall see, it was not so much the rules of the game, as the nature of the parties playing the game, that rendered proportional representation a serious liability for Weimar democracy.

Mary Fulbrook (2008). A History of Germany, 1918–2008. Wiley-Blackwell, p. 25.

Source B

 The final document… was in many ways a mirror image of the social dissonances of German society. The Weimar Constitution was a hodge-podge of principles drawn from Socialist and liberal agendas; it represented so much confusion in regard to economic objectives and unresolved class conflict that German democracy was stymied [impeded] from the beginning…

[It was] one of the most democratic documents in the world. In 1919, however, it was doubtful whether such a democratic constitution could work in the hands of a people that was neither psychologically nor historically prepared for self-government.

Klaus Fischer (1995). Nazi Germany: A New History. Continuum, pp. 56–59.

Source C

 [The] social and economic responsibilities [in the constitution] turned Weimar governments into uncritical upholders of the demands of workers and tenants in the eyes of industrialists and landlords. Many on the Right saw the new regime as a 'workers' government' and sought to undermine its authority. Furthermore, the political parties which contested the early elections and formed coalition governments were unused to operating on a national scale or to working with each other… the right-wing parties never gave the new parliamentary system their wholehearted support, although they were prepared to work through it to secure their particular interests.

Christopher Culpin and Ruth Henig (2002). Modern Europe 1870–1945. Longman, p. 265.

Conclusions on the constitution

In conclusion, the constitution contained several flaws that would contribute to the collapse of Weimar democracy.

Proportional representation

This enabled smaller parties, many of which were anti-Republican, to gain seats and hold influence in coalitions. The fact that proportional representation tended to lead to coalitions between parties with different aims and goals, meant that governments tended to be short-lived and this contributed to instability. As society became more polarized throughout the 1920s, so it became increasingly difficult for the centre, moderate parties to form stable coalitions.

Weimar Republic governments, 1919–1923			
Appointment	Chancellor	Party	Members of governing coalition
February 1919	Philipp Scheidemann	SPD	SPD, Centre, DDP (moderate socialist-centre)
June 1919	Gustav Bauer	SPD	SPD, Centre, DDP (from October) (moderate socialist-centre)
March 1920	Hermann Müller	SPD	SPD, Centre, DDP (moderate socialist-centre)
June 1920	Konstantin Fehrenbach	Centre	DDP, Centre, DVP (centre-right)
May 1921	Joseph Wirth	Centre	SPD, Centre, DDP (moderate socialist-centre)
October 1921	Joseph Wirth	Centre	SPD, Centre, DDP (moderate socialist-centre)
November 1922	Wilhelm Cuno	None	DDP, Centre, DVP, BVP (centre-right)
August 1923	Gustav Stresemann	DVP	SPD, Centre, DDP, DVP (centre-right with socialists – the 'Great Coalition'
October 1923	Gustav Stresemann	DVP	SPD, Centre, DDP, DVP ('Great Coalition')
November 1923	Wilhelm Marx	Centre	(centre-right)

Article 48

This was intended as a safety measure and it was not anticipated that it would be used other than in a situation of national emergency. However, Ebert ended up using it on 136 separate occasions. Although some of these, such as in the crisis of 1923, were emergency situations, it was also used in non-emergency situations where he wanted to override opposition in the Reichstag. As historian Stephen Lee puts it, *'The presidential powers meant the existence of a "reserve" or "parallel" constitution – which had no need of parliamentary parties'.*

The continuity of traditional institutions

The need for stability in the new constitution meant that there was a failure to reform the old traditional institutions of Imperial Germany; thus conservative forces were able to exert much influence.

The civil service: this was left in the hands of those who tended to conform to the anti-democratic, conservative values of Imperial Germany. These civil servants had a lot of power in the government, especially when ministers in coalition governments were frequently changing.

The judiciary: this was made up of judges who had held positions under the Kaiser. Article 54 of the constitution guaranteed the independence of the judges, but these men were conservative in nature and anti-democratic in their views. In their verdicts against those who threatened the constitution in the years after 1919, they handed out severe sentences to left-wing agitators, and acted leniently towards those on the right.

The army: as with the judiciary, the officer corps was made up of those who had trained under the Kaiser. Many of the generals were linked with the Prussian landowners and their sympathies were anti-Republican. It continued to have great status and influence in the new Republic.

Nevertheless, it is also important to note that the constitution was supported by many Germans who saw it as a great improvement on the undemocratic constitution that had existed before the First World War. It was perhaps the conditions in which it was created that would undermine its credibility and ensure that it faced an uphill battle in trying to establish its political legitimacy.

Activity 4
ATL Thinking skills

Refer back to the quotes at the start of this section by Troeletsch and Rathenau. What justification could be given for each of these verdicts on the Weimar constitution?

2. The Versailles peace settlement

Key to the credibility of the Weimar Republic would be the peace terms that it managed to secure with the Allies.

When the German government sued for an end to fighting, they did so in the belief that the Armistice would be based on Wilson's Fourteen Points (see page 5). In reality, the Armistice terms were very tough, and were designed not only to remove Germany's ability to continue fighting, but also to serve as the basis for a more permanent weakening of Germany. The terms of the Armistice ordered Germany to evacuate all occupied territory including Alsace-Lorraine, and to withdraw beyond a 10 km-wide neutral zone to the east of the Rhine. Allied troops would occupy the west bank of the Rhine. The Germans also lost all of their submarines and much of their surface fleet and air force.

When the German army returned home after the new government had signed the Armistice, they were still greeted as heroes. As already mentioned, however, for the German population, the defeat came as a shock. The German army had occupied parts of France and Belgium and had defeated Russia. The German people had been told that their army was on the verge of victory; the defeat did not seem to have been caused by any overwhelming Allied military victory, and certainly not by an invasion of Germany.

Several days after the Armistice had been signed, Field Marshal Paul von Hindenburg, the most respected German commander, made the following comment: '*In spite of the superiority of the enemy in men and materials, we could have brought the struggle to a favourable conclusion if there had been proper cooperation between the politicians and the army. The German army was stabbed in the back.*'

Although the German army was in disarray by November 1918, the idea that Germany had been '*stabbed in the back*' soon took hold.

Thus, at the start of the Versailles Conference, the German population believed that they had not been truly defeated. Furthermore, the new Weimar government still believed that Germany would play a part in the peace conference and that the final treaty, based on Wilson's principles, would not be too harsh. There was, therefore, a huge difference between the expectations of the Germans and the expectations of the Allies, who believed that Germany would accept the terms of the treaty as the defeated nation.

Germany was not involved in the treaty discussions and was not allowed to see the terms of the final treaty until 7 May. There was then national shock and outrage at the terms. The first Weimar government under Scheidemann resigned, but the Allies were not prepared to negotiate and so the Reichstag finally had to accept the treaty, which was viewed by Germans as a '**diktat**'. The signing ceremony took place in the Hall of Mirrors at Versailles, where the Germans had proclaimed the German Empire 50 years earlier following the Franco-Prussian War.

The terms of the Treaty of Versailles

The 440 clauses of the peace treaty covered the following areas:

War guit

The infamous Article 231, or what later became known as the 'war guilt clause', lay at the heart of the treaty:

> *The Allied and Associated Governments affirm and Germany accepts the responsibility of Germany and her allies for causing all the loss and damage to which the Allied and Associated Governments and their nationals have been subjected as a consequence of the war imposed upon them by the aggression of Germany and her allies.*
>
> **Article 231, Treaty of Versailles, 1919.**

This clause allowed moral justification for the other terms of the treaty that were imposed upon Germany.

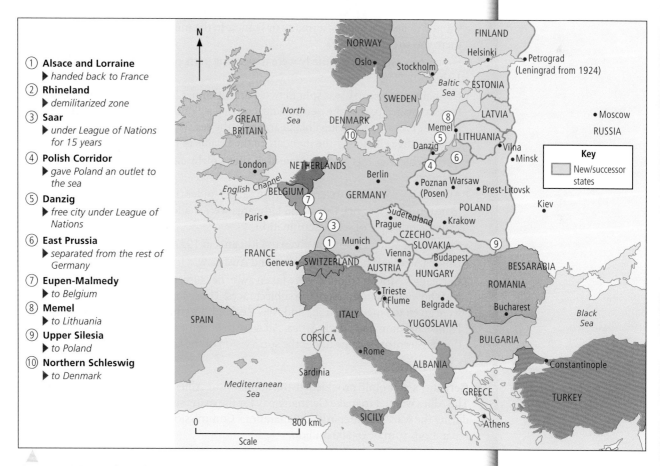

① **Alsace and Lorraine**
▶ *handed back to France*

② **Rhineland**
▶ *demilitarized zone*

③ **Saar**
▶ *under League of Nations for 15 years*

④ **Polish Corridor**
▶ *gave Poland an outlet to the sea*

⑤ **Danzig**
▶ *free city under League of Nations*

⑥ **East Prussia**
▶ *separated from the rest of Germany*

⑦ **Eupen-Malmedy**
▶ *to Belgium*

⑧ **Memel**
▶ *to Lithuania*

⑨ **Upper Silesia**
▶ *to Poland*

⑩ **Northern Schleswig**
▶ *to Denmark*

Key: New/successor states

The territorial changes that took place as a result of the Treaty of Versailles

Disarmament

It was generally accepted that the pre-1914 **arms race** in Europe had contributed to the outbreak of war. Thus the treaty addressed disarmament directly. Yet while Germany was obliged to disarm to the lowest point compatible with internal security, there was only a general reference to the idea of full international disarmament. In addition, the west bank of the Rhine was demilitarized (i.e. stripped of German troops) and an Allied army of occupation was to be stationed in the area for 15 years.

Territorial changes

Wilson's Fourteen Points proposed respect for the principle of **self-determination**, and the collapse of large empires gave an opportunity to create states based on the different nationalities. This ambition was to prove very difficult to achieve and, unavoidably, some nationals were left in countries where they then constituted minorities.

The following points were agreed upon:

- Alsace-Lorraine, which had been seized from France after the Franco-Prussian War in 1871, was returned to France.
- The Saarland was put under the administration of the **League of Nations** for 15 years, after which a **plebiscite** was to allow the inhabitants to decide whether they wanted to be annexed to Germany or France. In the meantime, the coal extracted there was to go to France.
- Eupen, Moresnet and Malmedy were to become parts of Belgium after a plebiscite in 1920.
- Germany as a country was split in two. Parts of Upper Silesia, Poznan and West Prussia formed part of the new Poland, creating a 'Polish Corridor' between Germany and East Prussia and giving Poland access to the sea. The German port of Danzig became a free city under the mandate of the League of Nations.
- North Schleswig was given to Denmark after a plebiscite (South Schleswig remained German).
- All territory received by Germany from Russia under the Treaty of Brest-Litovsk was to be returned. Estonia, Latvia and Lithuania were made independent states in line with the principle of self-determination.
- The port of Memel was to be given to Lithuania in 1922.
- Union (*Anschluss*) between Germany and Austria was forbidden.
- Germany's African colonies were taken away because, the Allies argued, Germany had shown itself unfit to govern subject races. Those in Asia (including Shandong) were given to Japan, Australia and New Zealand, and those in Africa to Britain, France, Belgium and South Africa. All were to become 'mandates', which meant that the new territories came under the supervision of the League of Nations.

Reparations

Germany's 'war guilt' provided justification for the Allied demands for reparations. The Allies wanted to make Germany pay for the material damage done to them during the war. The Inter-Allied Reparations Commission, in 1921, came up with the reparations sum of £6,600 million.

Activity 5   ▶ (ATL) Thinking skills

Review questions

1. Which clauses of the Treaty of Versailles were likely to be most problematic to enforce?
2. Which aspects of the treaty were most likely to a) annoy Germany, and b) damage Germany?

What was the contemporary response to the Treaty of Versailles?

Read through the source below and then address the questions following.

Source A

From John Maynard Keynes, *The Economic Consequences of the Peace*, 1919. Keynes was a British economist who worked at the Treasury during the First World War and was a chief representative at negotiations prior to the Treaty of Versailles, although he resigned from the British delegation.

> … the future life of Europe was not their concern: its means of livelihood was not their anxiety. Their preoccupations, good and bad alike, related to frontiers and nationalities, to the balance of power, to imperial aggrandisements, to the future enfeeblement of a strong and dangerous enemy, to revenge, and to the shifting by the victors of their unbearable financial burdens onto the shoulders of the defeated.

Source B

From Harold Nicolson's diary, 1919. Nicolson was a junior member of the British Foreign Office and was attending the Versailles Conference.

> Now that we see [the terms] as a whole, we realise that they are much too stiff. The real crime is the reparations and indemnity chapter, which is immoral and senseless. There is not a single person among the younger people here who is not unhappy and disappointed with the terms. The only people who approve are the old fire-eaters.

Source C

Extract from a German newspaper, *Deutsche Zeitung*, 1919.

> Today in the Hall of Mirrors of Versailles the disgraceful Treaty is being signed. Do not forget it! The German people will with unceasing labour press forward to reconquer the place among nations to which it is entitled. Then will come the vengeance for the shame of 1919.

Source D

A conservative DNVP deputy speaking in the Reichstag debate on the treaty.

> Our Fatherland finds itself in the most difficult hour of its history. … We in our party are aware of the results for our people which a rejection of the peace treaty will entail. The resulting harm, however, will only be temporary, but if we accept this treaty we will abandon countless generations of our people to misery. … For us, the acceptance of the treaty is impossible for many reasons. … In addition to making Germany defenceless, there is also the matter of the theft of our territory.

1. What are the main criticisms of the treaty put forward in sources A and B?
2. What were Germany's assessments of the treaty in sources C and D?
3. What common themes can you identify in these sources regarding the treaty?
4. With reference to its origin, purpose and content, analyse the value and limitations of Source D for historians studying the impact of the Treaty of Versailles on Germany.

Criticisms of the Treaty of Versailles

As you can see from the sources above, there was already strong criticism of the Treaty of Versailles at the time that it was signed, not just from the Germans but also from among the Allies. These criticisms, summarized below, became stronger in the 1920s, forcefully expressed by contemporary observers like Harold Nicolson and Norman H Davies, and economist JM Keynes.

The issue of war guilt

The 'war guilt' clause was particularly hated by the Germans, who felt that all countries should bear responsibility for the outbreak of war in 1914. It was especially harsh to put the whole guilt for the war on the new republic, which was already struggling for survival.

Disarmament clauses

These were hard for the Germans to accept. Germany now had an army of only 100,000, which was small for a country of this size. Germany was also very proud of its army. Germany's anger grew when, despite Wilson's call for disarmament in his Fourteen Points, efforts by the other European powers to disarm came to nothing in the 1920s and 1930s.

Reparations and loss of key resources

The economist J M Keynes led the criticisms of the treaty in the area of reparations. In *The Economic Consequences of the Peace*, he argued, *'The treaty ignores the economic solidarity of Europe and by aiming at the destruction of the economic life of Germany it threatens the health and prosperity of the Allies themselves.'* Not only could Germany not pay the huge reparations bill, but taking away the country's coal and iron resources meant that its economy would be unable to recover. The fact that Germany was to face hyperinflation in the early 1920s seemed to provide evidence for his predictions.

Territorial changes to satisfy the issue of self-determination

On this issue, Germany believed that it was treated unfairly. Thus, while the Danes were given the chance of a plebiscite in North Schleswig, the Germans in the Sudetenland and Austria were not given any such choice. Many German-speaking peoples were now ruled by non-Germans.

Removal of colonies

Wilson's reason for removing regions like South-West Africa and Rwanda-Urundi from German administration was to remove them from the harsh nature of German rule. Yet this action was clearly hypocritical. States that received German colonies – South Africa and Belgium, for example – could not themselves claim to be model colonial rulers.

League of Nations

The failure of the peacemakers to invite Germany to join the newly created body of the League of Nations, which was designed to deal with disputes between members and thus maintain peace, not only insulted Germany and added to its sense of grievance, but made it less likely that the League could be effective in promoting international cooperation.

Alternative views of the Treaty of Versailles

 Historians' perspectives

Many historians take a different view of the Treaty of Versailles, and its impact on the events of Europe after 1920, to that which was prevalent in the years after 1919. In fact, it is now argued that the treaty was *'relatively lenient'* (Niall Ferguson) and that, given the huge problems facing the peacemakers, it would have been difficult for them to have achieved a more satisfactory settlement. This is supported by historians such as Sally Marks, Anthony Lentin, Alan Sharp and Ruth Henig. The arguments of these historians are summarized below.

Compared to the treaties that Germany had imposed on Russia and Romania earlier in 1918, the Treaty of Versailles was quite moderate and the Allies can be seen to have exercised considerable restraint. The treaty deprived Germany of about 13.5 per cent of its territory (much of this consisted of Alsace-Lorraine, which was returned to France), about 13 per cent of its economic productivity and just over 10 per cent of its population. In addition, it can be argued that France deserved to be compensated for the destruction of so much of its land and industry. German land had not been invaded and its farmland and industries therefore remained intact.

The treaty in fact left Germany in a relatively strong position in the centre of Europe. Germany remained a dominant power in a weakened Europe. Not only was it physically undamaged, it had gained strategic advantages. Russia remained weak and isolated at this time, and Central Europe was fragmented. The peacemakers had created several new states in accordance with the principle of self-determination and this was to create a power vacuum that would favour the expansion of Germany in the future. Anthony Lentin has pointed out the problem here of creating a treaty that failed to weaken Germany, but at the same time left it 'scourged, humiliated and resentful'.

The huge reparations bill was not responsible for the economic crisis that Germany faced in the early 1920s. In fact, the issue of banknotes by the German government was a major factor in causing hyperinflation. In addition, many economic historians have argued that Germany could have paid the 7.2 per cent of its national income that the Reparations Schedule required in the years 1925–29, if it had reformed its financial system or raised its taxation to British levels. However, it chose not to pay the reparations as a way of protesting against the peace settlement.

Thus it can be argued that the treaty was reasonable, and not in itself responsible for the chaos of post-war Germany. Why, then, did the divisions over the signing of the treaty dominate German political life after 1919? The key issue is that while the treaty was not in itself exceptionally unfair, the Germans thought it was. Nationalist propaganda was very successful in persuading ordinary Germans that the diktat was the cause of the country's problems and that it was harsh and unjust. This meant that:

- Weimar socialist politicians were associated with the Treaty: they were called 'the November criminals' and were accused of 'betraying' Germany; this lost the Weimar Republic much support from ordinary Germans and it meant that democracy became associated with national humiliation (and later, economic ruin);
- it helped contribute to the recovery after 1919 of right-wing political forces, who now had ammunition with which to attack the Republic;
- it perpetuated the 'stab in the back' myth which again gave justification for continued Nationalist attacks on the Republic.

3. The threat from political extremism

Against the backdrop of resentment caused by the Treaty of Versailles, the Weimar government also had to face a series of political challenges from both the left and the right during the next few years. Violence on the street became the norm as politics became more polarized.

The influence of Karl Marx and Communism in Europe after 1917

In October 1917, the Bolshevik Party, which followed the ideas of Karl Marx , took control in Russia (see Chapter 7). Marx argued that a proletarian revolution was inevitable once society had become industrialized, due to the fact that the middle classes, or bourgeoisie, who dominated the means of production in an industrialized society, would always oppress the workers (proletariat) who would eventually rise up. Following the revolution there would be a dictatorship of the proletariat in order to put the factories and the means of production into the hands of everyone, to abolish the class system and deal with counter-revolution. Once that had happened, the dictatorship for the proletariat would no longer be needed and a communist society would have been reached in which everyone would work according to the principle, 'From each according to their ability, to each according to their needs'. The Bolsheviks hoped that their success in Russia would inspire the workers to rise up across Europe. Such a threat was terrifying to the middle and upper classes of Europe.

Rosa Luxemburg

CHALLENGE YOURSELF

(ATL) **Research skills**

Research more into the life of Rosa Luxemburg and her role in left-wing politics during this period. Also see if you can find out about other women who took an active part in politics during the Weimar era.

The Freikorps

These units were made up of right-wing nationalist soldiers who were mainly demobilized junior army officers – though the ranks were swelled with many others. They were given uniforms and weapons but they were not an official part of the army and so lacked the discipline of regular troops.

Threats from the left

	SPD (German Social Democratic Party)	USPD (German Independent Social Democratic Party); formed in 1917 as a breakaway from the SPD	Spartacists (Spartacus League); established in 1905
Aims	To establish a moderate *socialist republic* by having free elections to establish a parliamentary democracy.	To create a *socialist republic* governed by workers' and soldiers' councils alongside a national Reichstag.	They believed that Germany should enact a Russian-style revolution and create a *soviet republic* based on the rule of workers' and soldiers' councils.
Leaders	Friedrich Ebert Philipp Scheidemann	Karl Kautsky Hugo Haase	Rosa Luxemburg Karl Liebknecht
Support	Working class. In 1912 it became the largest party in the Reichstag and in 1919 had about 1 million members.	Working class. In 1919 it had membership of about 300,000 and it was in a coalition with the SPD in November and December 1918.	Working class. In 1919, it had membership of about 5,000.

The German left-wing movement; socialist groups and parties, 1918

On 5 January 1919, the Spartacus League, also known as the Spartacists, staged an uprising in Berlin. Their aim was to set up a revolutionary regime. However, the uprising had little support from the working class. Ebert called in the army but as General Groener could not rely on some of his units, he also used the **Freikorps** to put down the rebellion (see Information box). Ebert's reliance on the army and the Freikorps, along with the brutality used to suppress the revolt, caused bitterness within the left.

The Spartacist uprising was followed by other revolts by the left. However, none of these were successful. This was due to the fact that the activities of the left lacked effective coordination and, after its ablest leaders such as Liebknecht and Luxemburg were killed, it failed to find inspiring leaders. In addition, the brutal suppression of the rebels by the government made it difficult to make any headway. Thus the government was never seriously threatened by the left-wing revolts, though the continuing fear of a communist revolution, such as that which had happened in Russia, frightened many of the middle classes into supporting right-wing parties.

Threats from the right

A more serious threat to the Weimar Republic came from the right wing whose ideas were prevalent among the key institutions of the Republic. As we have seen, those on the right were united in their hatred of democracy and the values of the Weimar Republic, and their disgust with what they saw as a betrayal over the Versailles Treaty. They were also united in their hatred of **Marxism** and in a belief in the restoration of some kind of authoritarian regime. However, while some wanted a return to the monarchy others wanted some form of dictatorship. Such divisions weakened their ability to effectively challenge the Republic in the years 1919–23.

The first major crisis from the right was the Kapp Putsch in March 1920. In February 1920 the defence minister, Gustav Moske, ordered two Friekorps units to disband. General Walther von Luttwitz, the commanding general, refused to disband one of them; he was joined by the leader of the Fatherland Party, Wolfgang Kapp, and other disgruntled officers in a bid to overthrow the government. Crucially, however, the army refused to support the Freikorps – though it also failed to support the government, which was forced to withdraw to Dresden. However, the **putsch** quickly collapsed in the face of a general strike in Berlin which paralysed the capital. After four days, Kapp's government fled.

Although this was a victory for the government, which had retained the support of the people of Berlin, the events of the putsch highlighted the weaknesses of the Republic. The army had failed to actively support the government but no action was taken against its leaders. Indeed, Seeckt was appointed chief of army command and went on to remodel the army, continuing to uphold its independence, which placed it beyond government control. Meanwhile, those involved in the putsch were treated leniently by the courts; out of the 705 involved, only one was actually punished (with a five-year prison sentence).

Political assassinations

Right-wing nationalists also turned to political assassinations in order to weaken the Republic – a trend that was encouraged by the lenient sentences given out by the judges against the assassins. Between 1919 and 1922 there were 376 political assassinations. Of these, 354 were carried out by right-wing assassins and 326 went unpunished.

The most famous victim was Walther Rathenau, the foreign minister who was killed in June 1922. His involvement at Versailles and his Jewish background made him a target for right-wing nationalists. There was general dismay and revulsion, however, at this assassination, and 70,000 people demonstrated in Berlin. Despite this, Rathenau's killers and their accomplices received an average of only four years each in prison.

These murders did not succeed in overturning the Republic; however, the various revolts and assassinations helped to foster disillusionment with the government while the confidence of the anti-Republican right wing continued to grow.

The Munich Putsch

The leaders of the Munich Putsch, 1923

PERNET DR. WEBER KRIEBEL LUDENDORFF HITLER RÖHM WAGNER
FRICK BRÜCKNER

Following the ending of **passive resistance** in the Ruhr in 1923 by Gustav Stresemann (see page 24), there were again cries that the government had betrayed Germany. In Bavaria, the right-wing government declared a state of emergency and appointed Gustav von Kahr, who was an extreme conservative. Along with the army commander in Bavaria, General von Lossow, and Adolf Hitler, the leader of the National Socialist German Worker's Party (NSDAP), they called for '*a march on Berlin*' to overthrow the government.

Although Kahr and Lossow abandoned this plan, Hitler decided to continue. On 8 November, he took over a Munich beer hall where Kahr and Lossow were addressing a meeting and declared a '*national revolution*'. Under pressure, Kahr and Lossow cooperated and agreed to proceed with the march on Berlin, which would also involve installing Ludendorff as the new commander-in-chief. However, they quickly lost their nerve and support for Hitler's putsch melted away. Hitler's supporters, the SA (see page 31), were unable to gain control of the Munich army barracks and the march through Munich, on 9 November, ended in a gun battle in which 14 Nazis were killed and Hitler himself arrested on a charge of treason. Ludendorff handed himself into the police.

Once again the Weimar Republic had survived, and once again the army had stayed on the side of the government. However, the whole incident highlighted the importance of the army to the political survival of the regime and the judiciary's sympathy towards right-wing conspirators charged with treason. Hitler was only given a five-year sentence, which was the minimum possible for a charge of treason, but released after ten months. Ludendorff, meanwhile, was acquitted.

4. Weak coalitions

While the country struggled to deal with violence and extremism, the government itself struggled to create stable, strong coalitions that could deal with the threats and win public support. In the four years from 1919 to 1923, Weimar had six governments. The longest of these lasted for six months. It also became clear that public support was shifting from the centre parties to the more extremist parties.

Political parties in the Reichstag

The non-socialist parties in the Reichstag	
ZP *Zentrumspartei* (Centre Party)	Formed in 1870 to defend the interests of the Roman Catholic Church. Enjoyed a wide range of support from landowners to trade unionists. Supported the Republic (from late 1920s it became more sympathetic to the right wing).
DDP *Deutsche Demokratische Partei* (German Democratic Party)	A left-leaning liberal party that had support from professional middle classes. Committed to a democratic constitution.
DNVP *Deutschnationale Volkspartei* (German National People's Party)	A nationalist party based on the old Conservative Party. Support from landowners and some business owners. Monarchist and anti-Republican.
DVP *Deutsche Volkspartei* (German People's Party)	A right-leaning liberal party. Support came from upper middle class and business interests. At first voted against the new constitution, but under its leader, Gustav Stresemann, became a supporter of parliamentary democracy.

1. What does the table of elections 1919–20 (in the margin) indicate about the shift in public opinion between 1919 and 1920. What factor/s could have impacted on this change?
2. Review the political threats to the Weimar Republic in the years 1919–23. Create a timeline with the political challenges along the top of the line (you will add the economic challenges after the next section).
3. Which do you think was more dangerous for the long-term stability of the Weimar Republic: the threat from the left, or the threat from the right? Explain your answer.
4. Why might Republicans have been (a) dismayed, or (b) encouraged by the impact of the political crises 1919–23?

The 1919 and 1920 Reichstag elections		
Party	Seats in January 1919	Seats in June 1920
USPD	22	83
SPD	163	103
DDP	75	39
Centre	91	64
DVP	19	65
DNVP	44	71
KPD	0	4

What economic challenges did the Weimar Republic face, 1919–23?

The impact of war

Four years of **total war** had a serious impact on the German economy. Assuming that victory would provide the means to pay off Germany's debts, wartime governments had financed the war through increased borrowing and by printing money. Thus, defeat in 1919 left Germany with severe economic problems:

- a huge debt of 144,000 million marks;
- rising inflation;
- the cost of paying reparations (see page 14);
- the loss of industry and resources from areas such as the Saar, and Alsace and Lorraine;
- the loss of traditional trading links.

The causes and impact of the hyperinflation of 1923

Germany's economic problems reached a crisis point in 1923, when hyperinflation took hold. This meant that prices spiralled out of control and money became worthless.

Why did this happen? The long-term cause of this situation was the war which, as mentioned above, had created massive debts for Germany and started the process of inflation; however, the first years of the Republic also added to this situation. Unwilling to risk unpopularity by raising taxes or curbing government spending in areas such as benefits or salaries to civil servants, the Weimar government instead opted to keep taxation low and to continue to borrow and print money. This, they hoped, would not only shore up support for the government but would also allow economic growth to continue and unemployment to stay low.

In this situation, payment of reparations was not the primary cause of inflation. In fact reparations could only be paid in hard currency such as dollars or gold – not the deflated mark. Even so, reparations certainly contributed to the inflationary crisis because in order to buy hard currency to pay the reparations, the Weimar government continued to print millions of marks. This printing of money was also needed to pay wages to civil servants, to pay welfare benefits and to give the industrial sector subsidies to help it to readjust to peacetime and to continue to provide jobs.

The final factor that led to the hyperinflation of 1923 was the action of the French and Belgian governments, who ordered their troops to occupy the Ruhr in response to Germany's failure to keep up with reparations payments. The occupying troops, who eventually numbered 100,000, took over the mines, factories, steelworks and railways. In response, the German government, led by Wilhelm Cuno, stopped all reparations payments and ordered 'passive resistance'; no one was to cooperate with the French authorities. A general strike was also declared in the Ruhr area. This situation brought more economic burdens for the German government:

- It had to keep paying the wages of the striking workers.
- It lost tax revenue from closed businesses in the Ruhr.
- Deprived of deliveries of coal from the Ruhr to the rest of Germany, it had to pay for imported coal.

Within six months, the German currency had collapsed completely. Everyday items now cost millions of marks. Those with mortgages, debts or who had access to foreign currency made fortunes in this situation. However, the results of hyperinflation were devastating for those who had savings or fixed incomes; overnight they found themselves impoverished by the depreciation of the currency.

How did hyperinflation end?

In November 1923 the new Chancellor, Gustav Stresemann, took decisive action to end the crisis:

- He called off passive resistance in the Ruhr and promised to continue to pay reparations.
- He appointed the expert financier, Hjalmar Schlacht, to the Reichsbank.
- The old currency was replaced with a new stable currency, the Rentenmark.
- Government expenditure was cut sharply in order to reduce the deficit; 700,000 civil servants were sacked.
- He persuaded the Allies to hold an international conference to consider Germany's economic plight. This resulted in the Dawes Plan (named after the conference's chairman, the American banker Charles Dawes), which reduced the amount of reparations that Germany would have to pay each month and stated that Germany should receive a loan of 800 million marks from the US.

A German woman uses banknotes as fuel, 1935

Activity 8

The impact of hyperinflation

1. List the ways in which the hyperinflation of 1923 impacted on different groups of people and on the government.
2. Who were the 'winners' and who were the 'losers' of this situation?

ATL Thinking and self-management skills

1. Add the economic problems of the Weimar Republic to your timeline.

2. In pairs, use your timelines to review the threats and crises faced by the Weimar Republic in the years 1919–23. Which of these do you consider constituted the greatest threat to the Republic?

3. How strong was the Weimar Republic by 1924? Does the fact that it had survived so many crises indicate that in fact it had many strengths?

Essay writing

To what extent was the Treaty of Versailles responsible for the difficulties faced by the Weimar Republic from 1919 to 1923?

Intro:	You need to show that you understand the significance of the dates in the question and what exactly the 'difficulties' faced by the Republic during this time were.
	Also, you need to set out your main argument; was the Treaty of Versailles responsible or were other factors more important?
Paragraph 1:	Start with the focus of the question – the Treaty of Versailles – and make sure your opening sentence links directly to this issue e.g.
	The Treaty of Versailles played a key role in destablizing the new government. Firstly...
	You could consider the discontent among key sections of the German population regarding this treaty – particularly among conservatives and nationalist groups – and how this was directed against the new government, which had signed the treaty and was thus associated with it.
Paragraph 2:	*In addition, the issue of reparations demanded by the Treaty of Versailles led to the invasion of the Ruhr by French troops, which created a political and economic crisis.*
	Now move on to other factors to provide balance in your essay.
Paragraph 3:	*However the economic crisis of 1923 was also the result of the impact of the First World War and the politics of the Weimar government after 1919...*
Paragraph 4:	*The political instability of the Weimar Republic was also caused by other factors, including the nature of the constitution itself.* Here you could talk about the impact of proportional representation and also the failure to reform the traditional institutions. Give detailed evidence to support any points that you make.
Paragraph 5:	*In addition, many in Germany found it difficult to adjust to a republic after the autocratic rule of the Kaiser.* Here you could talk about the difficulties faced by political parties as identified by the sources on page 10.
Conclusion:	Make sure you answer the question directly and that your answer is based on the weight of your evidence in the main body of your answer, so that you have a consistent argument running through your essay.

Hints for success

Make sure you do not just write a long description of the terms of the Treaty; keep focused on how it created difficulties for the Weimar Republic.

The Golden Era under Stresemann 1924–29

Timeline of events – 1923–29		
1923	**Aug**	Stresemann becomes Chancellor
	Oct	Radical left-wing governments in Saxony and Thuringia are overthrown
	Nov	Hitler's Munich Putsch fails
		Hyperinflation is ended with introduction of Rentenmark
		New government: Stresemann becomes foreign minister
1924	**Apr**	Dawes Plan
	May	Election
	Dec	Election

1925	Feb	Ebert dies
	April	Hindenburg is elected president
	Oct	Locarno Conference
1926	Sept	Germany joins League of Nations
1928	May	Müller's Grand Coalition
	Aug	Kellogg-Briand Pact
1929		Young Plan
	Oct	Death of Stresemann
	Oct	Wall Street Crash

Gustav Stresemann

Key concepts: *Significance and change*

After the chaos and instability of the years 1919–23, the years from 1924 to 1929 are often seen as 'a golden age'. Indeed, there was improvement in Germany's economic position and relative political stability. In addition, there was great social and cultural progress and it seemed that Germany was once again being accepted as an equal on the international stage. Gustav Stresemann played a key role in this recovery.

How far was there economic recovery?

> *The economic position is only flourishing on the surface. Germany is dancing on a volcano. If the short-term loans are called in, a large section of our economy would collapse.*
> **Stresemann, 1928.**

The economic measures taken by Stresemann in 1923 and 1924 (see page 22) allowed the German economy to begin its recovery, and by 1925 Germany appeared more stable and prosperous. The American loans agreed in the Dawes Plan helped German industry to modernize, and cartels were established that had better purchasing power than smaller industries. Advances were also made in 'new' industries such as the chemicals, car and aeroplane industries. Between 1925 and 1929, German exports rose by 40 per cent and wages for workers correspondingly increased.

Alongside improved living standards caused by rising wages, the government also introduced generous pensions, and sickness and unemployment benefits. In addition, state subsidies helped to finance the building of housing, schools, parks and sports facilities. All of this gave the impression that the Weimar economy was in a healthy state.

Nevertheless, there were signs of weakness in the Weimar economy:

- Unemployment never fell below 1.3 million.
- Economic growth remained uneven and in 1926 actually declined. Imports continued to exceed exports.
- Not everyone benefited from the 'boom': the professional middle classes had been bankrupted by the inflation and did not see their wages rise in this period.
- Farmers continued to be hit by a worldwide agricultural depression, which kept food prices low; this situation worsened in 1925–26, when there was a global grain surplus leading to a price slump. Many were in debt, leading to an increase in bankruptcies in the late 1920s.
- The government continued to run a deficit despite the higher taxes.

How far was there political stability?

The period from 1924 to 1929 saw a much calmer time in politics. There were no attempted **coups** and no assassinations of key political figures. In addition, elections seemed to indicate a swing back in support to the parties of the middle ground; by 1928, this allowed a 'Grand Coalition' to be formed under Hermann Müller, the leader of the SPD. As this enjoyed the support of over 60 per cent of the Reichstag there seemed to be some hope for stable democratic politics.

Nevertheless, the weaknesses of Weimar politics remained very apparent during the years 1924–29. There were seven governments during this time, each one with a coalition that was a consequence of the proportional representation system, which we discussed earlier. As in the period 1919–23, the different parties found it difficult to cooperate; they tended to put self-interest before those of stable government. In addition, the parties themselves were often divided internally. This made it impossible to hold the coalitions together for any substantial length of time, or to allow any long-term planning. Minor issues, such as which flag to use, could bring about the collapse of a government. Most significantly, this situation discredited the political system in the eyes of many Germans, who viewed the continual political wrangling with increasing dismay and contempt.

Weimar Republic gopvernments, 1923–1930		
Time in office	Chancellor	Make-up of the coalition
1923–24	Wilhelm Marx	Centre, DDP, DVP
1924–25	Wilhelm Marx	Centre, DDP, DVP
1925	Hans Luther	Centre, DVP, DNVP
1926	Hans Luther	Centre, DDP, DVP
1926	Wilhelm Marx	Centre, DDP, DVP
1927–28	Wilhelm Marx	Centre, DDP, DNVP
1928–30	Hermann Müller	SPD, DDP, Centre, DVP

An indication of public attitudes came in 1925 during the presidential elections. These were due in 1925 and it was assumed that Ebert would be re-elected. His unexpected death in February 1925 brought forth a wide range of candidates; these included the war hero General Hindenburg, who went on to win in the second ballot.

Those who lacked confidence in the Weimar Republic were reassured by Hindenburg's election, seeing him as an authoritarian figure who might be capable of bringing stability to the Republic. However, for others, his election was a defeat for the Republic; the considerable powers of presidential office were now placed in the hands of a military figure, inexperienced in the ways of democracy and surrounded by army officers and fellow *Junkers*.

What were the achievements of Stresemann?

The one element of continuity in this period was Gustav Stresemann, who remained foreign minister between 1924 and 1929. Stresemann was a pragmatic nationalist. He wanted to restore Germany's position in Europe and to free Germany from the restraints imposed on it by the Versailles Treaty. However, he realized the best way of achieving these goals was to comply with the terms of the Versailles Treaty, in order to improve relations with Britain and France. This would then allow him to put pressure on them to revise the treaty.

As a result of this policy, Stresemann gained several successes:

- Locarno Pact, 1925: Stresemann guaranteed Germany's western borders, which reassured France and brought a degree of rapprochement between France and Germany. As a result, he was able to secure some withdrawal of allied forces from Germany (see below).
- League of Nations, 1926 (see page 14): Germany was accepted into the League of Nations and given great power status on the League council with veto power.
- The Treaty of Berlin, 1926: this renewed the earlier Treaty of Rapallo that had been signed in 1922 with Russia, thus continuing good relations with the USSR (which helped put pressure on the West to improve its relations with Germany as they did not want Germany moving closer to the USSR).
- The Young Plan: the US agreed to give further loans to Germany and a much reduced scheme of repayments for reparations was established to spread the cost over the next 50 years.

Stresemann's policy also secured the objective of removing foreign forces from German soil – an aim which was shared by all parties. Following Germany's cooperation in the Locarno Pact, by December 1925 the Allies had withdrawn from Zone 1, which was situated around Cologne. Once the reparation issue had been resolved in the Young Plan, the remaining Allied forces were withdrawn. The final zone was evacuated in June 1930, five years ahead of the schedule laid down in the Treaty of Versailles.

There is thus no doubt that by 1929 Germany was once more accepted on the international stage and that its relations with Britain and France had markedly improved. Indeed, Stresemann's contribution to the new atmosphere of cooperation, known as the Locarno Spring, earned him the Nobel Peace Prize in 1926 alongside his French counterpart, Aristide Briand.

Despite his achievements, during this period Stresemann was bitterly attacked by nationalist politicians, who claimed that his actions amounted to an acceptance of the Versailles Treaty. They believed that Locarno only benefited the French and that Germany should stay out of the League of Nations, which was associated with the victors of the First World War and thus with those who had imposed suffering on Germany via the Versailles Treaty. The Young Plan was also opposed as it confirmed the principal that Germany still had to pay reparations. They further condemned Stresemann for failing to secure the disarmament of the other countries.

As Stresemann died in 1929, it is not clear how far he meant to go in revising the Treaty of Versailles or what, for example, his aims were for the eastern borders of Germany, which had not been guaranteed by Locarno. The Wall Street Crash in 1929 in any case fundamentally altered the international atmosphere.

Society and culture in the Weimar Republic

Although this era of the Weimar Republic lasted only a few years, it was nevertheless marked by an explosion of creativity and experimentation in the sciences and the arts. There were also challenges to traditional norms in society during this period.

Activity 10   ▶ (ATL)   Research and communication skills

In groups, research the following aspects of Weimar culture and society: painting, literature, music and opera, theatre, architecture, film, cabaret, science, the status of women.

Prepare a presentation to the rest of your class on your topic. Make sure you show:

- the key developments/changes in this area and how they challenged traditional culture or norms (you may also want to consider areas where there was little change, or where in fact change had started before this period);
- reasons why these changes took place;
- the reaction to these developments within Germany;
- the influence that the developments had on other areas of Weimar society and culture, or on developments in other countries;
- the impact that these developments had on the Weimar Republic as a whole.

Essay writing

To what extent did the Weimar Republic experience a 'golden age' between 1924 and 1928?

For this essay, you will need to identify the positives and the negatives of this era for the Weimar Republic: the ways in which it saw a 'golden age' and the ways in which this was perhaps only a façade hiding more deep-rooted problems. Consider organizing your information thematically so that you have separate paragraphs for political, economic and social issues. Also remember that 'To what extent' questions require you to develop arguments for and against the assumption/assertion in the question.

Examiner's hint   Refer to the markbands for Paper 3 in the margin to check that you are meeting the criteria for the top markband

Essay frame

Intro: Set out why the period 1924–28 could be seen as a golden age and explain what this means regarding Weimar, i.e. political stability, economic upturn, acceptance on the international stage and a flowering of the arts. Set out your judgement as to whether this was a golden age or whether in fact this was only a superficial respite in a turbulent decade.

Here are some suggestions for opening or topic sentences; you need to add detailed evidence to support each point.

Paragraph 1:   *The years 1924 to 1928 saw a decrease in the political violence of the previous years and a return to more moderate stable politics, thus indicating a 'golden age' in the area of politics.*

Paragraph 2:   *However, despite these improvements, key areas of instability still existed.*

Paragraph 3:   *Economically, the reforms carried out by Stresemann in 1923 led to economic recovery.*

Paragraph 4:   *Despite the growing prosperity that allowed many Germans to experience a golden age financially, there were warning signs that this stability was quite fragile.*

Paragraph 5:   *In international affairs, there were clear signs that Germany was once more becoming accepted as a member of the international community. Thus, this was indeed a golden age in comparison to the position that Germany had held before, which had culminated in the invasion of the Ruhr in 1923.*

Paragraph 6:   *Despite Stresemann's success in restoring Germany's international position and gaining significant concessions, many in Germany criticized this and claimed that it was not in Germany's interest.*

Paragraph 7:   *Perhaps the most uncontroversial area in which Weimar Germany experienced a golden age was in the area of culture.*

Conclusion: Come back to the overall argument that you set out in your introduction; make sure you answer the question directly.

(!)

For top markbands for Paper 3 essays:

Introduction and main body paragraphs

Responses are clearly focused.

The question is fully addressed and implications are considered.

The essay is well structured and the material effectively organized.

Supporting knowledge is detailed, accurate, relevant to the question and used to support arguments.

Arguments are clear, well developed and consistently supported with evidence.

There is evaluation of different perspectives.

Conclusion

The conclusion is clearly stated and it is consistent with the evidence presented.

The crisis years and the rise of Hitler (1929–33)

Timeline of events – 1929–33		
1929	Oct	Wall Street Crash
1930	March	Collapse of Müller's Grand Coalition government
		Brüning appointed as Chancellor
	Sept	Reichstag election; Nazis and Communists make gains
1931		Financial crisis in Germany
1932	Apr	Ban on SA
		Hindenburg re-elected as president
	May	Brüning replaced by Papen as Chancellor
	June	Ban on SA lifted
	July	Election; Nazi Party becomes largest party in the Reichstag
	Sept	Reichstag passes vote of no confidence in Papen's government
	Nov	Election; Nazis still biggest party
	Dec	Papen forced to resign; Schleicher replaces Papen
1933	Jan	Hitler offered Chancellorship in a coalition government with Papen

Key concepts: *Causation and consequence*

The face of German politics was dramatically changed in the years 1929 to 1933. In October 1929, the New York Stock Exchange in America crashed, wiping tens of thousands of dollars off the value of share prices. This was to have a profound effect in America, leading to the Great Depression. However, the ramifications of this economic crisis were felt across the world, particularly in Germany, whose financial recovery had been based largely on US loans. These loans were rapidly called in by American banks with a catastrophic effect on industry which needed the money for investment. In addition, the US market for German goods ceased to exist as the US economy shrank. The result was closure of factories and spiralling unemployment. By 1932, the number of unemployed had risen to 6 million, with catastrophic effects on the living standards of millions of Germans.

The political implications of the economic crisis of 1929

The economic crisis put further strains on an already fragile political system. The coalition that had been formed following the 1928 election was led by Müller and was one of the most broadly based coalition governments in the Weimar period (see table, page 25). In the face of rising unemployment benefits, combined with falling tax revenues, the coalition fell apart: the DVP on the right wanted to reduce unemployment benefits, while the SPD on the left wanted to protect the level of benefits and raise taxes. In March 1930, Müller resigned.

President Hindenburg appointed Heinrich Brüning, leader of the Centre Party, as Müller's successor. Although it was a logical appointment, in that Brüning was leader of the second largest party in the Reichstag, it was also a crucial step towards the end of parliamentary government. In choosing Brüning, Hindenburg had been influenced by two key military figures: General Groener and General Kurt von Schleicher. This was an indication of the growing influence of the army in politics; these men were keen to see a more authoritarian government and saw Brüning as a respectable, conservative figure who would be prepared to take the Republic in this direction.

Brüning's coalition did not include the SPD and so he did not have enough support in the Reichstag to pass laws. Thus, Hindenburg used Article 48 to rule by presidential decree. However, when this was used to pass Brüning's budget, which aimed to solve the crisis by cutting spending and raising taxes rather than stimulating demand in the economy, there was a political crisis. The SPD won Reichstag support for a motion demanding that the decree be withdrawn on the grounds that Article 48 was to be used in an emergency, not for regular government matters. Brüning thus dissolved the Reichstag and called for new elections; these elections would be key in setting the stage for the rise of the Nazi Party.

The rise of the Nazi Party 1923–30

> Hitler's triumph on 30 January 1933 was at no stage an inevitable outcome of the failure of Weimar democracy.
>
> **Ian Kershaw (1990).** *Why Did German Democracy Fail?* **Weidenfeld & Nicolson, p. 25.**

The economic crisis and the failure of the government to tackle it effectively led to the German people turning to extremist parties on the left and on the right. In addition, there was once again an increase in violence on the streets. Two parties in particular benefited from this situation: the Communist Party (KPD) and the National Socialist German Workers' Party (NSDAP) – Nazi for short.

The Nazi Party, led by Adolf Hitler, had established a 25-point programme back in 1920 which stated:

1. We demand the union of all Germans in a Greater Germany on the basis of the right of national self-determination.
2. We demand equality of rights for the German people in its dealings with other nations, and the revocation of the peace treaties of Versailles and St Germain.
3. We demand land and territory to feed our people and to settle our surplus population.
4. Only members of the nation may be citizens of the State. Only those of German blood, whatever their creed, may be members of the nation. Accordingly, no Jew may be a member of the nation.
8. If it is impossible to sustain the total population of the State, then the members of foreign nations (non-citizens) are to be expelled from the Reich.
13. We demand the nationalization of all businesses that have been formed into corporations.
14. We demand a division of the profits of all heavy industries.
23. We demand that: a) all writers and employees of the newspapers appearing in the German language must be members of the race; b) Non-German newspapers must be required to have the express permission of the State to be published.
24. We demand freedom of religion for all religious denominations within the State, so long as they do not endanger its existence or oppose the moral senses of the Germanic race.
25. For the execution of all of this we demand the formation of a strong central power in the Reich.

Key to Hitler's ideology were **points 3 and 4**. Point 3 referred to the idea of *Lebensraum* (or 'living space') for Germans, which was to be gained to the east of Germany. Point 4 sums up Hitler's obsessive hatred against the Jews, which was to be found in all of his writings and which was translated into vicious discriminatory policies once he became leader of Germany.

Nazi election propaganda poster for the presidential elections of 1932.

Activity 11

1. Which aspects of the 25-point plan would have been most attractive to Germans in the early 1920s?
2. What would be the practical implications of such a programme?

As you read on page 20, the Nazis attempted to seize power in a coup in 1923, in what became known as the Munich Putsch, and its failure led to Hitler being sentenced to prison. It was while in prison that Hitler further developed his ideas in *Mein Kampf*; this was a combination of autobiography and political philosophy – it covered racist and authoritarian theories and ideas for the direction of Nazi foreign policy.

When he was released from prison, Hitler reorganized the Nazi Party and made a decision to use the parliamentary system to achieve power. However, with the increased economic and political stability of the Stresemann years, the Nazis failed to achieve any substantial electoral success, as can be seen in the graphs below.

Activity 12

1. What is the message of the graphs below?
2. What is the message of the Nazi propaganda poster in the margin to the left?

Graphs showing the numbers of Nazi voters in elections and the growth of support for the Nazi Party.

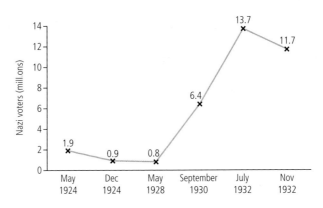

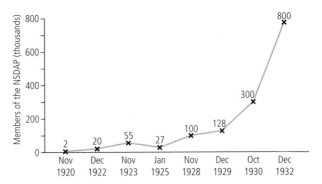

The economic crisis changed this situation and over the course of three elections, between September 1930 and July 1932, the Nazis more than doubled their electoral support. Why was this?

Brüning's only economic policy had been to cut spending, reduce the levels of welfare payments and increase contributions to the unemployment insurance scheme. This failed to improve the economic situation and, with parties on the left unable to put forward an alternative approach, the Nazis stood out as the one party prepared to pledge themselves to provide work for all Germans.

However, it was not just the Nazis' economic policy that got them support. The economic crisis led to a surge in support for the KPD among the workers. The middle and upper classes were terrified of a Bolshevik-style revolution taking place in Germany and the Nazi emphasis on a hatred of communism, along with their actual physical attacks on Communists in the streets, increased their electoral support.

In addition, Nazi ideology combined with calculated tactics succeeded in getting them support across a broad range of classes, as explained by Fulbrook below.

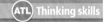

Activity 13 — ATL Thinking skills

> Nazi 'ideology' was a somewhat rag-bag collection of largely negative views combined with a utopian vision of a grandiose future coloured by nostalgic appeal to aspects of a mythical past. Thus Nazism opposed certain pernicious, potentially threatening tendencies of 'modern' capitalist society: the evils of big business (large department stores often owned by Jews), international finance ('Jewish'), and revolutionary communism. Nazis promoted a vision of a harmonious national community (Volksgemeinschaft) which would be racially pure… and which would overcome the class divisions which beset Imperial and Weimar Germany. Nazism claimed to be able to transcend the divisions and heal the wounds of capitalist society, and to be able to present a new way forwards to a great future… Hitler was able to appeal to a wide range of groups harbouring different resentments… precisely because he was never very specific about the details of the proposed new order.
>
> **Mary Fulbrook (2008). *A History of Germany 1918–2008*. Wiley-Blackwell, p. 44.**

1. According to Fulbrook, what aspects of Nazi ideology appealed to voters?

Hitler's personal leadership was also crucial to the success of the party. He was a charismatic speaker able to mesmerize his audiences. He was backed up by a brilliant propagandist, Joseph Goebbels. The Nazis had their own newspapers; they published posters and leaflets, organized rallies and marches. As indicated in the sources above, the Nazis were able to appeal to a range of different groups, and their propaganda was adapted accordingly for different audiences. The organization of the Nazi Party, which had been set up in the 1920s, also allowed it to distribute propaganda via its local branches; indeed, by the 1930s it had built up a formidable election machine. By this point, it also had financial solvency through the contributions it levied on its membership.

Finally, the party's paramilitary force, the SA or *Sturmabteilung*, gave the Nazis an image of order and strength (see Information box on the **SA and SS**). The SA grew dramatically in the years 1930–34 and it was responsible for the growing violence on the streets after 1930. This violence was encouraged by the Nazi leadership. Although street battles with the KPD were often started by the Nazis, the SA claimed that they were in fact keeping order on the streets by dealing with the Communists.

The SA and the SS

The SA or *Sturmabteilung*, also known as the Brownshirts, was a paramilitary wing of the Nazi Party. It played a key role in helping Hitler in his rise to power, providing protection for Nazi rallies and assemblies, disrupting the meetings of opposing parties, fighting the KPD (or Communist Party), and leading attacks against the Jews and other minority groups that the Nazis blamed for Germany's problems.

The SS or *Schutzstaffel*, also known as the Blackshirts, was considered to be an elite paramilitary force and was set up in 1925, initially to provide protection to Hitler. Members of the SS were expected to be totally loyal, obedient and racially pure. The SS went on to become one of the most feared and powerful organizations in Nazi Germany.

The political and economic crisis of 1930–33

Despite the strengths of the Nazis in campaigning and securing votes, the actual success of the Nazi Party in gaining political power was due to the political intrigues of 1932–33, which are outlined below.

March 1930 to April 1932: Brüning's government

Following the 1930 election, the Nazis obtained 107 seats in the Reichstag. The Communists also gained 23 seats, giving them 77 in total. With support from around only one third of the Reichstag's members, Brüning and Hindenburg now had to rely even more on Article 48. Brüning's economic measures continued as before and did little to reduce the impact of the economic crisis and growing unemployment. He also tried to persuade the Allied governments to cancel Germany's reparations; in this he was successful and reparations finally ended in 1932, but by this time German families were in a desperate situation.

With economic and political chaos escalating, a real fear developed that Germany was heading for revolution. In April 1932, Brüning banned the SA in an attempt to reduce street violence.

In March of 1932 there was a presidential election in which Hitler stood against Hindenburg. Hindenburg won the election but Hitler gained a respectable 37 per cent of the vote.

Hindenburg now lost confidence in Brüning and in May 1932 appointed Franz von Papen instead.

May to December 1932: Papen's government

Papen was a relative nonentity. In fact, the real power lay with Schleicher, who was appointed defence minister in the new cabinet.

General von Schleicher had turned against Brüning, believing that Brüning's opposition to the Nazis was wrong. Indeed Schleicher, along with other members of the conservative elite, started to believe the Nazis could be brought into government; this would give them the popular backing that they needed in order to replace the Weimar Republic with a more authoritarian government. However, Hitler was determined not to enter a coalition with anything less than the position of Chancellor. Schleicher would not agree to this and thus Papen took over as Chancellor for the time being in what became known as the 'cabinet of barons', none of whom were members of the Reichstag. As Culpin and Henig write, 'The Weimar Republic was now unquestionably dead'.

In June 1932, Papen lifted the ban on the SA. He also agreed to Hitler's demand to call for new elections. Once again, the Nazi Party gained from the economic crisis and, against a backdrop of violence, they achieved their greatest electoral success. They got 37.8 per cent of the vote and increased their number of MPs from 110 to 230, making them the largest party in the Reichstag. In such a position of power, negotiations now started in earnest with the Nazis over the terms by which they could be brought into power. However, President Hindenburg, who despised the upstart 'Bohemian corporal', refused to offer him anything more than the position of Vice Chancellor – which Hitler refused.

Papen did not, however, have the support of the Reichstag: as soon as it reopened following the election, on 12 September 1932, it passed a vote of no confidence against him, 512 to 42. Schleicher thus persuaded Hindenburg to allow new elections.

In the next election of November 1932, the Nazis lost 2 million votes. However, the KPD made further gains. To counter what conservatives saw as a dangerous situation, there was increased support for Hitler to be given a prominent role in government. In negotiations with Papen and then Hindenburg, Hitler continued to insist that he would only accept the position of Chancellor. Papen and Hindenburg refused; Papen wanted to continue as Chancellor and proposed to replace the Reichstag permanently and instead use the army, in order to suppress opposition.

Schleicher however was against this radical plan of a 'New State'. He convinced Hindenburg that a civil war, which the army would not be able to control, was likely, and persuaded him to dismiss Papen and appoint himself as Chancellor. He then tried to pull together various alliances, including trade unionists and the left wing of the Nazi Party led by Gregor Strasser. This failed and in fact alienated the industrialists, who were suspicious of his dealings with the unions.

Papen now took the initiative against Schleicher, seeking revenge for his early removal from power. He was now convinced that Hitler must be included in a coalition conservative–nationalist government and that, if necessary, Hitler would have to be Chancellor in order to achieve this. He was not alone in believing that as long as there were only a couple of other Nazis in the Cabinet, the Nazis could be controlled.

Finally, after a series of meetings, Hitler was offered the Chancellorship of Germany by a reluctant President Hindenburg.

As Ian Kershaw (2000) writes:

> Few… had Hitler as their first choice. But by January 1933, with other options apparently exhausted, most, with the big landowners to the fore, were prepared to entertain a Hitler government. Had they opposed it, a Hitler chancellorship would have been inconceivable. Hitler needed the elite to attain power. But by January 1933, they in turn needed Hitler as he alone could deliver the mass support required to impose a tenable authoritarian solution to Germany's crisis of capitalism and crisis of the state.
> **Hitler. Routledge, p. 55.**

Activity 14

 ATL Thinking and communication skills

Why did the Weimar Republic fail?

Task One

Most essay questions on this period focus on the overall question of why the Republic established in 1919 was unable to survive. Before tackling a question on this, consider how each of the following contributed to the collapse of the Weimar Republic. Work in pairs to make notes on the impact of each of these areas; look back through this chapter and also at any comments by historians. Then rank these factors according to how important you think they were in causing the downfall of the Weimar Republic. You may want to add to your notes when you have read the views of historians in Task Three.

- the Weimar constitution
- the political parties of the Republic
- the mindset of many Germans regarding Republicanism
- the Treaty of Versailles
- the Wall Street Crash
- the appeal of Nazism
- the skill of Hitler
- President Hindenburg
- the growth in support for the Communists after 1929.

Task Two

Discuss in pairs the *strengths* of the Weimar Republic.

Task Three

Identify the key points made in each of the following extracts regarding the collapse of the Weimar Republic. How far do you agree with each one?

Source A

Democracy was not strengthened by the performance of the political parties. … The traditional right – the DNVP – maintained a consistent hostility to the Republic and eventually welcomed its demise. Indeed, in collaborating openly with Hitler's NSDAP they actually accelerated the process. The more moderate Centre Party did manage to keep a respectable level of support from the Catholic population, but it lurched to the right under the leadership of Brüning and also assisted in the re-election of Hindenburg as president in 1932. It was certainly no defender of parliamentary democracy.

Stephen Lee (2008). *The European Dictatorships.* **Routledge, p. 148.**

Source B

[T]he real significance of [the 1923] inflation was that any future economic crisis would be bound to have a doubly serious impact. Hence from 1929 the Depression radicalized sections of the population which inflation had already rendered unstable, turning them either to the extreme right or to the far left. It also destroyed any possibility of political consensus and… returned Germany to the practice of authoritarian government.

Stephen Lee (2008). *The European Dictatorships.* **Routledge, p. 150.**

Source C

In the years before 1945, and indeed in some respects beyond this, the fatal successes of Imperial Germany's ruling elites, assisted by older historical traditions and new experiences, continued to exert an influence. In the widespread susceptibility towards authoritarian policies, the hostility towards democracy in education and political life, in the continuing influence of the pre-industrial ruling elites, there begins a long inventory of serious historical problems. A knowledge of the history of the German Empire between 1871 and 1918 remains absolutely indispensable for an understanding of German history over the last decades.

German historian Hans-Ulrich Wehler (1985). *The German Empire 1871–1918.* **Berg Publishers, p. 246.**

Essay planning

Work in pairs to plan out these essays:

Examine the reasons for the collapse of the Weimar Republic.

There are clearly many factors that you can choose to give as reasons for the collapse of the Weimar Republic in this essay, so an important part of your planning will be to identify about four key ones that you can analyse. It is better to choose fewer reasons that you can analyse in depth rather than just a list of many factors which you can only talk about briefly. Remember to stay focused on the question. So for each factor that you choose, ensure that you explain *how it contributed to the collapse* of the Weimar Republic. You may also want to decide which factor/s you think is/are most important and set this out in your introduction.

Discuss the reasons for Hitler's rise to power, 1929 to 1933.

The dates are key in this essay. You need to focus on the period from 1929 to 1933. Longer-term structural problems of the Weimar Republic may be relevant, but focus on the impact that these had after 1929.

Key for this essay will be:

- the economic crisis following the Wall Street Crash, the failure of the Weimar governments to deal with this and the impact it had on ordinary people;
- the rise of extremism as a result of the economic crisis;
- the appeal of the Nazi party after 1929;
- the political intrigues of 1932–33.

Hints for success

Look back at the last essay frame to remind yourself about how to write focused opening sentences for each paragraph.

▶▶▶ Historians' perspectives

Historians differ in their interpretations on what caused the collapse of the Weimar Republic. While some argue that the circumstances of its 'birth' were so dire that it was doomed from the start, others believe that the Republic was gaining in popularity during the 1920s and that it was the economic crash of 1929 that caused its downfall. Still others have looked for long-term trends in German history that led towards Hitler's dictatorship or have focused on the factors of chance, such as the intrigue of the Weimar Republic's last months.

02

Hitler's Germany: 1933–1939

Hitler's consolidation of power

Key concepts: *Causation and significance*

> The crisis of Weimar had gone so deep that Hitler only had to touch the remaining structures for them to fall apart.
>
> **Ian Kershaw (2000).** *Hitler.* **Routledge, p. 118.**

When Hitler became Chancellor in January 1933, there was no indication that he would soon be in a position of unassailable power. The Nazis only held three cabinet posts out of 12, they did not have a majority in the Reichstag and Hitler's post was still dependent on Hindenburg, who could easily sack him. Papen, who was Vice Chancellor, believed that the real decisions would be taken by the remaining members of the cabinet, who were all part of the old aristocratic elite. Nevertheless, Hitler was still leader of the largest political party in Germany and, significantly, the Nazis had control over the Prussian Ministry of the Interior under Göring, which gave them extensive powers over the law and order of two-thirds of Germany. Hitler's speech below indicates the speed at which he started using the resources at his disposal to strengthen his position.

After only two months, Hitler was well on the way to establishing a Nazi dictatorship; after 18 months this process was complete.

Essay questions:

- To what extent was Hitler's consolidation of power the result of legal methods?

- Examine the significance of the Night of the Long Knives in Hitler's consolidation of power.

- Evaluate the successes of Hitler's social and religious policies in transforming German society.

- To what extent had Hitler solved Germany's economic problems by 1939?

- To what extent was Nazi economic success the reason for the lack of opposition to Hitler's policies in the years 1933 to 1939?

- Discuss the impact of Nazi policies on the Jewish population between 1933 and 1939.

Activity 1

 Thinking skills

1. With reference to the content and tone of this speech, identify the ways in which Hitler discredits the Weimar Republic.
2. How else does he seek to gain support from the German people in this speech?

> Over fourteen years have passed since the unhappy day when, dazzled by promises made by those at home and abroad, the German people forgot its most precious possessions, our past, the Empire, its honour and freedom, and thus lost everything. Since those days of betrayal the Almighty has withdrawn His blessing for our people. Discord and hatred came among us. With the deepest sorrow millions of the best German men and women from all walks of life saw the unity of the nation founder and disappear in a confusion of politically egotistical [selfish] opinions, economic interests and ideological conflicts. ... The breakdown of the unity of mind and will of our nation at home was followed by the collapse of its political position abroad. ... With an unparalleled effort of will and of brute force the Communist method of madness is trying as a last resort to poison and undermine an inwardly shaken and uprooted nation. ... Fourteen years of Marxism have undermined Germany. One year of Bolshevism would destroy Germany. ... It is an appalling inheritance which we are taking over. The task before us is the most difficult which has faced German statesmen in living memory. But we all have unbounded confidence, for we believe in our nation and in its eternal values. Farmers, workers, and the middle class must unite to contribute the bricks wherewith to build the new Reich.

Hitler's 'Appeal to the German People', which was broadcast on the radio on 31 January 1933, immediately after he had been made Chancellor.

Timeline of events – 1933–34

1933	30 Jan	Hitler becomes Chancellor of Germany
	1 Feb	New elections called
	27 Feb	Reichstag fire
	28 Feb	Decree for the Protection of the People and the State
	5 Mar	Nazis win 43.9 per cent of vote in elections
	6–7 Mar	State governments taken over
	8 Mar	First permanent concentration camp set up at Dachau
	13 Mar	Ministry for Public Enlightenment and Propaganda established
	24 Mar	Enabling Act
	31 Mar	First Law for the Coordination of the Federal States
	7 April	Law for the Restoration of the Civil Service
		Second Law for the Coordination of the Federal States
	22 June	SPD outlawed
	14 July	Law against the Formation of New Parties
	12 Nov	Reichstag elections; Nazis win 92 per cent of the vote
1934	30 June	Night of the Long Knives
	2 Aug	Death of Hindenburg; Hitler combines offices of President and Chancellor. Army swears oath of allegiance
	19 Aug	Hitler takes title of *Führer*

The 'Legal Revolution', January–March 1933

The use of terror

As discussed in the previous chapter, the violence of the SA had already played a role in increasing support for the Nazi Party. Now, with the resources of the state at the party's disposal, Hitler was able to expand the activities of the SA and ensure that these gained legal authority. Gangs of the SA were able to attack the offices of trade unions and the KPD, to break up the meetings of the SPD and the KPD and to attack the homes of left-wing politicians. When the newspapers of the SPD and the Centre Party condemned these actions, they were banned. The first permanent **concentration camp** was established at Dachau in March 1933, and political prisoners were sent there and to around 70 other temporary camps. By the end of 1933, over 100,000 potential opponents had been arrested.

The Reichstag election, 5 March 1933

Within 24 hours of his appointment as Chancellor, Hitler had called new Reichstag elections believing that a new election would increase the Nazi vote and strengthen his own position. The election campaign gave the opportunity for an increase in terror by the SA; altogether 69 people died during the five-week campaign.

In this atmosphere of terror and repression, the Nazi Party continued to promote itself as the party that was combating the violence rather than creating it; the situation was blamed on the economic conditions and KPD terrorism.

A key moment of this campaign came with the burning down of the Reichstag building on 27 February. A Dutch Communist called Marinus van der Lubbe was arrested and charged with causing the fire. It has been widely assumed that the Nazis set der Lubbe up

Concentration camps

The first concentration or prison camp was set up in Dachau in 1933 and the first prisoners were political. However the camps were soon full of those who the Nazis saw as '*asocials*' and '*racially undesirable*' – such as Jews, Roma and homosexuals. Prisoners were classified into different categories denoted by coloured triangles worn on their uniforms. They experienced torture, killings, hard labour and every conceivable indignity at the hands of the SS units, known as the Deaths Head Units (see page 32), who ran the camps and who had been specially trained by Himmler. One camp commandant shouted to all new arrivals: '*Forget your wives, children and families, here you will die like dogs*'. Meanwhile, the gates of all camps were inscribed with the euphemistic slogan of '*Arbeit macht frei*' ('Work liberates').

to carry out the crime in order to be able to blame the Communists; however, no definitive evidence has actually emerged to prove this. Nevertheless, the incident certainly benefited the Nazis; they were able to claim that this was the onset of a Communist plot to start a revolution in Germany. Large numbers of Communists were arrested and, via the Decree for the Protection of People and State, most civil and political liberties were suspended. The decree was supposed to be temporary but in fact it remained in force until 1945.

What is the message of these election statistics for March 1933 regarding support for the Nazis?

Party	Left		Centre		Right		
	KPD	SPD	State Party	Centre Party	DVP	DNVP	NSDAP (Nazis)
Number of seats	81	120	5	73	2	52	288
% of vote	12.3	18.25	0.85	11.25	1.1	8.0	43.9

The election result saw the Nazis increase their vote from 33.1 per cent to 43.9 per cent, thereby gaining 288 seats in the Reichstag. However it is significant that, even with the intimidation and terror that accompanied the election campaign, they still failed to win the support of even half of the electorate, and could only claim a majority in the Reichstag with the help of the 52 seats won by the DNVP.

The Enabling Act, March 1933

Hitler decided to introduce the Enabling Act, which would allow him to make laws without the approval of the Reichstag, and without reference to the president, for a period of four years. However, as this was a change in the constitution, it needed a two-thirds majority to get it passed. The Communist Party delegates had already been excluded following the Reichstag fire and Hitler had the support of the DNVP. He just needed the support of the Centre Party, and this he secured by giving them the reassurance that he would not use his powers without first consulting the president. Only the SPD voted against the Enabling Act. Thus Hitler now had full executive and legislative powers.

1. Read through Sources A to C. In what ways did the Decree for the Protection of People and State (Source A) and the Enabling Act (Source C) undermine the Weimar Constitution?

2. How does Hitler justify the Enabling Act in Source B?

Source A

Decree for the Protection of People and State, 27 February 1933.

> *On the basis of Article 48, Section 2, of the German Constitution, the following is decreed as a defensive measure against Communist acts of violence that endanger the state:*
>
> *1*
>
> *Articles 114, 115, 117, 118, 123, 124, and 153 of the Constitution of the German Reich are suspended until further notice. Thus, restrictions on personal liberty, on the right of free expression of opinion, including freedom of the press, on the right of assembly and the right of association, violations of the privacy of postal, telegraphic and telephonic communications, and warrants for house searches, orders for confiscations as well as restrictions on property are permissible beyond the legal limits otherwise prescribed.*
>
> *2*
>
> *If any state fails to take the necessary measures to restore public safety and order, the Reich government may temporarily take over the powers of the highest state authority.*

Source B

A speech by Hitler given in the Sports Palace, March 1933.

66 For fourteen years the parties of disintegration, of the November Revolution, have seduced and abused the German people. For fourteen years they wreaked destruction, infiltration, and dissolution. Considering this, it is not presumptuous of me to stand before the nation today, and plead to it: German people, give us four years' time and then pass judgement upon us. German people, give us four years, and I swear to you, just as we, just as I have taken this office, so shall I leave it. I have done it neither for salary nor for wages; I have done it for your sake!

Quoted in Richard Evans (2004). *The Coming of the Third Reich*. Penguin Books, p. 324.

Source C

The Enabling Act, 24 March 1933.

66 Article 1. National laws can be enacted by the Reich Cabinet as well as in accordance with the procedure established in the Constitution.

Article 2. The national laws enacted by the Reich Cabinet may deviate from the Constitution as long as they do not affect the position of the Reichstag and the Reichsrat. The powers of the President remain undisturbed.

Article 3. The national laws enacted by the Reich Cabinet shall be prepared by the Chancellor and published in the Reichsgesetzblatt. They come into effect, unless otherwise specified, the day after their publication. Articles 68–77 of the Constitution do not apply to the laws enacted by the Reich Cabinet.

The consolidation of power, March 1933 to August 1934

The Enabling Act provided the basis for Hitler's dictatorship, which was established between March 1933 and August 1934. The process by which Hitler gained control was known as *Gleichschaltung* (coordination). It involved taking over or 'coordinating' as many aspects of German life as possible along Nazi lines so that the government had control of all key aspects of society. The priority in this process was to secure political supremacy, which meant that the first moves were made against the federal states, the political parties, the independent trade unions and the civil service. He then went on to deal with activists within his own party.

The federal states

There was a tradition of independence among the various states of Germany. Indeed, the Weimar constitution had agreed on a federal structure with 17 *Länder* (states) in which a large number of powers were devolved to regional governments. For Hitler, who wanted a strong unified Germany, this situation had to change. Thus, several laws were passed to centralize power:

- 31 March 1933: a law dissolved the regional parliaments and replaced them with Nazi dominated assemblies.
- 7 April 1933: Reich Governors were created to oversee the government of each state.
- 30 January 1934: regional parliaments were abolished; all state governments were formally subordinated to the central government.

The Nazi Party now used Nazi leaders called *Gauleiters* to control local government.

Political parties

Hitler's aim was a one-party state; political parties clearly could not be allowed to continue. In the course of the spring and summer of 1933 these were either outlawed or they dissolved themselves:

- The power of the Communists had effectively been destroyed since the Reichstag fire.
- The Social Democrats had been subjected to increasing repression and attacks by the SA since January 1933 and were officially banned on 22 June; following the attack on trade unionists, brutal acts of repression were carried out against Social Democrats all over Germany.
- The other major parties then agreed to dissolve themselves in late June.
- The Catholic Centre Party followed on 5 July.

The 'Law against the Formation of New Parties', 14 July 1933, formally established a one-party state. The sole function of the Reichstag was now just to approve the decisions of the Nazi government.

Activity 4　　　　　　　　　　　　　　　　 Thinking skills

In pairs, discuss the extent to which you agree with historian Klaus Fischer's verdict that, *'it is both amazing and appalling how meekly the German parties surrendered to Hitler's tyranny'* (1995. *Nazi Germany*. Constable, p. 280).

The trade unions

Hitler's policy of *Gleichschaltung* also meant that powerful rival organizations had to be eliminated. On 1 May, which socialists had already designated as International Workers' Day, the Nazis declared a national holiday, thus giving the impression to workers that they were prepared to accept and cooperate with the trade unions. However, the Nazis used the holiday to occupy trade union premises, confiscate funds and arrest leaders, destroying almost overnight the previously powerful German trade union movement. In the place of independent trade unions, the German Labour Front (DAF) was set up under Robert Ley, claiming to represent the interests of all Germany's workers (see page 49). However, this was more of an instrument of control, and rights such as negotiating wages and conditions of work were removed.

The civil service

As discussed in the previous chapter, the civil service had remained a conservative force within the Weimar government and it had opposed the more liberal, democratic ideas of the Republic. Many thus welcomed the arrival of the Nazis, seeing this as a return to the authoritarian rule of the Kaiser. However, the Nazis had no intention of being constrained by civil service officials. Many local officials were replaced by Nazi officials, and Nazi Party officials were placed in government offices to ensure that the others followed Nazi orders. The success of *Gleischchaltung* within the legal system can be seen by the oath taken at a mass meeting held in front of the Supreme Court building in Leipzig in October 1933; 10,000 lawyers gave the Nazi salute and publicly swore to *'strive as German jurists to follow the course of our Führer to the end of our days'*.

The Church

Nazi ideology posed fundamental challenges to the beliefs of Christianity. However, initially Hitler attempted to win over the support of the Protestant and Catholic Churches by indicating that they could be accommodated within the Nazi state. Key in this process was the Concordat that was signed between the papacy and the regime and which was an attempt to safeguard the position of the Catholic Church under the Nazis. In this agreement the Nazis guaranteed the Catholic Church religious freedom and full control over its own education and its property and legal rights. The papacy in return said that it would not interfere in politics and would give diplomatic recognition to the Nazi government.

The Nazi government had no intention of keeping to this agreement; however, it served the purpose of reassuring the Church while the dictatorship was being established.

Activity 5

1. Read the views of the historians in the two sources below and make a list of the factors that each one identifies for explaining Hitler's success by the end of 1933.
2. What other factors could you add to this list?

Source A

> By mid 1933, the 'organisational space' which any effective political opposition needs had been removed. Despite Nazi myths of a 'legal' revolution this had been done with a level of force, repression and brutality which had far exceeded the measures undertaken in consolidating Mussolini's rule in fascist Italy. The violence had destroyed the Left, and had impressed the ruthlessness of the new regime on the rest of society.
>
> **Ian Kershaw (2000). Hitler. Routledge, p. 71.**

Source B

> Why did the opposition give up? The most obvious reason is that it had no choice. The parties of the left were smashed by the government's emergency powers. The Communists, for example, were prevented from taking their seats in the Reichstag, and the SPD were banned outright in June. The Centre Party gave up any pretence of political opposition in return for a guarantee of religious freedom, and actually liquidated itself voluntarily. Even the DNVP was unable to keep itself afloat as its leaders found it increasingly obvious that they no longer had any hold on the political monster they had helped create. President Hindenburg, no admirer of the party system, made no attempt to interfere with Hitler's assault on the opposition, for fear of provoking a more violent and radical constitutional upheaval. But the middle of 1933 the only remaining obstacle between Hitler and total power was the German army.
>
> **Stephen Lee (2008). The European Dictatorships. Routledge, p. 160.**

The SA and the Night of the Long Knives

What is the message of this poster?

Photomontage by John Heartfield, published in Prague, 19 July 1934.

Hitler was increasingly concerned with the activities of the SA, who were determined to continue the process of *Gleichschaltung* from below. Hitler had supported and encouraged the actions of the SA during the process of gaining power and during the first half of 1933, when they played a key role in eliminating opposition. However, by July 1933 he was concerned that he could no longer control the activities of the SA, which had become a rather large, unruly organization. Maintaining control was essential if he was to keep the support of the conservative forces whose backing he still needed. He thus declared that the Nazi revolution was over and that the process of *Gleichschaltung* had been completed. For Ernst Röhm, the leader of the SA, however, this was most certainly not the case. He believed that it was time for a '*Second Revolution*'. Why was this?

The SA represented the more radical wing of the party. Its membership was drawn largely from the working class. It put more emphasis on the socialist elements of the Nazi Party programme and, unlike Hitler, was not concerned with upsetting the powerful conservative elites in German society, such as the industrialists. Having played such a key role in the Nazi rise to power, they had an expectation that they would gain more directly from the Nazi rule. Röhm also wanted to create a 'people's army', merging the SA with the German army. This last point meant that the SA was a threat to the army whose support Hitler needed if he was to attain his ultimate objective of military expansion and conquest.

Activity 7   (ATL) Thinking and communication skills

Read this extract – which is Ernst Röhm's viewpoint, taken from a conversation that he had with friends – and then answer the questions below:

> Adolf is rotten. He's betraying all of us. He only goes around with reactionaries. His old comrades aren't good enough for him. So he brings in these East Prussian generals. They're the ones he pals around with now. … Adolf knows perfectly well what I want. I've told him often enough. Not a second pot of the Kaiser's army, made with the same old grounds. Are we a revolution or aren't we? … Something new has to be brought in, understand? A new discipline. A new principle of organisation. … [we have] the chance to do something really new and great, something that will turn the world upside down – it's a chance in a lifetime, but Hitler keeps putting me off.
>
> **Quoted in Klaus Fischer (1995).** *Nazi Germany.* **Constable, p. 286.**

Work in pairs. Refer back to the 25-point programme of the Nazi Party on page 29, in the previous chapter.

1. Which of these points would Röhm have wanted to see implemented?
2. Why did Hitler no longer want to follow through with such aims?

When Röhm's opponents fabricated evidence of an SA plot against the government, Hitler instigated the Night of the Long Knives. On 30 June 1934, Röhm and other key members of the SA were murdered by the loyal SS. It was also the chance to settle old scores; Schleicher and Strasser, who had both plotted against Hitler in 1932, were killed; Papen was put under house arrest. The results of this coup are summarized below by the historians Ian Kershaw and Laurence Rees.

Activity 8 (ATL) Thinking skills

Source A

> The bloody repression of part of his own Movement was a critical moment in the consolidation of Hitler's power. In the first instance it removed the one force within the regime potentially capable of offering serious opposition from within or, more likely, of prompting opposition from other sources (especially the army) which could have toppled Hitler. After 30 June 1934, the SA amounted to no more than a useful but wholly loyal activist agency which… expended its violent energies in attacks on helpless minorities rather than tackling the wielders of state power. From the SA's loss of power, the main profit went to the SS – Hitler's pretorian guard, and unlike his mass army, an utterly loyal force. The power shift within the regime had, in other words, notably enhanced Hitler's own position.
>
> This was further consolidated in that the elimination of the detested and troublesome SA leadership bound the conservative power-groups more tightly to Hitler, and to the concept of the 'Führer state'. The mutual dependence of the traditional elites and the Nazi leader was reinforced.
>
> **Ian Kershaw (2000),** *Hitler.* **Routledge, p. 73.**

Source B

> The Night of the Long Knives was a breathtaking example of the total breakdown of the rule of law in Germany. None of those who suffered was tried in court. None of the alleged evidence against them was tested. None of them was given a chance to speak in their own defence. And yet Hitler's decision to order the murder of so many of his old comrades was widely welcomed. General Blomberg, in a statement on 1 July, said, 'The Führer with military decision and outstanding courage has himself attacked and destroyed the traitors and murderers'. … It was the most telling example yet of a paradox at the heart of Hitler's rule. Many people were frightened of the violence that abounded in German society – perpetrated both by the Communists and the SA. The majority longed for peace and stability. Now Hitler appeared to be about to deliver that peace and stability – but only by the use of more violence. Thus many who decried violence came to support it – even welcome it.

Because of his control of the media, Hitler was able to spin the events of 30 June 1934 in a way that was extremely advantageous for him. The fact that he had acted against elements of the Nazi Party enabled him to position himself as the proctector of all Germany, rather than the protector of just his own narrow self-interests.

Laurence Rees (2012). *The Dark Charisma of Adolf Hitler.* **Ebury Press, pp. 126–27.**

1. How, according to Sources A and B, did the Night of the Long Knives help to consolidate Hitler's power?

2. What factors allowed him to come out so completely unscathed from this act of violence?

When Hindenburg died on 2 August, there was no opposition when Hitler merged the offices of Chancellor and President, taking the title of *Führer* (leader). The army aligned themselves behind Hitler and agreed to take a personal oath of loyalty: '*I swear before God to give my unconditional obedience to Adolf Hitler, Führer of the Reich and of the German People, Supreme Commander and will be ready as a brave soldier to risk my life at any time for this oath.*' As Fischer writes, this secured '*the unlimited nature of Hitler's dictatorship*'.

Activity 9 Thinking and communication skills

In pairs, go back over pages 38 to 42 and discuss how each of the following factors contributed to Hitler's consolidation of power. Find evidence to support each factor and consider which one/s were the most important:

- terror and intimidation
- use of the law
- propaganda
- support from conservative forces
- weakness of opposition.

Essay planning

To what extent was Hitler's consolidation of power between 1933 and 1939 the result of legal methods?

Command term: To what extent

Topic: Hitler's consolidation of power

Concept: Causation

There is a temptation in this essay to write a chronological narrative of the key events that led to Hitler's consolidation of power. However, as you know, this approach will keep in you Levels 1 and 2 of the mark scheme! Make sure you base your paragraphs around the themes identified in the activity above.

Intro: Show your understanding of the relevance of the dates given in the question.

Identify the key themes around which you will structure your essay, and set out your key argument, i.e. which of these factors, other than legal methods, you think are the most important in allowing Hitler to consolidate his power.

Here are some possible paragraph headings. Decide what evidence you could give to support each point. Look back also at the views of the different historians included so far in this chapter; could you incorporate any of these views into your paragraphs?

Paragraph 1: Start with the theme identified in the question.

There is no doubt that Hitler was able to consolidate power by using legal methods. One of his first actions was to pass the Enabling Law...

Paragraph 2: *However, the Nazis combined legality with the use of violence, intimidation and terror...*

Paragraph 3: *Hitler was helped in his consolidation of power by the continued support of the traditional elites...*

Paragraph 4: *Hitler's success in getting rid of opposition was also key...*

The opposition groups also failed to take action because...

Paragraph 5: Are there any other factors that you consider important for explaining Hitler's consolidation of power?

Conclusion: Based on the weight of your evidence in the main body of your essay, answer the question directly. Were legal methods the most important or has your essay proved that other factors were equally or more important?

 For top markbands for Paper 3 essays:

Introduction and main body paragraphs

Responses are clearly focused.

The question is fully addressed and implications are considered.

The essay is well structured and the material effectively organized.

Supporting knowledge is detailed, accurate, relevant to the question and used to support arguments.

Arguments are clear, well developed and consistently supported with evidence.

There is evaluation of different perspectives.

Conclusion

The conclusion is clearly stated and it is consistent with the evidence presented.

The domestic policies of Nazi Germany

Timeline of events – 1933–39		
1933	30 Jan	Hitler becomes Chancellor of Germany
	1 April	National boycott of Jewish shops and businesses
	7 April	Civil service law permits removal of Jews and other opponents
	June	Marriage Loan scheme is introduced
	July	Law for Prevention of Hereditarily Diseased Offspring
		The SA are ordered to attend church services
		The Catholic Church and the government sign a concordat
1934		A protest Confessional Church breaks away from the state-supported Reich Church
	Sept	New Plan to control imports
	Oct	German Labour Front (DAF) replaces trade unions
1935	Sept	Nuremberg Laws
1936	April	Professional activities of Jews banned or restricted
	July–Aug	Olympic Games held in Berlin; anti-Jewish campaign temporarily halted
	Oct	Announcement of Four Year Plan
1938	Mar	Jews have to register their possessions
	July	Jews have to carry identity cards; Jewish doctors, dentists, lawyers forbidden to treat Aryans
	Aug	Jewish men have to take 'Israel' as a middle name and women have to take 'Sarah'
	Oct	Jews have 'J' stamped in passport
	Nov	Kristallnacht
		Jews excluded from schools and universities
1939		Start of plan to kill physically and mentally handicapped patients
	Jan	Reich Office for Jewish Emigration established
	April	Jews forced into ghettos

Nazi social policies: did the Nazis bring about a social revolution in Germany?

Key concepts: *Change and consequence*

> *Our age is once more acquiring creative momentum, it is gaining depth, direction and future. The creative dynamic, the basic quality of the Germanic-Western cultural soul is awakening in the dawn of its fourth day of creation in a new type of human being.*
>
> **A Nazi supporter.**

One of Hitler's key aims was to create a **Volksgemeinschaft** or people's community. This was partly based on an idealized past in which individuals were self-disciplined and put community before themselves. In the new Nazi community, Germans would be reunited through their blood, race and ideology and their loyalty to the German nation and its leader. In order to achieve this goal, the Nazis used blatant propaganda and indoctrination; however, they also attempted to reorganize society and the everyday experience of German people.

How far did German youth conform to Nazi ideals?

> *The Jews are aliens in Germany. In 1933 there were 66,060,000 inhabitants of the German Reich of whom 499,862 were Jews. What is the percentage of Jews in Germany?*
>
> **A mathematics problem from a school textbook.**

The starting point for inculcating German people with the skills and values needed for the *Volksgemeinschaft* was Germany's youth, who could be indoctrinated via education in schools and through the Hitler Youth movement

Within education, teachers were brought under the control of the Nazis. Anyone considered to be unreliable on political or racial grounds was dismissed and teachers were pressured into joining the National Socialist Teachers' League (NSLB). Meanwhile, the curriculum was controlled by the Ministry of Education to ensure that all aspects of a child's education were focused on the Nazi aim of producing *'politically-conscious people who sacrifice and serve with every thought and deed, who are rooted in the nation, and who are totally and indivisibly anchored to the history and destiny of its state'* (Wilhelm Frick, minister of the interior). This involved the following:

- the introduction of new areas of study such as racial sciences. This included studying the differences between races and the concept of evolution and the 'survival of the fittest';
- teaching traditional subjects to emphasize German superiority. For example, geography was used to develop the concept of *Lebensraum* (see page 30 in Chapter 1) and German racial superiority. In mathematics, students were given problems that promoted Nazi views on issues such as the inferiority of Jews (see quote at the start of this section) or the wastefulness of resources being spent on those with mental problems. In history, the emphasis was on war and the heroic actions of German soldiers as well as the betrayal of Germany at the end of the First World War and the evils of the Treaty of Versailles;
- devoting a large part of the curriculum to physical education to ensure that boys developed both fitness and aggression for future military service. For girls there was also an emphasis on physical education to ensure that they could fulfil their roles as healthy wives and mothers of workers and soldiers;
- putting emphasis on community service through various work schemes. This helped to encourage a sense of community as well as providing a source of cheap labour.

The Hitler Youth

The propaganda in schools was reinforced during activities in the Hitler Youth. By 1936, all youth organizations had been banned or taken over by the *Hitler Jugend* (Hitler Youth) for boys and the *Bund Deutscher Mädel* (League of German Girls). The aim of the Hitler Youth movement was to educate children *'physically, intellectually and morally in the spirit of National Socialism to serve the nation and the community'*. All members had to take an oath of loyalty to Hitler and activities included military drills for boys as well as sports and camping trips away from home.

Such opportunities provided new freedoms for many children as well as genuine feelings of comradeship and community, and were thus greeted with enthusiasm. By the late 1930s, however, there were signs that the Hitler Youth movement was losing its popularity; indeed, it seems that many young people conformed to avoid sanctions, while others developed their own youth subcultures; these consisted of local 'pirate' groups in the cities, and 'swing' groups who enjoyed dancing and music – in particular US swing music.

Activity 10 **ATL** Research and communication skills

Work in pairs or groups to investigate more about the young people in Nazi Germany and the impact of Nazi policies.

Task One

Find examples of activities for both the Hitler Youth and the League of German Girls. Also, find first-hand accounts from German children about the youth movements. Try to find both negative and positive accounts.

Task Two

Research the youth movements that challenged the Nazi drive for youth conformity. The most famous of these include:

- the Edelweiss Pirates
- the Swing movement
- the White Rose movement.

For each group, research its membership, its aims and its activities, and the reaction of the Nazi regime.

Task Three

What are your conclusions as to the success of the Nazi regime in indoctrinating the youth of Germany?

How did Nazis change the position of women in society?

> … *her world is her husband, her family, her children and her home.* … *We do not consider it correct for the woman to interfere in the world of the man*…
>
> **Hitler, 1934.**

Activity 11 **ATL** Thinking skills

1. What is the message of the poster in the left-hand margin regarding the roles of men and women in Nazi Germany?
2. What other messages does this poster convey about Nazi beliefs concerning the ideal German society that needed to be created/restored?

Under Weimar, women had enjoyed considerable political emancipation, education and employment opportunities. By 1933, women made up one-tenth of the members of the Reichstag; there were also 100,000 women working as teachers and 3,000 working as doctors. However, while Hitler stressed that women were very important to society, this importance lay in their roles as mothers and wives .Women were to be devoted to the three K's: *Kinder, Küche, Kirche* (children, kitchen, Church). This meant reversing any trends towards emancipation made during the Weimar era. Opportunities in education were reduced and they were barred from key professions.

A key priority for the Nazi regime was to raise the birth rate, which had dropped during the 1920s. This was essential if it was to expand German territory and populate these new lands with pure Germans. Thus various incentives were set up to encourage women to give up work and to have more children. Marriage loans were made to couples (with suitably **Aryan** characteristics) if wives stopped working after marriage; for each child born, the amount of the loan that had to be repaid was reduced by a quarter. Family allowances were increased dramatically and women who had four or more children received medals. In addition, birth control was discouraged and abortions were prohibited.

A Nazi poster. The caption at the bottom reads, '*A nation helps itself!*'

Aryan

The Nazis believed in a hierarchy of races. Hitler used the term 'Aryan' to describe what he considered to be the most superior and most 'pure' race on earth. The ideal Aryan was strong and lean and had pale skin, blond hair and blue eyes.

Research Nazi expectations for women with regard to fashion, lifestyle and their role in society. What methods were used by the regime to try to get women to follow these expectations?

How successful were Nazi policies towards women?

Germany's birth rate did increase in the 1930s; however, it still remained lower than it had been in the early 1920s. Meanwhile, the impact of economic recovery and rapid rearmament meant that there was a labour shortage. This had the effect of bringing more women into industrial employment; indeed, there were more women working in 1939 than there had been in 1933. However, highly qualified women never regained their former status and jobs.

How successful were Nazi policies towards workers?

The working class was the largest social group in German society. Given their previously strong attachment to trade unions (which had been abolished in 1933) and left-wing parties, it was an important challenge for the Nazi regime to get them to accept the *Volksgemeinschaft*.

The aim of the German Labour Front (*Deutsche Arbeitsfront* DAF), which was established in place of the trade unions, was not to fight for workers' rights or pay; its aim was to control workers and increase production, and also to win workers over to Nazism. Key to this last aim was the establishment by the DAF in November 1933 of two organizations. The first of these, the Beauty of Work (*Schönheit der Arbeit* or SdA) focused on providing good meals and new bathrooms, and making work areas more pleasant. Such changes allowed the DAF to show that workers were fit, happy and healthy and thus satisfied with the government and their work.

The second organization, '**Strength through Joy**' (*Kraft durch Freude* or KdF) improved workers' leisure activities by providing subsidized activities such as holidays, theatre and cinema visits with the aim that workers would '*gain strength for their work by experiencing joy in their leisure*'. However, by ensuring that workers would have both work and leisure time organized, Strength through Joy also ensured that workers had no time to involve themselves in anti-State activities. The belief was that if they were fully involved in community activities, they would increasingly come to see themselves as part of the *Volksgemeinschaft*. Nevertheless, Mary Fulbrook writes, '*Although many workers were prepared somewhat cynically to enjoy any holidays or outings offered to them by organizations such as Strength through Joy, few really swallowed much of the propaganda about the "harmonious factory community" and the like*'.

> **The reality of Strength through Joy.**
>
> One of the programmes set up by Strength through Joy was a scheme for workers to purchase a Volkswagen (or 'People's Car'). Workers made payments towards buying the car; however, none of them ever received one as the factories that were supposed to produce the Volkswagen were turned over to war work in the late 1930s. Only the military staff received the Volkswagens that had been built; workers' payments went towards the cost of the war.

How far did the Nazis integrate the Churches into the
Volksgemeinschaft?

Activity 13   (ATL) Thinking skills

John Heartfield, 'On the founding of the State Church' (June 1933). The caption reads: *'The cross was not heavy enough.'*

What is the message of this poster?

This issue provided a serious challenge for the Nazis since the Germans were divided by faith. As mentioned on page 42, the Nazis had initially taken measures to reassure the Protestants, who represented the majority of the Germans, and they had guaranteed the independence of the Catholic Church by signing the Concordat in 1933. However, even by mid-1933, it was clear that the Nazis were going to interfere in religion.

The Nazi regime gave support to a growing movement among Protestants that was known as the German Christians (*Deutsch Christen*). This movement believed that it was possible to reconcile Protestant and Nazi beliefs and it established a new Reich Church with the aim of combining all Protestants within one structure. Ludwig Müller was the first Reich Bishop; he abolished all elected bodies within the Church and reorganized it on the '*leadership principle*'. However, the actions of the German Christians created much opposition. In September 1933, over 100 pastors created the Confessional Church, which upheld orthodox Protestantism and rejected any attempt to link it to Nazi beliefs. This Church was led by Pastor Niemöller and it had the support of about 7,000 pastors out of 17,000.

By 1935, it was clear that the Nazis had achieved only limited success in gaining control over the Church. It was still difficult for the Nazis to attack the Churches head on, for fear of alienating large numbers of Germans; thus a war of attrition developed. The Ministry of Church Affairs, established in 1935 and led by Hanns Kerrl, now attempted to undermine both the Protestant and Catholic Churches through a series of anti-religious measures. These included discrediting church leaders by accusing them of crimes such as sexual abuse and financial misbehaviour, and reducing the Churches' influence over young people by closing church schools and youth groups. Less emphasis was put on religion in schools and in the mid-1930s the Nazi Party launched a 'Church Secession Campaign' to encourage Germans to abandon their churches.

However, the Nazis were not successful in coordinating the inclusion of the Churches in the *Volksgemeinschaft*. The German Faith movement was a failure, gaining only very limited support. The Confessional Church survived, and individual church leaders continued to speak out against Nazism; Niemöller was very outspoken (and as a result was put into a concentration camp in 1937) and Pope Pius XI attacked the Nazi system in 1937 and also spoke out against the euthanasia programme in 1940. This made it very difficult for the Nazis to launch an outright attack on religion. However, the Churches also failed to provide effective opposition and they refrained from a sustained attack on the Nazi regime.

Activity 14    Thinking skills

Read the source below. What reason does this historian give to explain the limited resistance of the Churches to Nazism?

> The churches' opposition was 'issue driven' (that is to say involving piecemeal reactions to individual, concrete actions such as the withdrawal of crucifixes form schools, the appointment of a German Christian as Reich bishop, or euthanasia) rather than rooted in a coherent, politically active anti-Nazi morality. The churches and their followers generally were more interested in defending their religious 'space' and surviving attack than in becoming society's moral guardians. They wanted to write themselves into the overall trajectory of the Third Reich rather than alter its direction per se.
>
> **Martyn Housden (1996). *Resistance and Conformity in the Third Reich*. Routledge, p. 64.**

Which groups were not included in the *Volksgemeinshaft*?

To be a member of the *Volksgemeinschaft* it was essential to be a '*true*' German, both in terms of loyalty and racial purity; the *Volksgemeinschaft* could not be contaminated by the '***Untermenschen***'. Such people included:

Asocials: These were people who did not follow the 'social norms' imposed by the Nazis and included beggars, criminals, prostitutes, and alcoholics. Between 1933 and 1938 such people were rounded up and sent to concentration camps.

Homosexuals: Homosexuals were regarded by the Nazis as degenerate and perverted, and a threat to the Nazi goal of increasing the population. Overall some 100,000 men were arrested for homosexuality, of whom about 50,000 were sent to concentration camps where they were treated particularly harshly. In addition, many were 'cured' by means of castration or were subjected to medical experiments.

The mentally ill or physically disabled: These people were regarded as a burden on society and a threat to the future of the Aryan race. Much of Nazi thinking was influenced by 'eugenicists' (see information box) who argued that a race could be

The Nazis, social Darwinism and eugenics

Nazi ideology was influenced by social Darwinism, an intellectual movement that developed in the 19th century. Social Darwinists applied basic principles from Charles Darwin's theory of evolution and the concepts of national selection and the *'survival of the fittest'* to society and politics. Thus the wealth and the power of the strong should be allowed to increase while that of the weak should decrease; in the case of Nazi ideology this meant that the Aryan race should be able to dominate the *'inferior'* races. Linked to this movement was the eugenics movement, which believed that society could be improved through the manipulation of its genetic makeup; in the case of the Nazis this meant first restricting and then eliminating those groups who were *'contaminating'* German society.

improved through selective breeding, which involved introducing measures such as birth control and sterilization of those with genetic disabilities. Thus, as early as 1933, sterilization was introduced for those with *'hereditary diseases'*. This led to over 400,000 people being sterilized. By 1939, however, this programme went a step further with the introduction of euthanasia for Germans who were mentally and physically disabled and who were thus an *'unproductive burden'*. The T4 programme, as it was known (due to its address in Berlin, Tiergarten 4), involved children with mental illnesses or physical deformities being sent to special hospitals where they were starved to death or given lethal injections; 5,000 innocent children were killed in this way. It was, however, halted in 1941 due to protests from the Catholic Church.

Religious sects: These were dealt with harshly. The Nazis were suspicious about their international links, and most were banned in November 1933. While some sects compromised with the Nazis in order to ensure their survival, the Jehovah's Witnesses were particularly hostile to the regime. As a result, many were arrested; about one-third of Germany's Jehovah's Witnesses died in concentration camps.

Racial enemies, in particular the Roma and Sinti, and the Jews: Following Himmler's 'Decree for the Struggle against the Gypsy Plague', Roma and Sinti were sent to camps, before being expelled to Poland when war broke out. They were sent to Auschwitz in December 1942 where 11,000 of the 20,000 Roma and Sinti were gassed.

The Jews were also subjected to increasing persecution from 1933; this is covered in full on pages 58–60.

A propaganda poster promoting the T4 euthanasia policy from the Office of Racial Policy's *Neues Volk* magazine. The wording says: *'This person suffering from hereditary defects costs the community 60,000 Reichsmark during his lifetime. Fellow German, that is your money, too.'*

How successful were the Nazis in changing society and in creating a *Volksgemeinschaft*?

As you have read in this section, the Nazis were not successful in winning over all Germans; quite often Germans conformed for reasons other than voluntarily wanting to become part of the *Volksgemeinschaft*.

Historians have mostly agreed that the *Volksgemeinschaft* ideal was not completely successful and that the Nazis failed to bring about any fundamental changes in society. Ian Kershaw (2015) writes:

 Some research… which paints an extremely complex picture of social behaviour and attitudes under Nazism, suggests strongly that it is easy to exaggerate the nature of changes in values and attitudes under Nazism and that here too there can be no suggestion of Nazism having effected a social revolution. … There was some penetration of Nazi values and attitudes [but] the regime's social propaganda made little serious dent in traditional class loyalties, particularly among older industrial workers. … The hold of the Church and clergy over the population, especially in country areas, was often strengthened rather than weakened by the 'Church struggle'. … Nazi policy failed categorically to break down religious allegiances. Even in their attempt to inculcate the German people with racial, eugenic, and social Darwinist values – the core of their ideology – the Nazis, it appears, had only limited success. Enhancement of existing prejudice against Jews and other racial minorities and 'social outsiders' unquestionably occurred… but… exposure to Nazi race values had come nowhere near completely eradicating conventional moral standards.

The Nazi Dictatorship. Bloomsbury Revelations, pp. 205–207.

Activity 15

ATL Self-management and communication skills

1. Create a mind map or other infographic to show the social policies used by the Nazi regime in their attempt to create a *Volksgemeinschaft*. Indicate on your diagram the groups that were targeted, which policies were successful and which were less successful or, indeed, a failure.
2. Which of these policies do you consider had the most radical impact on German society?
3. Which do you consider to be most successful and least successful in uniting Germans into a *Volksgemeinschaft*?

Essay planning

Evaluate the success of Hitler's social and religious policies in transforming German society.

Command term: Evaluate

Topic: Nazi social policies

Concept: Change

In this essay, make sure that you concentrate on the word 'evaluate'. It is not enough just to describe what Hitler did – you need to analyse the impact of his policies as you go through the essay.

Intro: Set out the aim of Hitler's policies in creating a *Volksgemeinschaft* and indicate the social policies to which you will refer. Set out your main argument regarding the success or failure of his policies.

Paragraphs: You may want to break down the social policies so that you have a paragraph each for women, youth and workers, in addition to a separate paragraph on religion. Within every paragraph focus on the extent to which the policies successfully transformed society – the ways in which radical change took place and the ways in which in fact there was little change overall.

Conclusion: Come back to the question and make sure you have a clear answer based on the evidence that you have provided.

How did the Nazi regime function?

Key concepts: *Change*

> The overall structure of the government was reduced to a shambles of constantly shifting power bases or warring factions.
>
> **Ian Kershaw (2015).** *The Nazi Dictatorship.* **Bloomsbury Revelations, p. 88.**

The role of Hitler

On the surface, it would seem that Hitler must have been an all-powerful dictator in control of all aspects of the Nazi state and indeed this was the image that was presented to the German people, as seen in the poster below. However, the reality was somewhat different. Hitler certainly provided the overall vision as to how Germany should be run, and as Kershaw writes, was '*the indispensable linchpin of the government*

▲
A German propaganda poster with the caption, '*One people, one empire, one leader*'.

apparatus', but he was surprisingly detached from the actual decision-making and from administrative matters. His work routine was rather haphazard, he rarely discussed detailed policy with his ministers and he spent much time away from Berlin, preferring to stay at his mountain retreat, the Berghof. From 1936, he grew increasingly focused on foreign policy.

The result of this was chaos, with ministers competing for power between themselves and decision-making often based on a conversation with the *Führer* rather than rational, clearly worked out policies. The historian Edward Peterson explains the confusion of the men working for him, who created:

> … *a literal anthill of aspiring and fearing people trying to please 'the great one' or escape his wrath or to avoid notice altogether; and never quite sure… what he wanted them to do after they had said 'Heil Hitler'… the result was the division of domination into thousands of little empires of ambitious men, domains that were largely unchecked by law [for this] had been replaced by Hitler's will, which was largely a mirage.*
>
> **Edward Peterson (2015).** *The Limits of Hitler's Power.* **Princeton University Press, pp. 432, 446.**

Two of the most powerful of these empires were led by Himmler, who was in charge of the police, and by Goebbels, who was in charge of propaganda.

However, while there was a certain level of chaos regarding the creation of policies, it is also clear that on issues that were important to Hitler, '*he pursued his aims with ruthlessness and appropriate brutality*' (Fulbrook). Thus, the polices of the regime became increasingly radicalized in line with Hitler's overall goals, as seen in policies towards the Jews.

Historians' perspectives

Historians such as Hans Mommsen, writing in the 1960s, argued that Hitler's lack of focus on the day-to-day running of events led to the key Nazis, such as Himmler and Göring, building up powerful personal empires. This meant that power was dispersed to several places and structures within Germany and this weakened Hitler's overall control. This is the **'structuralist'** interpretation.

However, Ian Kershaw has since argued that Hitler used the departmental infighting that developed between the 'empires' as a means of keeping control; Hitler remained the final arbiter in any dispute and thus the ultimate source of power. However powerful other groups or individuals became, it was still always Hitler's ideas that prevailed; for most of the time subordinates competed with each other to '*work towards the Führer*' (Kershaw). This view fits into the **'intentionalist'** interpretation (see Information box).

The police state: how was an atmosphere of fear created?

After 1933, there was no constitution in Germany. Hitler's word was law. There were no longer legal safeguards to protect individual citizens and judges were no longer an independent force; they were expected to make judgements in line with Nazi beliefs and aims. Individuals could be arrested and held without trial; new courts and police organizations were introduced to ensure that opponents to the regime were swiftly dealt with. In particular, the SS, with its secret police offshoot the Gestapo, became a powerful tool of control and of terror under Heinrich Himmler.

The SS

It was the SS that had carried out the Night of the Long Knives. Following this event, the role of the SS expanded. By 1936, it controlled the entire police system. It aimed to eliminate all enemies of the regime, whether political or racial, and was in charge of the concentration camps. It also established a vast economic empire.

Structuralist vs intentionalist?

This debate is a common one between historians. Those historians who argue that broader forces in a country, such as economic and political structures, have a powerful influence on the actions of individuals are known as structuralist historians. Others argue that individuals are more important in exercising an influence on historical development; these historians are known as intentionalists.

By 1939 there were 240,000 members organized into various divisions; the Death's Head formations administered the concentration camps and formed Panzer units; the Waffen SS was mainly a military organization.

Gordon Craig summarizes the significance of SS power:

> In the muddle of competing agencies that constituted the governmental system of the Third Reich, the SS was the effective instrument of domination. Unfettered by the normal restraints of law and accountable only to its commander, and beyond him the Führer himself, it exercised sovereign control over the lives and liberties of German citizens. … The knowledge of the enormities that the SS perpetrated daily, the knowledge that the camps were always waiting for new inmates, the knowledge that many who entered them were never heard of again was never absent from the minds of German citizens, and the fear that it induced was a potent force in maintaining their obedience to the dictatorship.
>
> **Gordon Craig (1980).** *Germany 1866–1945.* **OUP, p. 601.**

Activity 16    **Thinking skills**

According to Craig, what was the significance of the SS within the Third Reich?

The Gestapo

The Gestapo or *Geheime Staatspolizei* (Secret State Police) was a relatively small organization with only 20,000 officers in 1939. However, it managed to create an atmosphere of fear and suspicion among the German people by using Nazi informers in the general population to gain information. Each 'block warden' was in control of a block or unit of a town and would visit every home in their area each week, collecting donations and checking up on people. In addition, many of the public voluntarily denounced their neighbours, though in all probability this was inspired more by personal than political reasons. In fact, there were so many denunciations that the Gestapo were unable to investigate them all and so arrests and custody became increasingly random.

The propaganda state: what methods of indoctrination were used?

The other powerful department of the Nazi regime was the Propaganda Ministry under the control of Goebbels. In addition to influencing culture (see pages 57 and 58) Goebbels oversaw the press and radio. The radio in particular was a powerful means of indoctrination. This was helped by the mass production of radios, which were sold at subsidized prices; by 1939, 70 per cent of households owned one. There were also public loudspeakers in communal areas, which broadcast Hitler's speeches and important 'national monuments'.

Another aspect of the propaganda machine was the creation of a new social ritual: the 'Heil Hitler' greeting with the Nazi salute. Along with public festivals to celebrate key Nazi achievements, this was intended to strengthen the populations' identification with the Nazi regime.

Goebbels's propaganda machine was also crucial for creating the 'Hitler myth': that Hitler was uncompromising in his fight to defeat the nation's internal and external enemies; that he was a political genius who had masterminded the recovery of Germany after the post-war humiliations; and that, in addition to all of this, he remained a man of the people living a simple life and devoting himself to the welfare of his people.

As Ian Kershaw has argued, Hitler's popularity was key to securing his position and then allowing him to carry through his ideas:

> Without Hitler's massive personal popularity, the high level of plebiscitary acclamation which the regime could repeatedly call upon – legitimating its actions at home and abroad, defusing opposition, boosting the autonomy of the leadership from the traditional national-conservative elites who had imagined they would keep Hitler in check, and sustaining the frenetic and increasingly dangerous momentum of Nazi rule – is unthinkable. Most important of all, Hitler's huge platform of popularity made his own power position ever more unassailable, providing the foundation for the selective radicalization process in the Third Reich by which his personal ideological obsessions became translated into attainable reality.
>
> **Ian Kershaw (2001). *The Hitler Myth*. OUP, p. 1.**

How was culture affected?

Your investigation into the culture of Weimar Germany would have revealed that the 1920s in Germany was a time of experimentation and innovation in culture. This changed under the Nazi regime; cultural activity, like all other aspects of life, was to be controlled and 'coordinated' to fit the goals of the state.

The Reich Chamber of Culture was established in 1933 and it was supervised by the Propaganda Ministry. One of the first symbolic actions was the burning of books written by Jews, socialists and other 'undesirables' in Berlin, in May 1933. Over 2,500 authors emigrated between 1939 and 1945 including Thomas and Heinrich Mann and Bertolt Brecht. The art world was also attacked and Weimar's cultural awakening

'Working Maidens', painted by Leopold Schmutzler. This was approved Third Reich art following the rules of 'realism' (see Information box).

Romantic realism in Nazi art

Art in the Third Reich was to focus on the values of racial purity, militarism and obedience. It also glorified the simple and heroic virtues of rural life. This showed what Hitler called *'the true German spirit'*. Art was never to show true aspects of reality such as pain or distress.

Thus, the art that had been created under Weimar, such as Dada (much of which in fact did portray real-life suffering) was known as *'degenerate'*. Hitler wrote of this art, *'It is the sick production of crazy people. Pity the people who are no longer able to control this sickness'*.

labelled as '*degenerate*' and symbolic of the spiritual decline of Germany in the post-war years.

In the place of this era of experimentation Nazi culture was dominated by an emphasis on realism in painting and grandiose schemes in architecture. All art was expected to stress the values of Nazism, such as the glorification of war and the supremacy of the Aryan race.

Film played a special role under the Nazis; it was used for both relaxation and propaganda. It was an extremely effective way of showing the masses newsreels that glorified the achievements of Hitler and the Nazi state as they were shown before all feature films. However, Goebbels also realized the importance of film as an entertainment form. Between 1933 and 1945, over 1,000 feature films were produced, with only about one-sixth being overtly propagandist. It was probably only in this area that culture under the Nazis achieved anything notable due to the work, in particular, of Leni Riefenstahl. Her movies, such as *Triumph of the Will*, had a strong propagandist message, but one that was conveyed subtly using innovative cinematic techniques.

Activity 17 Research and communication skills

Task One

In groups, research one of the following aspects of culture under the Nazis. Each group should choose a different area of culture to investigate:

- cinema
- theatre
- literature
- music
- art and architecture.

Identify how Nazi ideology influenced your area of culture and how it changed from the Weimar era; find examples of work that was produced; and research the impact that Nazi ideology had on the artists.

Produce a presentation to the rest of the class on your theme.

Task Two

As a class discuss how successful the Nazi regime was in transforming German culture.

Activity 18 Thinking skills

Look through this chapter at the examples of Nazi propaganda. Identify the message of each poster/painting and how this message has been created. How effective do you find each piece of propaganda in conveying its message?

The racial state: how were the Jews affected by the Nazi regime?

Key concepts: *Consequence*

Underpinning Hitler's aims for Germany was his obsessive hatred of the Jews. Once in power he was able to translate his ideas into actual policy. Hitler's clear aims in this area led to increased radicalization between 1933 and 1939, which involved vicious persecution and legal discrimination backed up by government-inspired violence. At the same time, a relentless propaganda campaign was launched by Goebbels to convince the German population of the need to remove Jews from German society (see Information box on the next page).

CHALLENGE YOURSELF

 Research skills

Find and watch extracts from the following Nazi films on YouTube:

- *Jud suss*
- *Triumph of the Will*

1. What methods (either via cinematic techniques or storyline) are used in each of these films to strengthen Nazi values?
2. Which film do you find most successful in conveying its message?

The key measures taken against the Jews after 1933 are outlined in the timeline on page 46. The first of these, the boycott of Jewish shops and businesses, was quickly called off after it met with popular disapproval. However, the legalisation of discrimination with the Law of the Restitution of the Professional Civil Service met with little protest. This law had a severe impact on the middle-class Jews in Germany and led to increased numbers of Jews emigrating. At the same time, violence against the Jews continued at the hands of the SA with beatings, torture and killings. The burning of so-called Jewish books took place in Berlin in May 1933. Meanwhile, Nazi teachers took the lead in segregating Jewish children from other pupils.

Legal discrimination was stepped up with the Nuremburg Laws of 1935. The Reich Citizenship Law saw Jewish Germans being reduced to second-class citizens, which meant that they now lacked full civil and political rights. Under the Law for the Protection of German Blood and German Honour, Jews could no longer marry Aryan Germans; the employment of women under 45 in Jewish households was also forbidden. Germans were encouraged to denounce to the Gestapo anyone who continued with 'race defilement' or being a 'slave to the Jews'.

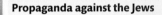

Propaganda against the Jews

Propaganda poster: 'The Eternal Jew'

A key goal of Goebbels' propaganda machine was to create an image of the German Jew as a distinctively different race rather than just Germans who were Jewish. This image of Jews as greedy, hideous and dangerous appeared not only in obvious propaganda, such as posters like this, but in more subtle areas such as children's textbooks, science books and encyclopaedias.

In the years that followed the Nuremburg Laws, Jews were systematically excluded from professions, education and from public and cultural life. From 1938, anti-Semitic policies moved into a more radical phase, which coincided with Hitler's expansion in Europe. New identification papers were marked with the letter 'J' for *Jude* (Jew) and women had to take the middle name of 'Sarah', while men had to take the middle name of 'Israel' to indicate their Jewish identity. The 'Aryanization' of the regime continued with Jews being forced to sell their shops and businesses for minimal prices, thus removing all forms of livelihood. By the end of the year, Jewish children had been excluded from German schools and Jews had been banned from public baths, theatres, cinemas and museums; in parks, they could only sit on certain benches.

In November 1938, the *Reichskristallnacht* (Night of Broken Glass) saw the biggest single outburst of organized violence against the Jews; on the night of 9 November, party radicals attacked 7,000 businesses and destroyed 267 synagogues as revenge for the shooting of a German Embassy official by a Polish Jew who was protesting at the mistreatment of his parents. Official party figures reported 91 Jews killed but many more died due to arrest and imprisonment. Many also committed suicide. Jews were forced to pay compensation for the destruction of property themselves and to forfeit their insurance claims. Many Germans were actually appalled by this level of violence; however, they did little to protest against the discrimination, which now continued apace.

Many Jews continued to emigrate and, indeed, emigration was actively encouraged by the Nazi regime both for German Jews and for the Austrian Jews who became part of the Reich with the takeover of Austria (***Anschluss***) in March 1938. However, Jews found it increasingly hard to find the money necessary for the 'emigration tax', while other countries made it clear that they were unwilling to take unlimited numbers of Jews. When war broke out in 1939, emigration became almost impossible and the persecution of Jews entered a new, far more radical phase. As Kershaw writes, '*The war… offered the opportunity, and created the context of brutalisation, in which [Hitler's key ideological issues] could… take genocidal shape*'.

The impact of *Anschluss*

In March 1938, Germany took over Austria in what was known as *Anschluss*. This brought 183,000 more Jews under Nazi control. They immediately lost their rights, property and employment, and they were subjected to humiliation and physical assaults. More than 1,500 were sent to Dachau and Buchenwald concentration camps in 1938.

Activity 19 (ATL) **Research and communication skills**

The 1936 Olympics in Berlin saw a brief respite in the increasing persecution of the Jews. In pairs, investigate:

- the aims of the Nazis with regard to these Olympic Games;
- how they put these aims into practice;
- the impact of the Olympic Games on international opinion about Nazi Germany.

The economy: How successful were Nazi economic policies?

Key concepts: *Consequence*

Nazi propaganda claimed that the regime's economic policies were a stunning success; by 1935, unemployment figures had fallen to 2 million from the 6 million of 1933, and by 1939 there were labour shortages in key industries.

What conclusions can you draw from this table about the success of Nazi economic policies?

Year	Pig iron (million tons)	Iron ore (million tons)	Steel (million tons)	Coal (million tons)	Arms budget (billion RM)	Unemployment (million)
1932	6.1	2.6	8.2	118.6	1.9	6.042 (January) 5.392 (July)
1935	12.8	6.0	16.2	143.0	6.0	2.974 (January) 1.754 (July)
1938	18.1	12.4	21.9	186.4	17.2	1.352 (January) 0.218 (July)

Nazi economic thinking

Although Hitler did not have a clear economic plan when he became Chancellor in January 1933, nevertheless, he had clear aims of what he wanted to achieve. These included:

- recovery from the Great Depression, in particular reduction in the number of unemployed;
- the creation of an economy that could allow Germany to rearm so he could pursue his goal of *Lebensraum*;
- economic self-sufficiency in the areas of food and essential raw materials, also known as 'autarky', which would allow Germany to survive a major war.

How successful was Schacht's economic strategy?

Until 1937, Nazi economic policy was in the hands of Hjalmar Schacht, who was president of the Reichsbank (1933–39) and minister of economics (1934–37). Schacht was a respected international financier and this reassured the conservative economic elite. Under Schacht, deficit financing was adopted in order to boost the economy and reduce unemployment.

Public works

In what the Nazis called the '*battle for work*', the state increased government expenditure and investment, and it tried to stimulate consumer demand. Large sums of money were spent on public work schemes, such as the building of *autobahns* (motorways) and public buildings, reforestation and **land reclamation**. This led to a dramatic increase in jobs.

In 1935, a Reich Labour Service was introduced under which unemployed men were forced to undertake six months of labour in farming or construction. The introduction of military service further reduced unemployment, as did Hitler's rearmament programme.

The 'New Plan' of 1934

By 1934, Germany was experiencing a trade deficit. It was importing more than it was exporting and so its foreign currencies, which were needed to buy the imports, were running low. To solve this problem, Schacht introduced controls on imports, which now had to be approved by the government. He also initiated a series of bilateral trade agreements with countries such as the Balkan states; through these agreements Germany paid for food and raw materials with German Reichmarks, which could then only be used to buy German goods.

The use of 'Mefo' bills

In order to finance rearmament, Schacht introduced 'Mefo' bills or credit notes. Companies that supplied goods or services to the government were given these Mefo bills, which they could then exchange for cash at the Reichsbank. However, there was an incentive to delay asking for this cash, as there was a 4 per cent annual interest rate on the Mefo bills if the companies kept them for five years. Thus, the government could start the rearmament programme without actually having to finance it, and it also prevented the danger of inflation by reducing the cost of government expenditure. This method also allowed the rearmament programme to go unnoticed because the expenditure did not show up in government accounts.

The Four Year Plan, 1936

> I consider it necessary that, from now on, with iron determination we attain 100 per cent self-sufficiency in all these areas such as steel and coal, so that we will not be dependent on foreign countries for these important raw materials, and that thereby we will also be able to save the foreign currency we require during peacetime in order to import our foodstuffs. I thus set the following tasks:
>
> I The German armed forces must be operational within four years.
>
> II The German economy must be fit for war within four years. … The extent of the military development of our resources cannot be too large, nor its pace too swift [underlining by Hitler].

An extract from the Four Year Plan Memorandum, August 1936

By 1936, there was still a balance of payments problem and a growing budget deficit. There were also food shortages. Schacht wanted to encourage exports in order to gain foreign exchange and also slow the increase in arms expenditure. However, this was not acceptable to the Nazi leadership. The debate over where priorities should lie within the German economy came to be summed up in the phrase, '*Guns or Butter?*'

The question was resolved, as you can see in the memorandum above, by Hitler himself. Schacht's caution was overruled. He was marginalized and Hermann Göring was put in charge of a Four Year Plan that would focus on economic autarky. For Hitler this was crucial if Germany was to be geared for war and avoid the crippling effects of an economic blockade such as had been imposed on Germany by the Allies in the First World War.

Autarky was to be achieved by creating a managed economy, which would control labour supply, prices, raw materials and foreign exchange. It would also involve cutting exports by increasing Germany's own production of key commodities such as iron, steel, and food, and developing substitutes for products such as rubber and coal. However, the Four Year Plan failed to meet production targets in key areas such as fuel and rubber, and by the time war broke out in 1939, Germany was still dependent on foreign supplies for one-third of its raw materials.

The Four Year Plan				
Industrial goods (in thousands of tons)	Target	Actual output 1936	Actual output 1938	Actual output 1942
Hard coal	213,000	158,400	186,186	166,059
Oil	13,830	1,790	2,340	6,260
Steel	24,000	19,216	22,656	20,480
Aluminium	273	98	166	260
Explosives	223	18	45	300
Rubber (buna)	120	0.7	5	96

Activity 21

 ATL Thinking skills

How successful were Nazi economic policies?

There is no doubt that Hitler's economic policies successfully restored full employment to Germany and allowed the country to be in a strong enough financial position to go to war in 1939. However, it is debatable as to how far Hitler was actually responsible for this success. The following sources give two very different interpretations as to the reasons for Nazi economic success.

Source A

Hitler explaining why the Nazis had been so successful economically in a speech to the Reichstag on 21 May 1935:

> What we have achieved in two and a half years in the way of a planned provision of labour, a planned regulation of the market, a planned control of prices and wages, was considered a few years ago to be absolutely impossible. We only succeeded because behind those apparently dead economic measures we had the living energies of the whole nation. We had, however, first to create a number of technical and psychological conditions before we could carry out this purpose; in order to guarantee the function of the national economy it was necessary first of all to put a stop to the everlasting fluctuations of wages and prices. It was further necessary to remove the conditions giving rise to interference which did not spring from high national economic necessities, i.e. to destroy the class organization of both camps which lived on the politics of wages and prices. The destruction of the Trade Unions, both of employers and employees, which were based on the class struggle, demanded a similar removal of the political parties which were maintained by these groups of interest, which interest in return supported them. Here arose the necessity of a new conservative and vital constitution and a new organization of the Reich and state.

Source B

> It was the exceptional decline of the depression years from 1929 to 1932 which gave the subsequent revival its rosy complexion. … The policies actually pursued in 1933 had much in common with those adopted in other countries, and with the policies of the pre-Hitler governments. …
>
> By any long-term measurement the achievement of the 1930s was not very remarkable. Even by 1937 the economy was only just above the level reached some 25 years before. From 1936 onwards all the indices of growth began to slow down. If the short-term recovery had been achieved with remarkable speed, the longer term prospects for growth were more muted. The switch to war preparation did not produce a real crisis in the economy before September 1939, but it did increasingly compromise the achievements already made.

> **Richard Overy (1982). *The Nazi Economic Recovery 1932–1938*. The Macmillan Press Ltd, pp. 2–3, 63.**

1. What factors does Hitler identify as the reasons for his success?
2. Compare and contrast the views on the success of Nazi economic policies in these two sources.

1. In what ways was the building of *autobahns* a useful source of propaganda for the Nazis?

2. What practical benefits would the building of motorways have for Hitler?

The poster reads:
'23.9.1933 First '*spatenstich*' (or breaking of the ground)
23.9.1936 1000 km of *autobahn* completed'.

Why was there no effective resistance to the Nazi regime before 1939?

In the years following 1933, many Germans did not see the need for opposition or resistance to the Nazi regime. They saw the Weimar Republic as having been ineffective and they had suffered too much under the impact of the Great Depression; the provision of work under the Nazis was key for winning many people over to the regime. In addition, the power of the SS and the work of the Gestapo made it difficult to express opposition, while propaganda was relentless in highlighting the success of the Nazi state and in glorifying the role of Hitler. Therefore, many Germans just got on with their lives and kept out of trouble; they may not have wholeheartedly supported Nazi policies but they were not prepared to openly attack or oppose the regime.

There were of course significant exceptions to this. You have already read about opposition from some individual Church leaders, and researched the rebellious nature of some youth groups and the brave resistance of the White Rose movement. Socialists and Communists were of course opposed to the regime, but both organizations were brutally dealt with by the Nazis and, in addition, failed to organize themselves effectively or work with each other. As you have read, there were also specific reasons why the Churches failed to successfully challenge the regime.

Interestingly, the only effective opposition came from the upper classes, who dominated the civil service, and in particular from the highest ranks of the army. The conservative elites had initially supported Nazism because of its attacks on the Socialists and Communists, its restoration of authoritarian rule and its overturning of the Treaty of Versailles. The army was also won over to the regime following the Night of the Long Knives. However, from 1937 they became concerned with Hitler's foreign policy aims, which they feared might result in Germany having to fight a war on two fronts. Hitler's purge of conservative army leaders in 1938 and his increasingly personal control over the army intensified concerns, and some army leaders considered the possibility of a coup during 1938–39. However, any attempts at resistance were deflected by Hitler's success in foreign policy from 1938 to 1939, and then, after 1939, by the need to support the government in time of war.

Activity 23

ATL Self-management skills

Refer back to the section on Hitler's consolidation of power, your work on youth resistance, the position of the Churches, the impact of propaganda, and the work of the police state. Create a mind map to show the reasons for the limited opposition to Hitler in the years 1933–39.

Essay writing

To what extent had Hitler solved Germany's economic problems by 1939?

Command term:	To what extent
Topic:	Nazi economic policies
Concept:	Change
Intro:	It is necessary to give some context here and to explain the 'problems' that Hitler faced regarding the economy in 1933 and how he planned to solve them. Also, set out your main argument regarding the extent of Hitler's 'success'.
Section One:	Deal first with the ways that Hitler had solved Germany's economic problems. Identify the ways in which Nazi policies contributed to the economic recovery; key here are Schacht's policies. You may also want to consider the positive impact of the 1936 Four year Plan in increasing production of key materials and reducing imports. Make sure you explain how these policies helped to solve Germany's economic problems
Section Two:	As this is a 'To what extent...' question, you need to give the other side of the argument by identifying failures in the economic recovery and in the impact of Four Year Plan. You may also want to consider other factors that contributed to Germany's economic recovery other than Hitler's policies
Conclusion:	Make sure you come back to the question and answer it directly based on the weight of evidence in the main body of your essay.

Essay planning

Work in pairs to plan these essays on Nazi Germany. Refer back to the essay planning grid to remind you of the structure to follow and check that you understand the meaning of the command terms by referring back to the Introduction.

To what extent was the Night of the Long Knives the main factor in Hitler's consolidation of power?

Evaluate the extent to which Hitler established a *Volksgemeinschaft* in the years 1933 to 1939.

To what extent was Nazi economic success the reason for the lack of opposition to his policies in the years 1933 to 1939?

Hints for success

When planning, it is useful practice to write out an introduction in full and to provide the opening sentence to each paragraph to indicate the key theme for that paragraph.

03 Italy: 1918–1922

That a man with Mussolini's lack of experience and vague programme could become the head of the Italian government reflected the profound social, economic and political crises in post-war Italy.
Sheehan, J (2007). *The Monopoly of Violence.* **Faber & Faber, p. 98.**

Italian infantry in the First World War, 1915.

Essay questions:

- To what extent was Mussolini's rise to power due to the weaknesses of Liberal Italy?
- Examine the role of ideology in the rise of Mussolini in Italy between 1918 and 1922.
- 'The devastating impact of the First World War led to Mussolini's acquisition of power in 1922.' To what extent do you agree with this statement?
- Discuss the reasons for the rise to power of Mussolini in Italy in 1922.

Timeline of events – 1903–1922

1903–14		Giovanni Giolitti is prime minister
1910		Benito Mussolini joins Socialist Party
1911		Italy defeats the Ottomans/Turkey and gains Libya
1912		Mussolini leader of radical Socialists and editor of Socialist newspaper *Avanti!*
		Majority of men get the vote/franchise
1914		Widespread unrest. 'Red Week'
	Aug	The First World War begins. Italy initially remains neutral
	Nov	Mussolini shifts to pro-war and intervention stance and is expelled from Socialist Party
		Mussolini sets up new newspaper, *Il Popolo d'Italia*
1915	Apr	Treaty of London sets down major gains by Entente Powers
	May	Italy enters war against the Central Powers
1917	Oct	Mussolini wounded in the war. Italy defeated in Battle of Caporetto
1918	Oct	Italy wins the Battle of Vittorio Veneto
	Nov	Austria sues for peace
	11 Nov	Germany signs Armistice. The First World War ends
1919	Mar	Mussolini establishes the Italian Fascist movement
	Jun	Versailles Settlement: Italy does not secure all of its territorial claims
	Sept	The Italian Nationalist Gabriele D'Annunzio seizes port of Fiume
	Nov	Italian elections; Socialists and Catholic Party gain majority of votes
		Failure to form a stable government
1919–1920		Widespread Socialist unrest; *Biennio Rosso*
1920		D'Annunzio position weakened when expelled from Fiume
	Sept	Northern factories taken over by workers
		Centre-right and conservative groups move further right
		Support grows for fascism
1920–22		Widespread Fascist violence against opposition groups
1921	May	Italian elections; Fascists gain 7 per cent of vote
		Mussolini and 34 Fascists elected
	Nov	Fascist Party established under control of Mussolini
		Anti-clerical position dropped by Fascists
1922	Oct	Mussolini rejects government post
		Fascists seize northern cities
		Fascists plan to march on Rome
		King appoints Mussolini prime minister

67

The rise of Mussolini

Key concepts: *Causation, consequence and significance*

Mussolini came to power in Italy in 1922. Between this time and his demise in the Second World War, he dominated Italian politics. He was the most popular leader that Italy had ever seen and he attempted to transform Italy into a Fascist state as well as to establish a New Roman Empire in Africa and the Mediterranean. However, ultimately his Fascist revolution failed: '*Mussolini neither achieved a profound consensus, nor created a new civilisation, nor created a totalitarian state*' (Ipsen, C 1996. *Dictating Demography: The Problem of Population in Fascist Italy*. Cambridge University Press, p. 12).

Italy after 1870

In order to understand the rise of Benito Mussolini we must consider the context in which Italian **Fascism** emerged and the conditions in which he attained power in 1922. It is necessary in fact to go back to the aftermath of Italy's unification, which had taken place during the years 1861 to 1870.

Map showing the different states of Italy before the country was unified in 1870.

The process by which the various states had been unified (see map on previous page) has been called the 'Risorgimento' or 'rebirth' of Italy. Prior to this there had been a number of independent states; Rome was garrisoned by French troops, and Lombardy and Venetia were part of the Austro-Hungarian Empire.

Italian unification had been achieved through the military and diplomatic efforts of the Nationalist Giuseppe Garibaldi and the prime minister of Piedmont Sardinia, Count Camillo Benso Cavour. Rome and some of the papal states had been the last to join the new Italian kingdom in 1870. The era between this date and Mussolini's attainment of power in 1922 is usually known as 'Liberal Italy', and the rise of Fascism can be traced back to the problems and divisions of this period, in particular the impact of the First World War.

To what extent was Mussolini's rise to power due to the weaknesses of Liberal Italy?

Key concepts: *Causation and significance*

What were the long-term problems facing Liberal Italy after unification in 1870?

After unification there remained a lack of a national identity. Few Italians had been directly involved in the *Risorgimento*, and many felt stronger loyalty to their local towns and families than to the state. In addition, the Italian language was actually the local dialect of Tuscany and fewer than 2 per cent of the population spoke it.

Politically, Liberal Italy was controlled by the northern and central ruling elites. Although the political system was similar to the British system, it lacked defined political parties. The masses were not involved, as the elites feared a social revolution and offered no clear agricultural reform programme. The urban and rural poor did not have the vote. There developed what some historians have termed as two separate Italys: the 'legal' Italy was the King, parliament and bureaucrats and the 'real' Italy was the mass peasant population. Successive governments failed to address the grinding poverty of the peasants in the south, whose conditions led to periodic violence.

The ruling classes of Liberal Italy also faced opposition from the Catholic Church. The 'Roman Question', as it was known, developed when the Liberal post-unification modernizing programme took control of marriage law and education from the Church, and limited its property and privileges. Pope Pius IX refused to recognize the Kingdom of Italy, and instructed Catholics to boycott elections.

The lack of party politics meant that governments were formed through, and depended on, temporary allegiances; when these broke down, governments fell. The lack of political stability can be seen in the fact that between 1870 and 1922 there were 29 different prime ministers.

Peasant leagues and cooperatives existed in the countryside, and Italian 'agrarian socialism' was one of the strongest of this type of movement in Europe. The urban workforce had grown by the end of the 19th century, as had Italian working-class movements such as trade unions. The Italian Socialist Party was founded in 1892; however, the party was often divided ideologically between reformist socialists, who advocated working through parliament, and the revolutionaries, **anarchists** and syndicalists, who wanted to overthrow the government. To take on the challenge posed by the socialists there were rival Catholic trade unions and peasant leagues. The Church removed its ban on Catholics voting in an attempt to stem the socialist movements, and in 1909 even permitted Catholic candidates to stand for parliament.

Italy was also economically behind other European countries like Britain and Germany, which had become industrialized, as it lacked raw materials and had poor communications. The north, close to the rest of Europe, had some commercial and industrial activity; however, the south was mainly agricultural, and was impoverished. Around 68 per cent of the population relied, at least in part, on the land. Although, Liberal Italy made some clear economic progress up to the outbreak of the First World War, its relative economic weakness meant that it was viewed as a 'minor player' by the other European powers.

In the last decade of the 19th century, Italy descended into an 'end of century crisis', where bad harvests, a global economic recession and heavy taxation led to unrest in both the countryside and cities. Banks collapsed and there were corruption scandals involving leading political figures such as Francesco Crispi and Giovanni Giolitti. The response of 'legal Italy' to the outbursts of violence by 'real Italy' was repression. Francesco Crispi's government believed that the whole of Italy was on the brink of revolution and Crispi sent 40,000 government troops to restore order in Sicily. Many of the Catholic movements were disbanded, and the Socialist Party newspapers were closed down and their leaders arrested. However, this attempt to create an 'authoritarian state' was unsuccessful; it revealed how fragile the Liberal state was.

The Fascist movement that emerged after the First World War had some features in common with the reactionary Italian state at the turn of the 20th century; it pursued imperial expansion both as a means to achieve international respect and in an attempt to solve economic and social problems. It also championed the monarchy, the armed forces and certain elements on the right of the working classes.

In foreign policy Italy failed to take Tunisia during the great 'scramble for Africa', but Crispi was determined to gain 'great power' status for Italy alongside Britain and France. Italy was finally able to gain territory on the East African coast in Somaliland and Eritrea in 1885. Crispi attempted to extend its control into Abyssinia but was defeated disastrously at the Battle of Adowa in 1896. There were 5,000 Italian soldiers killed, and Italy became the only European power to have been beaten in a war by an African people.

Activity 1 　　　　　　　　　　　(ATL) Self-management and thinking skills

Review the material we have covered thus far and answer the following questions:

1. Identify the main political issues that faced Liberal Italy up to 1900.
2. Discuss with a partner Liberal Italy's economic problems.
3. In small groups discuss why Liberal Italy might not have been considered 'a great power' by the other European powers.

Did the Giolitti era and the attempts to pursue *transformismo* improve the situation in Liberal Italy?

After the decade of turmoil at the end of the 19th century, Giolitti was part of a more progressive bloc that led the opposition to the oppressive measures of the previous government. He also attempted to perfect the politics of *transformismo*. The idea of a '*transformismo*' had been initiated in the 1870s, and it aimed to transform political parties and to bring together all moderates under a Liberal parliament and government of national unity.

Thus Giolitti attempted to address the division between real and legal Italy and to bring the masses into the political system. He did this by introducing electoral reform that gave the vote to most adult males in 1912. He sought the support of the Socialist ministers and also introduced reforms for working conditions and benefits.

Giovanni Giolitti

Nonetheless, Giolitti's policies had been buoyed by a period of economic boom, which by 1909 was slowing, leading to a renewal of social unrest. In addition, Giolitti's own policy of launching a colonial war in Libya in 1911 destroyed his alliance with the Socialists. Italy had ambitions to gain territory in North Africa and, in September 1911, Italy invaded Libya in an attempt to take control of this Ottoman colonial territory. The French had taken Tunis and, when they started to consolidate their positions in Algeria and Morocco, Italian Nationalists feared France's next target would be Libya. Giolitti, following public pressure to act, hoped it would be a quick campaign in Libya; indeed, compared to the disaster in Abyssinia the war was a success, and in October 1912 Turkey formally ceded the territory to Italy.

However, at the Socialist Party Congress in 1912 members who had supported Giolitti were defeated in a hail of criticism and condemnation of the '*imperialist war*', and the Socialist Party adopted a policy of non-cooperation with the '*capitalist-bourgeois*' parties of parliament. It was also at this congress that a radical leader, Benito Mussolini, came to the fore.

Giolitti also failed to appease the Nationalists with his war in Libya. Although they had supported colonial conquest and the war in Libya, they condemned the Liberals for failing to make Italy a great power. The Nationalists also strongly promoted *irredentism*, which aimed to seize the Italian-speaking territories of the Austro-Hungarian Empire, South Tyrol, Trentino and Istria (*terre irredente* means unredeemed lands). The Nationalists resented Italy's economic weakness and the fact that millions had emigrated to escape poverty at home. More than five million Italians had emigrated between 1890 and 1914, most heading for the US or South America.

Thus, Giolitti had not only failed to gain working-class support for the Liberal state, he had further alienated those on the left and the right. In the 1913 elections it was only with the mobilization of Catholic votes that the government was saved. The Nationalists on the right had gained six seats in the election of 1913 and it was clear as the First World War broke out that Italian politics was polarizing between the right and the left. In June 1914 there was rioting in northern and central Italy during leftist-inspired uprisings in what became known as 'Red Week'.

Anti-clerical radicals, appalled at Giolitti's agreement with the old enemy Catholicism, withdrew their support from his coalition government; Giolitti resigned.

CHALLENGE YOURSELF

 Research skills

Who were the Futurists?

The Futurists were a group founded by Filippo Marinetti in 1909. It was a literary and artistic movement and its manifesto glorified war, youth and violence.

'The City Rises' by the Italian painter Umberto Boccioni, 1910.

In small groups, research the Futurist movement and its role in Italian society and politics prior to the outbreak of the First World War in 1914.

Activity 2

 Self-management and thinking skills

Read through the bullet points and economic data below and discuss what evidence there is for a) growth in the Italian economy during the pre-war period and b) limitations in the Italian economy in the pre-war period.

- GDP (gross domestic product) increased by 4 per cent in Italy compared to Britain, which increased 40–50 per cent;
- 57 per cent of the Italian population was rural in 1910;
- low agricultural yield – 9 hectolitres of wheat per hectare compared to 25 hectolitres per hectare in Britain;
- limited raw materials – lack of coal and iron.

	Italy 1890	Italy 1910	Britain 1910	
Steel production	0.1	0.7	6.5	[million tonnes]
	Italy 1860	Italy 1913	Britain 1913	
Foreign trade	0.3	1.8	7.5	[$ billion]
	Italy 1880	Italy 1913	Britain 1913	
Railways	9,290	18,873	38,114	[km]

Activity 3   ATL Thinking and communication skills

1. In pairs read through the chart below. Add detail to each heading to provide evidence to support the point.

2. In pairs, discuss the extent to which Giolitti had addressed the key problems facing Liberal Italy by 1914.

3. Identify which problems remained or had become worse under Giolitti.

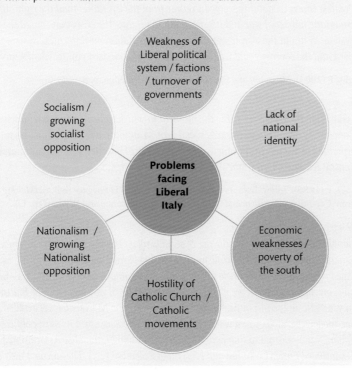

Activity 4   ATL Thinking and communication skills

Read through the sources below and answer the questions that follow.

Source A

Giovanni Giolitti addressing the Italian parliament in 1900.

> *The country is sick politically and morally, but the principal cause of its sickness is that the classes in power have been spending enormous sums on themselves and their own interests, and have obtained money almost entirely from the poorer sections of society… When in the financial emergency of 1893 I had to call on the rich to make a small sacrifice, they began a rebellion [in parliament] against the government even more effective than the contemporary revolt of the poor Sicilian peasantry, and Sonnino who took over from me [as prime minister] had to find the money by increasing still further the price of salt and tax on cereals. I deplore as much as anyone the struggle between classes but at least let us be fair and ask who started it.*

> **Quoted in Adler, FH (2002). *Italian Industrialists from Liberalism to Fascism: The Political Development of the Industrial Bourgeoisie, 1906–34.* Cambridge: CUP, p. 22.**

Source B

❝ There is no doubt that Italy's weaknesses in 1914 were greater than its strengths, but this is not to say that they were sufficient to bring about the collapse of the political system. They help explain why Italy after 1919 was susceptible to Fascism, which promised to end weak government and restore Italian greatness. But they do not explain the emergence and rapid growth of the Fascist movement. Right-wing parties were relatively insignificant in 1914 and the greatest threat to stability seemed to come from the left rather than the right. It required the traumatic impact of war and its aftermath to produce the crisis that caused the demise of the system. Without the war, it seems likely that the Italian parliamentary system would have survived and the country could well have evolved into a modern political democracy.

Knight, P (2003). *Mussolini and Fascism*. London: Routledge, p. 8.

Source C

❝ The Giolittian period was possibly the moment in which radical changes, representing a fundamentally new strategy towards social protest, might have occurred and been incorporated in the political framework of liberalism. That they were not, ultimately destroyed the central feature of that framework – parliamentary democracy.

Corner, P (1986). 'Liberalism, Pre-Fascism, Fascism'. In D Forgacs (ed), *Rethinking Italian Fascism: Capitalism, Populism and Culture*. London: Lawrence and Wishart, p. 17.

Source D

❝ National humiliation […] and the rise of socialism […] inspired a vociferous minority of Italian intellectuals to attack liberalism in terms that carried appeal for a growing number of the educated young. The poet Gabriele D'Annunzio, for example, thrilled his readers with his assaults on supposed liberal decadence and his exaltation of violence. […] the Futurists, a literary, artistic and semi-political movement led by Filippo Marinetti, […] extolled physical power, modern technology and war. […] This restlessness assumed its most political form […] in Italian Nationalism. Leading figures within the Italian Nationalist Association, founded in 1910, included Enrico Corradini and […] Luigi Federzoni […]. They accused their country's liberal political class of weakness and corruption [and] 'ignoble socialism'. The Nationalists' proposed cure for the alleged ills of liberalism was its replacement by openly authoritarian government, presiding over unrestrained capitalist development and an imperialist foreign policy. Enforced solidarity among all social classes within a 'proletarian nation' like Italy would, they insisted, make possible the maximization of the country's productive energies and enable it, through imperialism, successfully to challenge 'plutocratic' nations like Britain and France.

Blinkhorn, M (2006). *Mussolini and Fascist Italy*. Methuen & Co. Ltd, pp. 12–13.

Source E

❝ Where Giolitti was a politician seemingly devoid of ideals, whose power was rooted in his ability to manipulate parliament rather than in any emotional engagement with the masses, at once cynical, utilitarian, calculating and unscrupulous – the 'minister of the underworld' as Gaetano Salvemini famously branded him in 1910 for this willingness to broker electoral deals with criminal elements in the South – the new leader would be inspired by faith and conviction [and] connect directly with the people… It was from this context of simultaneous condemnation and messianic hope that the cult of Mussolini was eventually to emerge.

Duggan, C (2013). 'The Cult of the Duce'. In S Gundle, C Duggan and G Pieri (eds), *Political Cults in Liberal Italy, 1861–1922. Mussolini and the Italians*. Manchester: Manchester University Press, p. 24.

1. Read Source A. Who was Giolitti attempting to appeal to in this speech?
2. Discuss how Source B and Source C present contrasting views of the impact of Giolitti's regime in Italy.
3. According to Source D what was the response in Italy to 'national humiliation and the rise of socialism'?
4. What criticisms does Source E make of Giolitti's leadership?

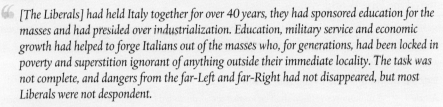

Activity 5

 **Thinking skills**

Read the sources below to find the perspectives of different historians.

Source A

> [The Liberals] had held Italy together for over 40 years, they had sponsored education for the masses and had presided over industrialization. Education, military service and economic growth had helped to forge Italians out of the masses who, for generations, had been locked in poverty and superstition ignorant of anything outside their immediate locality. The task was not complete, and dangers from the far-Left and far-Right had not disappeared, but most Liberals were not despondent.

> **Robson, M (1992).** *Italy: Liberalism and Fascism.* UK: Hodder, pp. 34–35.

Source B

> It is no exaggeration to say that Giolitti's failure to launch Italy on the path of representative, mass democracy in the pre-war years helped open the way for Mussolini and Fascism in the post-war period.

> **Pollard, J (1998).** *The Fascist Experience in Italy.* UK: Routledge, p. 17.

Source C

> … pre-1914 Italy was not a [nation state]… Most people still spoke only dialect; nearly 40% of adults were illiterate… The social and economic gap between North and South was all too evident; so too was the chasm between town and country… Italy was still run by a small elite, with little title to rule except its belligerent patriotism and it historical myths.

> **Clark, M (2008).** *Modern Italy, 1871 to Present.* UK: Routledge, p. 177.

1. According to Source A, what were the positive achievements of Liberal Italy before the First World War?
2. According to Source B, what was the main failing of Liberal Italy before the First World War?
3. According to Source C, what were the limitations of Liberal Italy before the First World War?

How did the First World War lead to greater divisions in society and foster the rise of Mussolini?

Key concepts: *Consequence*

Italy's reasons for joining the Allies

Italy's politicians were divided during the 'Intervention Crisis' that developed when the First World War broke out in Europe in August 1914. Despite its membership of the Triple Alliance with Germany and Austria–Hungary, Italy at first remained neutral. The government had declared that the alliance was defunct and the majority of Italians were satisfied with this decision as there was historic hostility towards Austria–Hungary due to its opposition to Italian unification and its control of Trentino and Istria.

However, right-wing liberals and many of the supporters of Antonio Salandra, who had succeeded Giolitti, were concerned that a Triple Alliance victory would strengthen Austria's determination against any revision of its borders. They also hoped that if Italy joined the Entente (the Alliance bloc of Britain, France and Russia established in 1907) they might be able to gain the Italian-speaking territories of the Austro-Hungarian Empire on its defeat. Prime Minister Salandra favoured this action.

Negotiations in 1915 revealed that Austria–Hungary would not concede Trentino and Trieste, whereas the Entente powers promised these territories and more: South Tyrol,

Istria and Dalmatia, which would give Italy dominance in the Adriatic. There was also the promise of colonies, the exact locations of which were unspecified, in either Africa or the eastern Mediterranean. Thus, Prime Minister Salandra persuaded the King to back the Entente Treaty. Italy duly signed the Treaty of London in May 1915 and entered the First World War.

Activity 6 · ⒶⓉⓁ Thinking skills

Read the source and answer the questions that follow.

Extracts from the Treaty of London, 26 April 1915.

Article 1   A military convention shall be immediately concluded between the General Staffs of France, Great Britain, Italy, and Russia...

Article 2   On her part, Italy undertakes to use her entire resources for the purpose of waging war jointly with France, Great Britain, and Russia against all their enemies.

Article 3   The French and British fleets shall render active and permanent assistance to Italy...

Article 4   Under the Treaty of Peace, Italy shall obtain the Trentino, Cisalpine Tyrol with its geographical and natural frontier, as well as Trieste, the counties of Gorizia and Gradisca, all Istria as far as the Quarnero and including Volosca and the Istrian islands of Cherso and Lussin, as well as the small islands of Plavnik, Unie, Canidole, Palazzuoli, San Pietro di Nembi, Asinello, Gruica, and the neighbouring islets...

Article 5   Italy shall also be given the province of Dalmatia within its present administrative boundaries...

Article 6   Italy shall receive full sovereignty over Valona, the island of Saseno and surrounding territory...

Article 7   Should Italy obtain the Trentino and Istria in accordance with the provisions of Article 4, together with Dalmatia and the Adriatic islands within the limits specified in Article 5, and the Bay of Valona (Article 6), and if the central portion of Albania is reserved for the establishment of a small autonomous neutralized State, Italy shall not oppose the division of Northern and Southern Albania between Montenegro, Serbia, and Greece...

Article 8   Italy shall receive entire sovereignty over the Dodecanese Islands which she is at present occupying.

Article 9   Generally speaking, France, Great Britain, and Russia recognize that... in the event of total or partial partition of Turkey in Asia, she ought to obtain a just share of the Mediterranean region adjacent to the province of Adalia...

Article 11   Italy shall receive a share of any eventual war indemnity corresponding to their efforts and her sacrifices.

Article 13   In the event of France and Great Britain increasing their colonial territories in Africa at the expense of Germany, those two Powers agree in principle that Italy may claim some equitable compensation...

Article 14   Great Britain undertakes to facilitate the immediate conclusion, under equitable conditions, of a loan of at least 50,000,000 pounds...

1. In pairs, read through the terms of the treaty and identify the key gains that were offered to Italy.

2. With reference to its origin, purpose and content, analyse the values and limitations of this source for historians studying Italian intervention in the First World War.

Italian intervention in the First World War was supported by the Nationalists and the Futurists. Indeed the poet Gabriele D'Annunzio had declared in May 1915:

> ❝ ... here is the dawn. Our vigil is over... After so much wavering the incredible has happened. We shall now fight our war, and blood will flow from the veins of Italy. We are the last to enter the struggle but we will be among the first to find glory. Here is the dawn.

However, it was not popular among the poor in the south, who were not motivated by potential territorial gains in the far north of the country. The Catholic Church's support was limited by its refusal to condemn the enemy: Catholic Austria. Giolitti and many Liberals, including most of the Chamber, opposed the war. In addition, intervention caused division on the left; the PSI (*Partito Socialista Italiano*) was against intervention, viewing the conflict as a war of the 'imperialists' or 'bosses', while others on the left supported intervention because they believed that it would destroy 'Liberal Italy' and would facilitate revolution. 'Revolutionary action groups' (*fasci di azione rivoluzionaria*) were set up by left-wing interventionists to support the war. Benito Mussolini, a leading member of the PSI, changed his opinion during the intervention crisis from initially opposing the war, to then arguing in favour of intervention. When Mussolini expressed his support for the war, from October 1915, he was expelled from the PSI and from his editorship of its newspaper, *Avanti!*

The impact of the First World War: 1915–18

The Italians fought the Austrians and the Germans across a front in Northern Italy. Between 1915 and 1918, 5 million men were engaged in military service, mainly as conscripts. Most of the conscripts were drawn from rural areas, as industrial workers tended to be engaged in the production of war materials. Similar to the practices on the Western Front in France and Belgium, trenches were developed on the Italian front and for most of the ensuing three years the war was static and was a war of attrition. Italian troops fought bravely, endured appalling conditions and were on low pay. At the Battle of Caporetto in October 1917 the Italians were surprised by an Austro-German offensive and suffered huge losses; 700,000 troops were pushed back by more than 100 km. The commander-in-chief blamed the cowardice of his troops and had thousands executed. However, the Nationalists blamed the government.

Despite the catastrophe at Caporetto, the Italian lines held, and Italy finally achieved a victory at the Battle of Vittorio Veneto, against the Austrians, in October 1918. By this time the German army was exhausted by the Anglo-French offensives on the Western Front. Austria then sued for peace and an armistice was signed on 3 November 1918.

On 11 November, Germany surrendered and the First World War came to an end. However, victory came at a huge human cost for the Italians: more than 650,000 had been killed and hundreds of thousands wounded.

Italian alpine units, 1916.

The war increased the political divisions in Italy. The 5 million men that served in its army were politicized by their experience, and many deeply resented the Liberal government for what they saw as the mismanagement of the war. Some veterans also resented the socialist PSI's anti-war stance. The government had mobilized the population to fight a total war and this led to an increase in the number of industrial workers and in turn an increase in trade union membership and syndicalism.

Activity 7 · (ATL) Thinking skills

According to this source, what was the impact of the First World War on Italy?

> *The final figure for the cost of the whole war had been 148 billion lire, that is to say twice the sum of all government expenditure between 1861 and 1913.*
>
> *This total is a symbol for an enormous consumption of energy and natural resources, in return for which Italy obtained little joy and much grief. A great deal of idealism had gone into the war on Italy's part, and much elevated patriotism, but one need not look many years beyond 1918 to see that it had been one of the great disasters of her history. [As a result] Italy suffered 25 years of revolution and tyranny.*

An extract from the academic book, *Italy: A Modern History*, by the British historian Denis Mack Smith (1969). University of Michigan Press, p. 313.

Why did support for fascism grow in Italy after the First World War?

What is fascism?

In the inter-war period, Europe was dominated by dictatorial regimes. Dictatorships were more common than democracies, and many countries had fascist-style movements. The word *fasci* – meaning group – had been used to describe Sicilian rebels in the 1890s and, indeed, the rebels held some ideas that were similar to those later espoused by the fascists in Italy and other European movements before the war. However, Mussolini overtly suggested the term was related to a Roman symbol of authority (which consisted of rods bound around an axe) in order to link his Fascist movement with the classical Roman period.

Fascism itself did not have a coherent founding doctrine and it therefore manifested differently around the world. Fascists promoted nationalism, a one-party state, a strong leader or dictator, **imperialism** and war. At its core, fascism was an ultranationalist ideology. It sought to mobilize the masses to bring about the 'rebirth' of a nation and establish a new modernist culture that rejected the decadence of liberal democratic societies. The nation state, which is central in fascism, could be defined on historical and/or racial grounds. Roger Griffin argues that fascism aimed to establish an '*alternative modernity to that of the liberal societies of the 1920s*'. Whereas liberals promoted ideas of the rights of the individual, and the power of reason and science, those on the right promoted emotion, instinct and the primacy of nations and races. These ideas on race often adopted the British writer Herbert Spence's ideas. He took Darwinian theories of evolution and applied them to human society, drawing conclusions about the inevitability of conflict: the notion that violence and war were part of 'God's plan', were necessary in order to weed out the 'unfit' and establish the domination of the 'fittest', and would ensure the 'survival of the fittest'. However, in pre-war Italy the left had been more powerful than the right; thus, according to Patricia Knight, '… *the problems resulting from the war made it possible for these "pre-fascist" ideas to be developed and to attract a much wider audience*'.

Fasci – Roman rods bound together.

Fascist ideology: Key elements of fascist doctrine

In 1932 Mussolini declared, '*For the Fascist, everything is in the State, and nothing human or spiritual exists, much less has value, outside the State. In this sense Fascism is totalitarian.*'

It has been argued that to fully understand fascism it may be easier to consider what it was opposed to. Fascists were anti-communist and denounced the idea of a class struggle. They were against multi-party liberal democracy and against the idea of 'internationalism'. Fascists were opposed to pacifism. Mussolini himself outlined what fascism stood against in *The Doctrine of Fascism* in 1932:

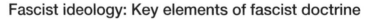

66 *Fascism [is] the… negation of that doctrine which formed the basis of Marxian Socialism.*

> *After Socialism, Fascism attacks the whole complex of democratic ideologies… Fascism denies that the majority, through the mere fact of being a majority, can rule human societies… Fascism is definitely and absolutely opposed to the doctrines of liberalism, both in the political and economic sphere.*

Nevertheless, some fascist intellectuals themselves suggested that the Fascist movement lacked a 'central idea'. The British historian AJP Taylor argued, '*Fascism was… revolution by fraud: talk without action*' and Mussolini's British biographer Denis Mack Smith suggested that fascism was primarily a '*vehicle for power*'.

Activity 8

 Social skills and self-management skills

Read through the key elements of fascist doctrine on the chart below.

In small groups discuss the ideas that were the foundations for the post-war Fascist movement and consider which groups in Italian society might have been attracted to such ideas in post-war Italy.

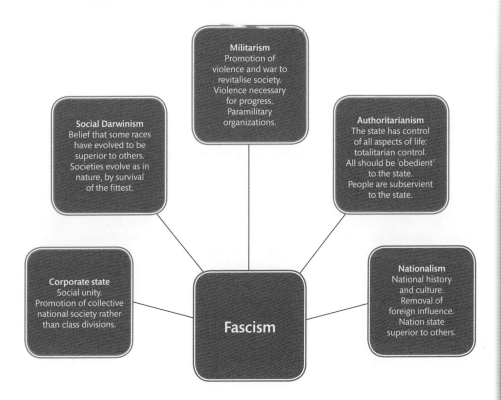

Militarism
Promotion of violence and war to revitalise society. Violence necessary for progress. Paramilitary organizations.

Social Darwinism
Belief that some races have evolved to be superior to others. Societies evolve as in nature, by survival of the fittest.

Authoritarianism
The state has control of all aspects of life: totalitarian control. All should be 'obedient' to the state. People are subservient to the state.

Corporate state
Social unity. Promotion of collective national society rather than class divisions.

Fascism

Nationalism
National history and culture. Removal of foreign influence. Nation state superior to others.

Activity 9

 Self-management and thinking skills

1. In pairs, review the material on fascist ideology on pages 78 and 79. Discuss and identify the key ideas of fascism.

2. In small groups compare the Italian Fascist and the German Nazi movements. Review Chapter 2 on Germany and discuss the comparisons below. In pairs identify examples from these chapters to support each of the comparisons.

    - Both called for national unity and regeneration.
    - Both promoted the idea of a strong leader.
    - Both vehemently opposed socialism and communism.
    - Both opposed liberal pluralist society and democracy.
    - Both began as left-wing groups, and although both moved to the right they both retained socialist ideas that could appeal to workers.
    - Both viewed their groups as movements rather than political parties.
    - Both recruited the First World War veterans into violent paramilitaries.
    - Both despised discussion and debate, and promoted action.
    - Both showed the power of their movements in huge rallies and parades.

3. In the same groups, now attempt to identify contrasts between the two movements. Are there more comparisons or contrasts between the ideologies of Italian Fascism and German Nazism?

In March 1919 Mussolini created the *Fasci di Combattimento*, the first Fascist units, which had around 100 members. They wore the *fasci* symbol, intended to symbolize strong bonds between the men in the militia units, black shirts and saluted with a straight arm (the style of salute given by the ancient Romans). The initial members were a mixture of Futurists, Nationalists, ex-soldiers, former Socialists and trade unionists. Some of the early members were from the elite military unit, the black-shirted *arditi*. These units became known as the Blackshirts.

Mussolini was careful not to articulate a clear **manifesto**, as he wanted to create a 'movement' not a party. However, when he decided to contest the elections of 1919, the limitations of his new movement were revealed. The Fascists did not win a single seat.

⟩⟩⟩ Historians' perspectives

To what extent was the rise of fascism due to the weaknesses of Liberal Italy?

Some historians, including the British historian GM Trevelyan, writing before the First World War, argued that Liberal Italy had many positive achievements, and was relatively stable before the outbreak of war in 1914. He suggested that the Italian kingdom was safe, stable and rested on firm foundations of liberty. The Italian liberal historian Benedetto Croce also suggested that the rise of fascism was not the fault of the Liberal regime and was primarily caused by the socioeconomic impact of the First World War, along with the political backlash and fear of communism caused by the Bolshevik Revolution. However, other historians have suggested that the failures of Liberal Italy, and in particular the leadership of Giolitti, did lead to the rise of fascism and, ultimately, Mussolini.

The Socialists argued at the time that the regime was merely a cover for the capitalist exploitation of the Italian working classes. The Marxist historian Antonio Gramsci argued that it was due to the failings of the Liberal Italian state, which had failed to include the masses, had used violence against discontent and revolts, and had maintained the role of the elites as the dominant force in politics.

The Nationalists also viewed the regime as an abject failure because it had not made Italy a great power. The Catholic view was divided between those who could support liberalism and those who could not forgive the Liberals for their attack on papal power and authority.

Activity 10 ATL Thinking skills

Read Source A and Source B and answer the questions that follow.

Source A

Extract from Mussolini's speech to the first meeting of the Milan Fascio in March 1919. Quoted in Delzell, CF (ed) (1971). *Mediterranean Fascism, 1919–45 (selected documents)*. London: Macmillan, p. 10.

❝ *I have the impression that the present regime in Italy has failed. It is clear to everyone that a crisis now exists. During the war all of us sensed the inadequacy of the government; today we know that our victory was due solely to the virtues of the Italian people, not to the intelligence and ability of its leaders.*

We must not be faint hearted, now that the future nature of the political system is to be determined. We must act fast. If the present regime is going to be superseded, we must be ready to take its place. For this reason, we are establishing the fasci as organs of creativity and agitation that will be ready to rush into the piazzas and cry out, 'The right to the political succession belongs to us, because we are the ones who pushed the country into war and led it to victory!'

Source B

The national programme of the *Fasci di Combattimento*, Milan 1919.

Italians!

Here is the national programme of a soundly Italian movement. Revolutionary... and highly innovative...

For the political problem

What WE WANT:

> *a) Universal suffrage in the regional list ballot, with proportional representation; voting and eligibility for women.*
>
> *b) The minimum age for voters lowered to 18; for the deputies lowered to 25 years.*
>
> *c) The abolition of the Senate.*
>
> *d) The convening of a National Assembly for a term of three years, whose first task is to determine the form of the state constitution.*
>
> *e) The formation of National Councils technical labour, industry, transport, social hygiene, communications etc. elected by the professional community, with legislative powers, and with the right to elect a Commissioner General with ministerial powers.*

For the social problem:

WE WANT:

> *a) A State law that enshrines for all workers the legal day of eight hours of work.*
>
> *b) Minimum pay.*
>
> *c) The participation of workers' representatives in the technical operation of industry.*
>
> *d) The award to proletarian organizations of the management of industries or public services.*
>
> *e) The rapid and complete arrangement of railway workers and all transport industries.*

For the military problem:

WE WANT:

> *a) The establishment of a national militia.*
>
> *b) The nationalization of all weapons and explosive factories.*
>
> *c) A national foreign policy aimed at enhancing the Italian nation in the world.*

For the financial problem:

WE WANT:

> *a) A strong progressive tax.*
>
> *b) The seizure of all assets of the religious congregations.*
>
> *c) The review of all war supplies contracts, and the seizure of 85% of the profits of war.*

1. Discuss in small groups what Mussolini presented as the key ideas of his Fascist movement.

2. Discuss which groups in Italian society he wanted the Fascist movement to appeal to.

Who was Benito Mussolini?

Before the First World War Mussolini was a radical socialist who had condemned the moderate socialists for working with the Liberal state. He supported the use of violence and he had been sent to prison in 1911 for attempting to incite a rising against the Italian war in Libya. After his release from prison in 1912 he became editor of the socialist newspaper, *Avanti!* He then resigned from *Avanti!* in 1914 because he switched to a pro-war stance, which was opposed by the Socialists who condemned the war as an 'imperialist' conflict and who favoured a policy of neutrality (see page 77).

Mussolini then set up a new newspaper, *Il Popolo d'Italia*, which – although it claimed to be socialist – promoted Italian intervention in the First World War. He believed that war would purge society and facilitate revolution, and key industrial companies, for example Fiat, gave his newspaper financial support. Subsequently, he was expelled from the Socialist Party.

Mussolini was conscripted into the army, but after being injured in a training exercise in 1917 he was invalided home. He once again took over editorship of *Il Popolo*. The

newspaper promoted both nationalism and social reform and, as editor, Mussolini heavily criticized the government. He accused it of '*defeatism*' and held it responsible for the Italian defeat in the Battle of Caporetto. He also claimed that Italy needed a '*dictator*' to effectively direct the war. As you have seen, following the defeat of the central powers, Mussolini founded the Fascist movement in 1919 during the post-war crisis that gripped Italy.

Activity 11 **ATL** Thinking skills

In small groups, read through Source A and Source B and discuss the reasons why Italians might have been attracted to fascist ideas.

Source A

> The fasci of Milan are composed, in the very great majority, of employees, small renters and lesser and middling professional men… Fascism is composed in the large cities of new men. They formed the crowd which before the war watched political events with indifference and apathy and which has now entered the contest. Fascism has mobilized its forces from the twilight zones of political life, and from this derives the unruly violence and juvenile exuberance of its conduct.

Extract from *The State and the Post-War Social and Financial Crisis*, by a founder member of the Fascist Party, Agostino Lanzillo; published in 1920.

Source B

> Fascism had elements of both [left and right] … It was revolutionary, but could also sometimes claim to be conservative. It was Monarchist but also republican, at different times. It was Catholic, but also anti-clerical; it claimed to be Socialist, but could also be strongly Capitalist whenever it suited the Duce to be so… Fascism was not a doctrine, not ideas, not ideology, but was really a means for winning power by a single man.

An extract from a lecture given at Oxford University in 1990 by the British historian Denis Mack Smith: 'Sleeping Car to Power, Mussolini's Italy 1922–43'.

The post-war crisis 1918 to 1922

Italy entered into a period of crisis following the First World War, and the Liberal governments (between 1918 and 1922) began to lose control of the situation.

• Politically, the franchise was extended but this resulted in the Liberals not faring well in the post-war election of 1919 where they won less than half the seats in the chamber. Indeed, the main political parties were unable to form coherent coalition governments; governments were short-lived and this further undermined the credibility of the democratic parliamentary system.

• Economically, the government had borrowed heavily from Britain and the US during the war and was 85 billion lire in debt by 1919. It had also resorted to printing money to cover the cost of intervention. This led to high inflation and workers' wages did not keep up with the cost of goods. The war had meant high profits for industrialists who were paid by the government to produce weapons and supplies, but after the war government expenditure was severely cut back. Unemployment soared to over 2 million in 1919 as employers cut jobs and returning soldiers swelled their numbers. Membership of Socialist trade unions increased to 2 million as war restrictions were relaxed and workers went on strike to protest against pay and conditions. More than a million workers went on strike in 1919 alone. New US restrictions on immigration meant that the southern poor could no longer emigrate to escape their poverty. High inflation not only hit the fixed-wage workers, but also the middle classes who had their savings wiped out. This dire economic situation fuelled political division and radical ideologies.

- In addition, the role of the left was significant in the post-war crisis. The Bolshevik Revolution in October 1917 in Russia had led to widespread fear that communism would spread across Europe. It had inspired the Italian Socialists to call for the overthrow of the Liberal state and in the 1919 Socialist Congress new aims were set down that suggested that the workers must now have '*recourse to the use of violence*' to achieve a '*dictatorship of the **proletariat***'. In the elections of November 1919 Socialists were successful across the northern cities and won a total of 156 seats, becoming the largest party in parliament. This horrified the middle classes. To oppose the Socialists the Italian People's Party, the *Popolari*, was founded in 1919 by a Catholic priest and was backed by Pope Benedict XV. It took 20.5 per cent of the votes in the general election in 1919 and achieved a similar result in the election of 1921. It became the second largest party in parliament.

- In what became known as the *Biennio Rosso* or 'Two Red Years' there was mounting unrest in Italy between 1919 and 1920, as the Socialists advocated a Russian-style revolution. In September 1920 a wave of strikes swept northern cities, and within days 400,000 people were on strike. The Socialist occupation of factories, including some armaments producers, led to intense fear among the middle classes and ruling elites that Italy was on the brink of violent upheaval. In addition, landowners were outraged by the government's failure to stop the land seizures that continued in the countryside.

- On 21 January, 1921, the Italian Communist Party (*Partito Comunista Italiano* – PCI) was established. The landowners and conservative groups decided to take action against the threats to their interests from the left. Some turned to local Fascist groups for support against the Socialists. In Bologna in November 1920, at the inauguration of the Socialist council, Fascist activists turned the occasion into a riot. The violence spread and Socialist buildings were burned down. Widespread violence continued into 1921.

• Nevertheless, Socialists and the other left-wing groups lacked effective and strong leadership and they did not have a coherent plan to seize power in Italy. Although their language was inflammatory and violent, the Socialists were usually timid in action. They refused to collaborate with the government against fascism and some historians view this failure as making a '*right-wing victory inevitable*' (Mack Smith). It seemed that many Socialists believed that they could simply wait for liberalism to collapse now that universal suffrage had been achieved. One northern Italian newspaper commented in September, 1920: '*Italy has been in peril of collapse… [but] there has been no revolution… as the General Confederation of Labour has not insisted on it*'. As the historian Denis Mack Smith argues: '*One must conclude that Socialism did not believe wholeheartedly in either revolution or collaboration, and hence it was merely going to provoke Fascism.*'

Activity 12

Read Sources A to C and answer the questions that follow.

Source A

❝ *The First World War… radicalised a large part of a previously politically illiterate and inert mass electorate. A number of different factors were responsible for this: President Wilson's demand… for a more democratic future; the promises made by wartime leaders in order to rally support for the war effort, for example 'Save Italy and she is yours', which was specifically interpreted as a promise of land reform; the impact of the Bolshevik revolution of October 1917; and the remarkable process of informal political 'education' which took place in the trenches as peasant soldiers from remote regions rubbed shoulders with more politically sophisticated comrades from urban areas.*

The radical mood created in the trenches transferred itself to civilian, peacetime society and was manifested most obviously in a general demand for radical economic, social and political change.

Pollard, J (2005). *The Fascist Experience in Italy*. London: Routledge, p. 22.

Source B

❝ *The Italians had been divided before, but by November 1919 they were more divided than ever: 'combatants' against 'shirkers', peasants against workers, patriots against defeatists. No conceivable form of government could suit them all.*

The war left other major legacies. They included a thirst for justice ('land for the peasants') and a transformed economy. The war also produced tens of thousands of new officers, drunk with patriotism and greedy to command. They had won the war, and did not intend to let anyone forget it.

Clark, M (2008). *Modern Italy 1871 to Present*. UK: Routledge, p. 200.

Source C

❝ *Italy's difficulties were not unique; they were common to most European nations which had participated in the war, with the difference that Italian governments were less equipped than most to resolve them. In particular they seemed impotent to deal with the unrest in town and countryside, impose law and order or curb Fascist violence. Also, unlike other European states, Italy had no effective right-wing parties to provide an alternative to the Fascists.*

Knight, P (2003). *Mussolini and Fascism*. London: Routledge, p. 22.

1. Compare and contrast the views expressed in Source A and Source B regarding the impact of the First World War on the attitudes and expectations of Italian society.

2. According to Source C, although Italian difficulties 'were common to most European nations', what was different in other post-war European states?

The Versailles Settlement and the 'mutilated victory'

Key concepts: *Consequence*

Unable to redress the economic situation or the escalating violence in the cities and towns, the government seemed impotent. To make matters worse for the Liberals, they not only faced opposition from the left Socialists, but they also incited outrage and criticism from the Nationalists. When it became clear that the Liberal Prime Minister Vittorio Emanuele Orlando had failed to obtain the territory Italy had claimed at the peace settlement meetings at Versailles, the Nationalists, who had criticized the Liberals' management of the war, now accused the government of failing to defend Italian interests. As you have read, Italy had been persuaded to intervene in the First World War by promises of territorial gains in the Treaty of London. However, although the **Treaty of St Germain** gave Italy the province of Tyrol, the Istrian Peninsula, the port of Trieste, the Dodecanese Islands, and a protectorate and a port in Albania, it did not receive the port of Fiume or Dalmatia. The latter territories had not in fact been clearly cited in the Treaty of London, but the Italians had assumed these would be awarded to them too. Britain and the US refused to cede Fiume as they believed it was vital for the economy of the newly created state of Yugoslavia.

Prime Minister Orlando had been willing to renounce Italian claims to Dalmatia in return for the acquisition of the port of Fiume. However, his foreign minister, Sidney Sonnino, had disagreed. In the end the other powers refused to comply to Italian demands for either territory, claiming that Dalmatia had too few Italians to justify its handover.

The outcome of the settlement was greeted with widespread disgust in Italy. It was deemed that Italy's great sacrifices – 650,000 killed, 1 million injured, and a casualty rate higher than that of Britain – had been for nothing. The poet and Italian Nationalist Gabriele D'Annunzio declared it to be '*a mutilated victory*'.

It was within this political, economic and social post-war crisis that support for fascism began to grow. As its doctrines were loosely defined, fascism could appeal to groups across the class divide. Its demands for law and order, and its willingness to take direct action against the Socialists on the streets, were increasingly appealing to a broad section of Italian society. Many former conservative supporters of the Liberal regime had now lost faith in the ineffectual parliamentary system.

Activity 13

Source A

A map of Italy showing Italian borders between 1914 and 1920.

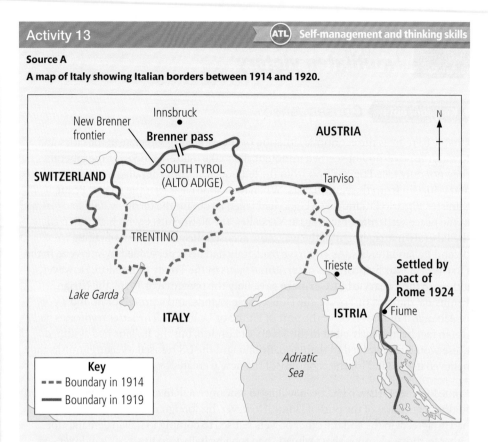

Source B

Italy and the peace settlement		
What Italy claimed	Promised at Treaty of London, May 1915?	Did Italy receive it in the St Germain Treaty, 1919?
South Tyrol	yes	yes
Trentino	yes	yes
Istria	yes	yes
Fiume	no	no
Dalmatia	yes	no
Colonies	yes	no

Look at Source A and Source B and refer back to the terms of the Treaty of London on page 76. In small groups, discuss the extent to which you agree that Italian gains from the Versailles Settlement represented a 'mutilated victory' for Italy.

Gabriele D'Annunzio and the Fiume affair

Key concepts: *Significance*

The Nationalist Gabriele D'Annunzio decided to redress the '*mutilated victory*', and with an army of 2,000 ex-soldiers and *arditi* occupied Fiume by force in September 1919. This was against the Italian government's agreement to hand over the port to Yugoslavia. However, the Liberal government was impotent to stop D'Annunzio until the return of Giovanni Giolitti as prime minister in December 1920. Giolitti ordered the Italian navy to blockade Fiume and only then did D'Annunzio's support collapse. The importance of the 'Fiume affair' to the rise of Mussolini was that the Fascists would later copy many of D'Annunzio's methods; this decisive act of force was seen as more effective than parliamentary discussion and debate. D'Annunzio's use of parades, public speeches and uniformed militias were all adopted by Mussolini. As historian Denis Mack Smith argues:

> *Although it was a petty and ridiculous affair, its example was an inspiration and a dress rehearsal for fascism… The black shirts of the arditi were to be seen in Fiume as people shouted the future fascist war cry 'A noi… eja, eja, alala.' Here, too, was seen the first sketch of the 'corporate state'. All this was later copied without acknowledgement by Mussolini.*
> **Mack Smith, D (1997). *Modern Italy – A Political History*. USA: Yale University Press, pp. 292–93.**

In addition, the affair had again undermined the credibility of the liberal democratic system.

Gabriele D'Annunzio in Fiume, 1920.

Activity 14 **ATL** **Thinking and self-management skills**

Prepare for a class debate on the following resolution: *'Liberal Italy was doomed to fail by 1921.'*

You need to organize one team who will support the motion and another team who will argue against it.

Liberal Italy was doomed to fail:

Point 1 *Liberal Italy faced serious political issues by 1914...* (add evidence and explain). Is there a historian you could add here?

Point 2 *In addition, politics seemed to be polarizing and becoming more radicalized after the First World War... failure at Versailles...* (add evidence and explain)

Point 3 *The economic situation was also deteriorating in industry and agriculture...* (add evidence and explain)

Point 4 *Furthermore the economic situation had become acute after the First World War...* (add evidence and explain) Can you find a historian to support this side of the argument?

Liberal Italy was not doomed to fail:

Point 1 *There had been relative political stability and the extension of the franchise... the Roman Question...* (add evidence and explain)

Point 2 *Indeed, there were also clear economic indicators that Liberal Italy was modernizing the country...* (add evidence and explain)

Point 3 *Liberal Italy had been victorious in the First World War... and gained...* (add evidence and explain)

Point 4 *It was Fascist violence and agitation that destabilized post-war Italy...* (add evidence and explain). Can you find a historian for this side of the argument?

How was Mussolini able take power in October 1922?

The growth of Fascist support

Having failed miserably in the election of 1919 it seemed that the Fascist movement might be doomed. However, Mussolini began to understand that his movement would need to move more clearly to the right to gain popular support. He ordered his Fascist regional bosses, the *Ras*, to organize the Blackshirts on paramilitary lines. In rural areas Fascist squads developed, and although they were not directed by Mussolini, their leaders looked to him for inspiration. Fascist support increased due to the apparent inability of the government to deal with the 'Socialist threat'; indeed, Mussolini realized that the authorities were reluctant to arrest his Blackshirts as they violently broke up strikes and factory occupations. By the spring of 1921, the movement had been transformed from an urban to a rural one. National Fascist membership had increased from 80,000 to 187,000 by May 1921. Between this date and October 1922, Mussolini continued to grow in strength:

• In the May 1921 elections, the Fascists won 35 seats, including a seat for Mussolini himself. The Catholic Party took 108 seats, and 138 seats went to the Socialists and Communists. It was at this point that Prime Minister Giolitti hoped to bring fascism into mainstream politics. Giolitti gave the movement much credibility and legitimacy when he invited the Fascists to join his Nationalist bloc in the May 1921 elections. It gave the Fascists a foothold in parliament and gave Mussolini a platform from which to criticize the political system. Giolitti believed that he needed the Fascists to secure a stable government. This was a terrible mistake as the election was blighted by Fascist violence: 40 people were killed on one polling day alone and, despite the intimidation, the Socialist vote held up quite well. It was clear that Italian politics was polarizing, and Giolitti resigned in despair.

Activity 15

 ATL Thinking skills

Mussolini's first speech in Parliament, 21 June 1921:

> *I am not unhappy to be delivering my speech from the benches of the extreme right... [this speech will be] clearly anti-democratic and anti-socialist... if you present a bill for the eight-hour day, we shall vote for it... indeed we shall vote in favour of all measures intended to improve our body of social legislation... But let me warn you at once that we shall resist with all our strength any attempt at socialization, collectivism and state socialism!... Fascism does not preach and does not practice anti-clericalism... I believe and affirm that the Latin and imperial traditions of Rome are today represented by Catholicism... and that the sole universal idea that exists in Rome is that which radiates from the Vatican.*

With reference to the source, identify which groups Mussolini was attempting to appeal to in this speech.

- At the end of 1921 the Fascist Party had around 250,000 supporters. Almost half of these were ex-servicemen, but there were also landowners, businessmen, teachers and workers. The movement also attracted the young. There was clear complicity from the police and the army, who did not restrain the Blackshirts from their excesses. In addition, the new pope, Pius XI, gave Mussolini his tacit support, as he saw the Fascists as a key weapon against the secular Socialists and Communists. The Pope also believed that fascism would be a means of improving the position of the Church. As we have seen, the Catholic Church was a significant political force in Italy and a valuable potential ally for Mussolini in his attempt to gain power.

- Mussolini wanted to wrest more direct control of the Fascist movement from the regional bosses. In October 1921 he established the National Fascist Party. This set up a more structured organization and put Mussolini's own Milan faction, personally loyal to him, into key positions in the party. He attempted to reassure conservatives and the Catholic Church that he was a man they could trust. Nevertheless, Fascist violence against the left continued to escalate.

- The fear of communism was a key factor in the rise of Mussolini and fascism. In the countryside, Fascist squads were deployed to protect wealthy landowners who feared Communist-inspired peasant land-seizures; Fascist squads were also active in violently attacking strikers and those taking part in factory occupations in the cities during the *Biennio Rosso*.

Mussolini speaking to Fascists in Bologna, April 1922:

> *However much violence may be deplored, it is evident that we, in order to make our ideas understood, must beat refractory skulls with resounding blows... But we are violent when it is necessary to be so.*

Mussolini and the March on Rome, October 1922

Key concepts: *Significance*

Mussolini and Blackshirts march on Rome, 28 October 1922.

By 1922, it was clear that Liberal Italy had failed to bring about a 'victor's' peace, was unable to establish a strong and stable post-war economy, and could not stem the violence on the streets. Indeed, a state of virtual civil war existed in the north and central parts of Italy. However, Mussolini was unsure whether to attempt to gain power through legal means or to seize power by force. He made it clear in a speech in September that he backed King Victor Emmanuel III, and he engaged in negotiations with conservative politicians hoping that they would agree to make him prime minister. Meanwhile, however, Fascist squads had gained ground and removed Socialist councils in several towns, and rumours circulated that there would be a Fascist coup.

Significant individual: King Victor Emmanuel III (1869–1947)

King Victor Emmanuel III had ascended the Italian throne in 1900 after the assassination of his father. Despite the fact that Italy was a constitutional monarchy with established parliamentary rule, the King retained significant power within the constitution. The monarch had the right to appoint the prime minister even if the majority in the Chamber of Deputies did not support the choice. King Victor Emmanuel had indeed intervened, due to political instability in Italy, on ten separate occasions up to 1922. In addition, when parliament was reticent about Italy entering the First World War on the side of the Triple Entente, the King had taken the decision to go to war himself. Victor Emmanuel would play a key role in Mussolini's acquisition of power in 1922.

Nevertheless, Mussolini continued to explore a legal route to power and attempted to arrange a formal truce with the Socialists, as he was concerned that the level of violence was alienating the Liberal politicians. However, the still powerful regional Fascist bosses (the *Ras*) refused to agree to this truce with the Socialists.

A coalition government led by the first Italian Socialist prime minister, Ivanoe Bonomi, had collapsed in February and was succeeded by a weak conservative coalition led by Luigi Facta. Both governments failed to contain the violence on the streets. In July 1922, Socialist trade unions called a general strike in an attempt to force the government to act against the Fascists. When, in August 1922, this general strike began, the middle classes panicked and looked to the Fascists to restore law and order. Mussolini declared that if the government did not break the strike then his Fascist squads would do it. Fascists took over the running of public transport and communications, Socialist strikers were beaten and, in the end, the general strike was a total fiasco for the Socialists. It was badly organized and they had managed to get only partial support from the workers. When the strike collapsed it left the Socialists in total disarray and Mussolini was able to present the Fascists as the only capable defenders of law and order. Conservative forces in Italy were impressed.

By September 1922 there were three political groups that were preparing to take action to address the situation. Prime Minister Luigi Facta was planning to militarily reinforce Rome and to garner support using D'Annunzio as a national hero at a 'stop Mussolini' rally on 4 November (the anniversary of Italy's victory in the First World War). The traditional political establishment was another bloc; they expected Facta to resign and a new government to be formed – under either Giolitti or Salandra – which would include some Fascists in order to 'tame' Mussolini. The third group were the Fascists themselves, who now controlled many local governments. The *Ras* were pressing for action and Mussolini knew he had to make a move before 4 November. Nevertheless, his call for the 'March on Rome' was not because he held any political sway in parliament. Indeed, some historians believe this decision was to prevent an anti-Fascist alliance developing.

Mussolini continued to engage in talks regarding the formation of a new government that would include Fascists. Even though there was some agreement on cabinet posts for Fascists, Mussolini demanded a more major role. On 16 October he met with leading Fascists in Milan. They decided that the time was ripe to seize power. Then, on 24 October, Mussolini declared at a Fascist conference in Naples, '*Either they will give us the government or we shall seize it by descending on Rome.*' In response, it is said that 40,000 Blackshirts chanted '*A Roma*' (to Rome). The *Ras* were the architects of the March on Rome, planning to seize key buildings on 27 October. Mussolini, however, was dubious about the plan and remained in Milan. Indeed, only 10,000 of the planned 50,000 Fascists assembled at three different positions outside Rome on the night of 27 October. The terrified local officials panicked when Fascist squads attempted to take control of government buildings and sent urgent calls for assistance. Prime Minister Facta was asked to stay, but the rest of the government resigned. Facta called on the King to impose **martial law** and use the army to crush the revolt. At first the King agreed, but then he changed his mind; instead he decided to ask Mussolini to form a government. On 29 October, Mussolini received a telegram from King Victor Emmanuel III: '*Very urgent. Top priority, Mussolini, Milan. HM the King asks you to proceed immediately to Rome as he wishes to confer with you.*'

Mussolini, the leader of a violent and undemocratic party that had only 35 Members of Parliament, accepted the King's offer and became prime minister.

> *The March on Rome… was a show of strength against a parliamentary majority. This show of strength would have failed if the King had opposed it. But… the King felt it was right not to oppose it.*
> **Carocci, G (1974). *Italian Fascism*. UK: Penguin, pp. 126–27.**

Historians have debated the reasons for the King's decision to hand power to Mussolini. He seems to have been motivated by a variety of reasons, including the fear of Italy collapsing into a civil war and the fear that he might be personally deposed in favour of his pro-Fascist cousin, the Duke of Aosta.

Mussolini arrived in Rome by train on 30 October and was sworn in as prime minister. He had been given power by conservative forces and politicians who thought he could serve their own interests.

Activity 16 Thinking and self-management skills

Look at the source and answer the questions that follow.

Italian postcard depicting Mussolini leading the March on Rome, 1922.

1. What is the message of the image on the postcard?
2. Discuss with a partner the ways in which this source differs from the account of Mussolini's March on Rome given in this chapter.

Historians' perspectives

Why was Mussolini able to take power in October 1922?

As you have already read, the Italian Liberal historian Benedetto Croce suggests that the rise of fascism was not the fault of the Liberal regime and was primarily caused by the socio-economic impact of the First World War, and the political backlash and fear of communism caused by the Bolshevik Revolution. It was the product of very specific circumstances. Croce follows the 'parenthesis' line of argument, which suggests that fascism represented a 'gap' in Italy's development and had little relation to what had happened in Italy beforehand or what happened there afterwards.

One of the most controversial historians of Italian fascism is Renzo de Felice, a prominent historian who, between 1965 and 1990, wrote a vast seven-volume 'life and times' biography of Mussolini. He argues that Fascist Italy was a *'freakish deviation'* which split the period from Liberal Italy to post-war Italy. Fascism could not be explained by what had come before it, and it was dislocated from the Liberal governments that preceded and succeeded it. He denied that his *'anti-anti-fascist'* approach to Mussolini's regime was not in fact pro-fascist. Felice argued that Italian Fascism was specific and unique and could only exist in the period between 1919 and 1945. He argues that fascism was not *'bad'* or *'evil'*, and has suggested that historians should look at the movement more objectively.

The Marxist historian Antonio Gramsci, however, argued in line with the left-wing perspective on the rise of fascism, that it was due to the failings of the Liberal Italian state. It had failed to include the masses in politics, it had used violence against discontent and revolts, and it had maintained the role of the elites as the dominant force in politics. This perspective suggests a 'revelation' line of argument; fascism was '*the autobiography of the nation*' and was the inevitable outcome of the flawed political and socio-economic developments in Italy following the *Risorgimento*. Reactionary forces funded the Fascists in order to retain their wealth and power, and to destroy the political and economic gains made by the working class up to the end of the First World War.

The US historian Alexander De Grand asserts that fascism developed as a response to the growth of socialism after the First World War, which had deepened class conflict in Italy. In 1919 the Socialists were the largest party in parliament and this panicked the middle classes and conservatives. As the government seemed impotent in the face of strikes in the cities and land seizures in the countryside, the anti-Socialist violence of Fascist squads was important for the growth of support for the movement.

Some contemporaries believed that the success of fascism in Italy was a result of its charismatic leader, Mussolini. In 1932, Italo Balbo, a Fascist leader in Ferrara wrote, '*Many in those days turned to socialism. It was the ready-made revolutionary programme and, apparently the most radical... It is certain, in my opinion, that, without Mussolini, three quarters of the Italian youth which had returned from the trenches would have become Bolsheviks.*'

The British historian, Denis Mack Smith, supports De Grand's view of the significance of the violence of Fascist squads; however, he also emphasizes, like Balbo, the importance of Mussolini himself. Mussolini made great political capital on the growing disorder in his newspaper, and promoted the image of the Fascist squads as the 'saviours' of Italy. Mussolini was a capable politician, and managed to shift his 'message' to appeal to different audiences. He would rally Fascist squads with calls for violent and radical change, but he also reassured the liberals and middle classes that he was a moderate.

Activity 17

 **Self-management skills**

Whose views?

With a partner match the following views on why fascism was successful in Italy after the First World War to one of the historians' perspectives outlined above:

1. It was caused by the socio-economic impact of the First World War.
2. It was the failings of the Liberal Italian state.
3. It was a '*freakish deviation*' from the liberal politics that came before and after it.
4. It was successful as it was based on popular support.
5. The middle classes feared socialism and the anti-Socialist violence of the Fascist squads led to increasing support.
6. It was the result both of Fascist squad violence and the abilities of their leader Mussolini.

Activity 18

 Thinking and self-management skills

Using the information in this chapter, complete the following grid:

Factors in rise of Mussolini	Evidence	Historian/ contemporary views	Significance
Political issues			
Economic problems			
Impact of the First World War			
Actions of the left wing			
Actions of conservatives			
Popularity of fascism			

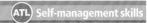

Activity 19 — ATL Self-management skills

Get into groups of four students. Each student takes one of the following 'lines of argument' regarding the rise of Mussolini, a) through to d). Add evidence to support your line of argument from this chapter.

Present your 'view' with supporting evidence to your group. Review the historians' perspectives and attempt to find a historian whose work you can use as additional supporting evidence.

a) **Leadership of Mussolini**
   - use of *Il Popolo d'Italia* for propaganda;
   - moves away from socialist principles in 1920;
   - enters parliament in 1921;
   - engages in talks with Liberal politicians;
   - encourages Fascist violence;
   - declares the March on Rome 1922.

b) **Popular appeal of fascism**
   - strong government;
   - anti-socialist;
   - promises an end to class conflict;
   - nationalism;
   - focus on action;
   - propaganda.

c) **Weakness of Liberal Italy**
   - weak political parties/factions;
   - short-term governments;
   - corruption;
   - failure to address economic issues, high inflation, unemployment, and industrial and rural unrest.

d) **Weakness of the left**
   - instilled fear in the elites, conservatives, Church, landowners and industrialists;
   - limitations of *Bienno Rosso*;
   - failure of the general strike.

Essay planning

In pairs plan the following essay questions.

1. **Examine the role of ideology in the rise of Mussolini in Italy between 1918 and 1922.**

2. **'The devastating impact of the First World War led to Mussolini's acquisition of power in 1922.' To what extent do you agree with this statement?**

Remember to address the command terms of the question when planning how to structure your essay. Begin each paragraph with an analytical point, and include detailed evidence to support this point. Attempt to identify relevant historiography where possible, and evaluate the different perspectives you present. Your conclusion should be based on the evidence and arguments you have developed.

Share your essay plans with another pair of students. Have you met the higher markband descriptors for Paper 3?

Essay writing

Practice essay question:

To what extent was Mussolini's rise to power due to the weaknesses of Liberal Italy?

Command term: To what extent

Topic: Mussolini's rise to power – the weakness of Liberal Italy, and other key factors.

Concept: Causation

Command term: For 'To what extent' questions you need to develop arguments for and against the theme set down in the question.

Introduction: Set down how the weakness of Liberal Italy had been a factor in the rise of Mussolini and suggest counter-claims: the popular support for fascism, the leadership of Mussolini, and the relative weaknesses of the left in Italy in the post-war period.

Paragraph 1: *Weaknesses of Liberal Italy in the long-term [political and economic problems up to the outbreak of the First World War] led to the rise of Mussolini...* (add evidence and explanations).

Paragraph 2: *The political weaknesses of Liberal Italy in the First World War and in the post-war crisis (1915–22) led to the rise of Mussolini...* (add evidence and explanations).

Paragraph 3: *Furthermore, the economic weaknesses of Liberal Italy in the First World War and in the post-war crisis [1915–1922] led to the rise of Mussolini...* (add evidence and explanations).

Paragraph 4: *However, there was also considerable public support for fascism after the First World War, which fostered the rise of Mussolini...* (add evidence and explain).

Paragraph 5: *In addition, the effective leadership of Mussolini himself facilitated his rise to power...* (add evidence and explain).

Paragraph 6: *Nevertheless, the weaknesses of the left in Italy in the post-war period also was a factor in the rise of Mussolini...* (add evidence and explain).

Conclusion: Answer the question, concisely and clearly, and develop a well-reasoned conclusion based on the weight of evidence and analysis presented. Was the rise of Mussolini primarily due to the weakness of Liberal Italy, or popular support for the Fascist movement and its charismatic leader?

For top markbands for Paper 3 essays:

Introduction and main body paragraphs

Responses are clearly focused.

The question is fully addressed and implications are considered.

The essay is well structured and the material effectively organized.

Supporting knowledge is detailed, accurate, relevant to the question and used to support arguments.

Arguments are clear, well developed and consistently supported with evidence.

There is evaluation of different perspectives.

Conclusion

The conclusion is clearly stated and it is consistent with the evidence presented.

04 Mussolini's Italy: 1922–1939

> *The nation is in our hands now and we swear to lead her back to her ways of ancient greatness.*
> **Mussolini.**

After his appointment as prime minister, Mussolini went on to consolidate his control and create the dictatorship of the **Duce**. But, despite having control over the institutions of state he never established the same degree of personal control as Adolf Hitler in Germany or Joseph Stalin in the USSR.

 Duce means leader in Italian, and from 1925 Mussolini was known as *Il Duce* or 'the leader'.

How did Mussolini consolidate his power between 1922 and 1926?

> **Key concepts:** *Significance and consequence*

Essay questions:

- Discuss how Mussolini consolidated his control in Italy between 1922 and 1926.
- To what extent were Mussolini's economic, social, and political policies successful up to 1939?
- Examine the nature of the Fascist state established in Italy between 1922 and 1939.

Timeline of events – 1922–1928

1922	Oct	Mussolini appointed prime minister of a coalition government
	Nov	Mussolini gains parliament's approval to rule by decree for 12 month period
	Dec	Mussolini creates the Grand Council of Fascism to strengthen his control over the Fascist movement
1923	Jan	National militia formed from Fascist squads
	Jul	The Acerbo Law changes the electoral system. Most popular party now gets majority in parliament
1924	Apr	First general election with Acerbo Law in place. Fascists win a majority in parliament
	Jun	Leading Socialist Matteotti is murdered by Fascists and his murder leads to a political crisis for Mussolini
	Jul	Press censorship introduced
1925	Jan	Mussolini announces that he intends to form a dictatorship
	Dec	All opposition parties are banned. Trade unions are banned
1926	Jan	Mussolini gains right to pass laws without parliamentary approval
1928		King no longer to select prime minister. A list would be drawn up by the Grand Council of Fascism and the King would have to choose a candidate from this

When Mussolini was appointed prime minister in October 1922, he understood that he would have to bide his time before attempting to consolidate his control. The Fascists did not have a majority in parliament, which meant he would have to form a coalition government – at least at first. Mussolini's initial government had only four Fascists, and most were ministers from the Liberal and *Popolari* parties. This coalition reassured the conservatives, many of whom did not think fascism would last for very long.

However, Mussolini had a political strategy. He would pursue, on the one hand, policies designed to reassure the conservative forces and to persuade them to give him dictatorial powers as this would be in their own interest; on the other hand, he would continue to use his Blackshirts to intimidate his opponents.

Step 1: Rule by decree, November 1922

Mussolini claimed that if he was given the power to rule by decree, this would be a *temporary* measure until the situation in Italy had been stabilized and parliamentary government could resume. In actual fact most of the violence at this time was being perpetrated by Fascist squads, but the Conservatives and Liberals remained terrified by the potential of a Socialist upheaval. The idea of 'rule by decree' was not new in Italy and had been used since 1870 during periods of political crisis. In November 1922 parliament gave Mussolini the power to rule by decree for one year, and this was supported by leading Liberals such as Giolitti, Facta and Salandra. The Socialists and Communists were the only members to oppose it.

Activity 1	 **ATL** Thinking skills

Mussolini's speech to parliament, 16 November 1922.

    … I am here to defend… the revolution of the 'black shirts'… With three hundred thousand young men, fully armed… [ready] to obey any command of mine, I could have punished all those who have slandered the Fascisti… I could have shut up Parliament and formed a Government of Fascisti exclusively; I could have done so, but I did not wish to do so, at any rate at the moment…

I have formed a Coalition Government… in order to gather together in support of the suffering nation all those who, over and above questions of party… wish to save her.

… I thank all those who have worked with me… [and] I pay a warm tribute to our Sovereign [king], who, by refusing… to proclaim martial law, has avoided civil war and allowed the fresh and ardent Fascista… to pour itself into the sluggish main stream of the State…

Quoted in Quaranta di San Severino, B (trans and ed, 1923). *Mussolini As Revealed in his Political Speeches.* JM Dent & Sons, pp. 208–209.

1. According to this source, what had Mussolini done to maintain parliamentary cooperation after he came to power in October 1922?
2. In pairs identify where in the speech Mussolini seems to be a) persuasive and b) intimidating.
3. With reference to its origin, purpose and content, analyse the value and limitations of this source for historians studying the aims of Mussolini in the early 1920s.

Step 2: Creation of the Grand Council of Fascism, December 1922

Having gained extraordinary powers in parliament, Mussolini now moved to consolidate his control over the Fascist Party by establishing the Grand Council of Fascism. The Grand Council became the supreme body within the Fascist movement; it discussed all proposals and made all key appointments within the Fascist Party. Mussolini, however, made the appointments to the Grand Council, and this meant he had direct control over Fascist policy. He then moved to limit the power of the *Ras* by converting the Fascist squads into a national militia in January 1923. The new national Fascist militia (*Milizia volontaria per la sicurezza nazionale*, MVSN) was to be paid by the state, and this in effect gave Mussolini a private army of over 300,000 men.

Step 3: Broadening his support base, 1923

In January 1923, the Pope's secretary had a secret meeting with Mussolini to discuss the 'Roman Question' and the relationship between the Church and the state. Mussolini offered to assist the struggling Catholic bank *Banca di Roma* and suggested that he would make religious education compulsory in schools and would ban contraception. In addition, he declared that fascism was incompatible with Freemasonry. The Pope was thus persuaded to remove his support from the *Popolari*. By the middle of 1923 the *Popolari* had lost the backing of conservative Catholics and had been dropped from the coalition government.

Mussolini's first cabinet included the Nationalist leader, Luigi Federzoni, in the post of colonial minister. Although a small party with only ten deputies, the Nationalists had influence with industrialists and had an 80,000-strong blue-shirted militia. The Blueshirts had regularly clashed with Fascist Blackshirts on the streets. In February 1923 the Nationalists were persuaded to merge with the Fascist Party. This merger gave Mussolini more support in parliament, strengthened the Fascists' position on the streets and gave Mussolini support in the south of Italy where fascism was weakest.

In addition, Mussolini courted the powerful conservative industrialists and their organization, the *Confindustria*. He promised not to pursue widespread tax evasion, and he lowered taxes. Price and rent controls were also abolished and government regulation of corporate finance was relaxed. Mussolini further appeased their concerns about the 'syndicalist Fascists' (Fascists who supported the power and influence of trade unions) by allowing the industrialists to create their own syndicates, separate from those of the workers. By 1923, the *Confindustria* had swung its support behind his premiership. Mussolini also pursued good relations with the landed elites by suspending the law on land reform and reducing death duties; in addition, government subsidies to agricultural collectives were ended.

Step 4: The Acerbo Law, July 1923

Mussolini, now strengthened by support from conservatives, the Church and leading Liberals, moved for outright electoral reform. He proposed that the party that won the most votes in an election should be given two-thirds of the seats in the Chamber of Deputies. He claimed this was necessary for the decisive rule that was needed to redress the problems Italy faced. He argued that previous weak coalition governments had all failed as they could not agree on what to do. However, what Mussolini did not make explicit in his speeches was that if this Acerbo Law was passed, the Fascists would become the majority party and then they could intimidate voters and attack opposition newspapers. Mussolini had already put leading Fascists in control of many local governments.

Nevertheless, when the Acerbo Law was presented in parliament for debate, a large majority of voters supported it. Armed Fascist squads had patrolled the chamber when the vote was taken to threaten those who might have been undecided, but in fact many Conservatives and Liberals believed that strong repressive leadership was needed to quell the Socialist threat. Giolitti and Salandra backed the Acerbo Law. The Liberals continued to hope that Mussolini and his party were not enemies of the parliamentary system and that due process would resume after this period of 'crisis' was over.

Step 5: The general election, April 1924

In the general election of April 1924 the Acerbo Act was put into practice. In fact, the Fascists and their Liberal allies attained 66 per cent of the vote and therefore would have had a two-thirds majority in the chamber regardless of the act. Although Mussolini's public profile had grown and he had gained much popular support, the result, an increase in Fascist seats from 35 to 374, was also due to ballot rigging and to intimidation carried out by Fascist squads. Despite this, 2.5 million Italians still turned out to vote for the Socialists and Communists, and they won 46 and 19 seats respectively, while the *Popolari* won just 39 seats. The results were based on a turnout of 7.5 million; 4.5 million of those eligible did not vote.

Step 6: The murder of Giacomo Matteotti, June 1924

Significant individual: Giacomo Matteotti (1885–1924)

Giacomo Matteotti was born into a wealthy family in Veneto. He graduated with a law degree and became an active member of the Socialist movement. He opposed Italy's entry into the First World War. When the Italian Socialists split he became leader of the United Socialist Party. He was elected to parliament in 1919, 1921 and 1924, and he spoke out against fascism, the National Fascist Party (*Partito Nazionale Fascista*, or PNF) and Mussolini. In 1921 he condemned Fascist violence in a pamphlet called 'Socialist enquiry on the deeds of the Fascists in Italy'. After the general election, on 30 May 1924, he denounced the Fascists' use of violence, intimidation and fraud to gain votes. Matteotti was kidnapped and murdered 11 days later by Fascist militiamen.

Although Mussolini had a majority in parliament, he was not yet powerful enough to be a dictator. He still had to get parliament to approve any new law; there were still opposition parties; and the King had the power to remove him as prime minister. Indeed, when parliament reopened after the election, opposition MPs, led by the well-known and respected Socialist Giacomo Matteotti, wanted to hold the Fascists to account for the violence they had perpetrated during the campaign.

On 30 May, Matteotti called for the election result to be declared invalid in parliament. A few days later, on 10 June, a group of Fascists abducted Matteotti and stabbed him to death. His murder sent shock waves across Italy. The Liberals were horrified. Mussolini denied any knowledge of the murder and attempted to distance himself from events. However, the main suspects in the murder were a personal assistant to Mussolini's press secretary, Amerigo Dumini, and the head of his press bureau, Cesare Rossi. Also implicated in the murder was a senior Fascist official, Giovanni Marinelli. There were even allegations that Mussolini himself had been involved. As the press released details of the crime, public opinion appeared to turn against Mussolini. Leading Fascists, including Rossi, were forced to resign.

A cartoon published in an underground Italian newspaper, 1924.

In pairs, discuss the message of the cartoon above.

The situation appeared to become more serious for Mussolini when 100 opposition MPs walked out of parliament and set up an alternative parliament, the **Aventine Secession**, at the end of June (see Information box). These MPs hoped their action would prompt the King to dismiss Mussolini. However, by removing themselves from parliament they destroyed the possibility of the Chamber of Deputies voting to remove Mussolini. In response, Mussolini again attempted to distance himself from the murder by ordering the arrest of Fascist suspects and appointing a Conservative minister of the interior. He claimed he wanted a transparent investigation. However, he also put more Blackshirts onto the streets to quell protests over the murder.

The withdrawal of the Aventine ministers in fact gave the King an excuse to do *nothing*, as there was no coherent pressure from parliament to act. The King was also apparently appeased by Mussolini's actions and refused to dismiss him. He was afraid that the removal of Mussolini would strengthen the radical left and could even lead to civil war. In addition, some Liberals also saw the affair as an opportunity to gain more control over Mussolini and so supported the King's position.

The army could have posed a threat to Mussolini during the Matteotti crisis, but it supported the regime's attacks on the left-wing opposition. Nevertheless, its leadership, concerned about the nature of the MVSN (see Step 2), wanted to use the Matteotti crisis to gain concessions from Mussolini. In June 1924 Mussolini sent six legions of the militia onto the streets to put down protests against his regime. The army gave the militia weapons but in return they forced Mussolini to place ex-army men in the MVSN as officers and made him agree that the MVSN's oath would be to the King, not just to Mussolini.

In July 1924 Mussolini attempted to silence his critics with press censorship and he banned political meetings of opposition parties. In October 1925 an assassination attempt on Mussolini gave him the justification to ban Matteotti's Socialist party, the PSU (*Il Partito Socialista Unitario*). These moves alienated some of the Liberals who had

The original **Aventine Secession** occurred in ancient Rome when citizens had withdrawn from the city to the Aventine Hill in a bid to oppose unjust rule. This secession had been successful.

supported him and they then joined the opposition. In November, when parliament resumed, leading Liberals, including Giolitti and Salandra, withdrew their support for Mussolini. The Matteotti affair was not going away.

Now leading radical Fascists wanted Mussolini to take decisive action, end the 'Matteotti scandal', and set up a dictatorship. At a Fascist rally in Florence, at the end of December 1924, Mussolini was called on to take '*dictatorial action*'. Then, on 27 December the 'Rossi Memorandum' was published. Rossi, arrested over the Matteotti murder, made a statement in which he claimed he was being made a 'scapegoat' and accused Mussolini of ordering attacks on his opponents (although not Matteotti specifically). Under increasing pressure, Mussolini was finally pushed into action by a visit from 33 militia leaders on 31 December. The leaders demanded that he either set up a dictatorship or they would withdraw their support.

On 3 January 1925, Mussolini made a dramatic speech in parliament in which he accepted responsibility for Fascist actions, although he stopped short of admitting responsibility for the death of Matteotti:

> ❝ I declare… that I, and I alone, assume the political, moral and historical responsibility for all that has happened… If Fascism has been a criminal association, if all the acts of violence have been the result of a certain historical, political and moral climate, the responsibility is mine.

One press report asserted that the speech was the '*Caporetto of the old parliamentary liberalism*'. Mussolini then promised decisive action against his opponents. The chamber lacked coherent leadership and many of its members had been compromised by previously supporting Mussolini. Parliament was impotent as Mussolini dared it to remove him. The King refused to sanction his dismissal.

Activity 3    **(ATL) Thinking skills**

> ❝ Mussolini lost his confidence for months. By the end of the year he had recovered it partly because of the hopeless divisions among his enemies. Most of them left the actual Chamber to form the Aventine Secession… but most of the Liberals disapproved of this as contrary to parliamentary principles. The King disliked the Aventine people because most of them were Republicans. The decisive voices, however, were those of the Church and industry. The Pope expressed approval for the regime… Industrialists were opposed to another fresh beginning, all the more so since Mussolini had gone all out to propitiate them [win them over] by reducing the state's interference in the economy.

An extract from *Fascism in Italy, Its Development and Influence*, written by the historian Elizabeth Wiskemann (1969). Macmillan, p. 16.

Discuss in pairs the reasons identified in this source for how Mussolini survived the Matteotti crisis.

Step 7: Mussolini gains the right to make law without parliament, January 1926

After Mussolini's speech on 3 January, Blackshirts were mobilized to attack opposition groups. Opposition meetings were closed down and there were widespread arrests. In December a new press law meant that only registered journalists could publish their work. Mussolini was given the title 'Head of Government' in the same month, and set up a committee to draft a reform of the constitution. In December 1925 the *Leggi Fascistissime* were passed, which banned opposition parties, organizations and trade unions. Local government came under tighter Fascist control as elected mayors were replaced with chosen officials. In addition, a new secret police force was established and a special court was set up for political crimes. Four attempts to assassinate Mussolini, between 1925 and 1926, were used to justify further repression. Finally, in January 1926, Mussolini was given the right to make laws without having to consult parliament and by the end of the year parliament had lost the right to even debate issues or new legislation. By November 1926 all opposition parties had been dissolved. In 1928 the King lost the right to select a prime minister; from this point on he could only chose from a list drawn up by the Grand Council of Fascism.

It was not only the weakness of parliamentary opposition that facilitated Mussolini's creation of a dictatorship. Many of the Italian public were prepared to either support or tolerate Mussolini's regime as it was preferable to the chaos and instability of the post-war years. The army tolerated Mussolini's dismissal of the minister for war in 1925 and his taking of the position himself, and it tolerated Mussolini assuming the role of political head for each of the armed forces. The military was appeased by Fascist promises of an assertive foreign policy and Mussolini's ambition to develop Italy's military capabilities. Furthermore, as Mussolini was fully committed in his other roles, the generals and admirals believed they would be free to make the direct decisions regarding their forces. The powerful industrialists continued to support Mussolini as they were benefiting from a period of economic growth and the policies of the finance minister, Alberto De Stefani, who had limited government interference, lowered taxes and abolished price controls. Industrialists, blighted by memories of the *Bienno Rossi*, were delighted when the Vidoni Palace Pact of 1925 was implemented, which only permitted Fascist trade unions. In April 1926, strikes were banned through the Syndical Law, which laid the foundations for the Corporate State. The Charter of Labour in April 1927 forced Fascist trade unions and employers into collective legally binding contracts. Mussolini also had the support of some of Italy's leading intellectuals, such as Giovanni Gentile, who described himself as the *'philosopher of fascism'*.

A law passed in 1928 ended universal suffrage and this cut the electorate by two-thirds. Only those who paid a tax of 100 lire or who were members of a fascist organization were eligible to vote. In any case, even those who could vote were unable to change the regime; Italy was a single-party state, and the 400 members of parliament were selected by the Fascist Grand Council. Mussolini had purged the PNF between 1925 and 1926 of *Ras* power and influence. In 1929 Mussolini completed the process of consolidating his control when he signed the Lateran Pacts (see pages 111 and 112) with the papacy, through which he hoped to neutralize the power of the Church in Italy. The agreements guaranteed a separate sphere for the Catholic Church and its youth movement, Catholic Action.

Mussolini had now created his dictatorship.

Activity 4

(see pages 111 and 112)

(ATL) **Thinking and self-management skills**

> *Mussolini was an extraordinary political tactician, but his skill in manoeuvring was due in part to the absence of any ethical foundation or an overall political vision. Every individual or institution became an instrument to be used only as long as it served his immediate purpose.*

An extract from *Italian Fascism: Its Origins and Development*, by the historian Alexander De Grand (1982). University of Nebraska Press, p. 42.

In pairs discuss the extent to which you agree that Mussolini's political success was due to the *'absence of any ethical foundation or an overall political vision'*.

Activity 5

 Thinking and self-management skills

In small groups discuss how each of the following factors helped to destroy Liberal Italy and to consolidate Mussolini's control:

- rule by decree
- creation of the Grand Council of Fascism
- broadening his support base
- the Acerbo Law
- the general election
- Matteotti Crisis, 1924
- measures taken to resolve the crisis, 1925
- the end of parliamentary politics
- the establishment of a dictatorship.

Activity 6

 Thinking and self-management skills

In pairs discuss the two perspectives on the chart below regarding what Mussolini aimed to achieve between 1922 and 1926. Add evidence from this chapter to support both opinions. Which perspective do you and your partner agree with most?

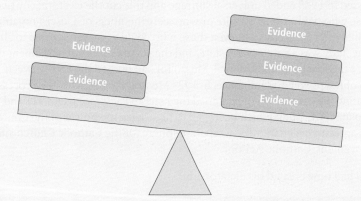

> Mussolini aimed to establish a strong government within the Italian parliamentary system. He wanted to restore stability. It was only after the Matteotti crisis developed and when he was under pressure from Fascist extremists that he moved to create a dictatorship.

> Mussolini aimed to create a dictatorship after his successful March on Rome. He needed total control of the human and material resources to be able to establish a Fascist state.

Essay writing

Discuss the factors that led to the establishment of a dictatorship in Italy by 1926.

Command term: Discuss

Topic: Factors that led to the establishment of a dictatorship in Italy by 1926.

Concept: Causation

Essay plan

Command term: 'Discuss' questions require you to develop a balanced view of the question. For this essay you need to identify thematic reasons for Mussolini's establishment of a dictatorship by 1926.

Introduction: Set down your key themes: the thematic strengths of Mussolini and his Fascist movement, support from significant groups within Italy and the weaknesses of the opposition.

Paragraph 1: *Mussolini was a capable politician, and he effectively used a combination of persuasion and coercion to garner support for his regime and took decisive action after the Matteotti crisis...* (evidence and explanations).

Paragraph 2: *Mussolini gained the support of different conservative forces in Italy... the King, the Catholic Church, Conservative politicians, the Confindustria (industrialists)...* (evidence and explanations).

Paragraph 3: *Fascism was popular with the Italian public... and Fascist violence intimidated opponents...* (evidence and explanations).

Paragraph 4: *However, the opposition was hopelessly divided...* (evidence and explanations).

Paragraph 5: *In addition, political opposition in parliament was ineffective...* (evidence and explanations).

Conclusion: Based on the evidence presented, offer a clear and concise conclusion regarding the main factor in establishing a dictatorship in Italy by 1926.

How successful were Mussolini's domestic policies?

Timeline of events – 1923–1939

1923	Pope withdraws support from *Popolari*
1925	Vidoni Palace Pact bans independent trade unions
	At the final Congress of the Fascist Party internal arguments are banned
	Dopolavoro, the Fascist leisure organization, is established
	The Battle for Grain policy is launched
1926	Mussolini able to make laws without consent of Parliament
	Right to strike abolished
	Ministry of Corporations established
	Opposition newspapers pushed underground
	The youth organization ONB is set up
	Cult of personality developing
1927	Revaluation of the lira
	The Battle for Births policy is launched
1928	All positions in Fascist Party assigned by headquarters in Rome
1929	Wall Street Crash in USA. Global economic depression begins
	Lateran Agreements with Roman Catholic Church
	Teachers forced to take oath of loyalty
1931	The Fascist Teachers Association is created
1935	Mussolini drives for autarky
1938	Anti-Jewish race laws introduced
1939	Chamber of Fasces and Corporations replaces parliament

When we consider the successes and failures of a leader we need to begin by considering what it was they were aiming to achieve. Mussolini's domestic policies were focused on consolidating and maintaining his control in the 1920s. However, he also had specific economic, social and political aims and he used a variety of methods and policies to achieve them.

Economic policies

As you have read, initially, Mussolini pursued economic policies that would garner support from influential groups. He was not an economist, and at first he did not have a coherent economic policy. Nevertheless, as his political position became more secure Mussolini became more confident in pursuing a transformation of Italy. His 'radical' new way of organizing the economy was to establish the first 'Corporate State'. This system was, according to Mussolini, superior to capitalist economies like that of the US and the Communist economy of the USSR. After he had established the Corporate State, Mussolini aimed to make Italy an autarky, or an economy that was self-sufficient.

Policies for Industry

At first Mussolini's regime benefited from a period of relative economic growth as exports of cars, textiles and agricultural goods doubled between 1922 and 1925. The appointment of an academic economist, Alberto De Stefani, as treasury minister, reassured skeptical big businessmen and his policies gained further support as he limited government spending, which kept down inflation. As you have read earlier, his other policies of broadly reducing government intervention and outlawing Socialist and Communist trade unions (in the Vidoni Palace Pact of 1925) meant that the leading industrialists swung their support behind the regime. However once his position was more secure, Mussolini moved away from courting the industrialists. He dismissed De Stefani, and revalued the lira (the Italian currency). The exchange rate for the lira had been falling, as the period of boom slowed in Italy from 1926. Mussolini was appalled when its value dropped to 150 lira to 1 British pound. In response he announced the Battle for the Lira and declared that '... *our lira, which is a symbol of our nation… our sacrifices… our blood… will be defended*'. Mussolini revalued the lira between 1926 and 1927. In December 1927 he set the value of the lira at 90 lira to 1 British pound, which was the value it had been when Mussolini came to power in 1922.

This policy was popular at home and it increased Mussolini's prestige. It was also supported abroad as it suggested to international bankers that the regime intended to restrict government spending further. The owners of heavy industry benefited, as they depended on importing raw materials, which were now far cheaper. However, although the Battle for the Lira had some positive political outcomes for Mussolini, the policy caused significant economic problems. The revaluing made Italian exports twice as expensive for foreign buyers, and industries such as textiles went in to sharp decline. The policy had a knock-on effect regarding unemployment, which trebled between 1926 and 1928. In addition, although the policy could have benefited Italian consumers as imported goods became cheaper, this did not happen because Mussolini imposed high tariffs on imports in an attempt to protect the domestic market for Italian products. Thus, companies producing armaments and those making goods for the domestic market profited from the *Duce*'s Battle for the Lira, whereas export industries stagnated and declined.

The Corporate State was the key new idea of the Fascist regime (see the previous chapter for earlier ideas about the Corporate State and its function). Essentially, the Corporate State was a model for the economy within which all industries would be part of a Fascist-led corporation that would arbitrate and resolve all disputes between owners, managers and employees. The system would assist with the organization of production, pay rates and working conditions. From 1926 Mussolini wanted to move forward with this revolutionary concept for transforming the economy. Each industry was to have a corporation which contained both employers and Fascist trade unions representing the workers. If the Fascist trade unions and employees could not find agreement, the dispute would be passed to a labour court. These courts, overseen by the new Ministry of Corporations, would find a quick and workable solution. The philosophy behind the Corporate State was that by collaborating, workers and employers would maximize productivity for the good of the nation as a whole. This contrasted with capitalist economies, as prolonged industrial disputes would be avoided; it also contrasted with communist economies as there would still be the value added by profit incentives and the entrepreneurial skills of the businessmen.

Initially, the Fascist trade unions seemed to offer a voice for the workers. Indeed, the head of the Fascist trade unions had attempted to champion the union members, but it soon became apparent that workers' interests would be subordinated to those of the industrialists and big business. Mussolini did not want to alienate these powerful groups who rejected any power being given to unions. In addition, the head of the Ministry of Corporations, Giuseppe Bottai, did not trust the Fascist trade unions and wanted the corporations to be dominated by the employers and his own technical experts from the ministry. He believed this was the most effective means to increase productivity.

In 1927, Mussolini clarified the roles he wanted for his new Corporate State: he sided with Bottai's vision and gave him the task of developing a 'Labour Charter' that would set out the rights of workers. The resulting charter stated:

- Private ownership of businesses and industries was the most efficient way to run an economy.
- Employers could change working hours without consultation.
- Employers could offer annual holidays for workers, but this was not compulsory.

In 1928, the influence of the Fascist trade unions was further reduced when the single confederation of trade unions was divided up into six smaller confederations. In 1929, The Ministry of Corporations proclaimed the new Corporate State system a success. The economy was entering a new era and class conflict had been removed. By 1934, 22 corporations had been set up and these had influence over nearly every aspect of the economy. For the workforce this new system meant:

- Workers could not choose their own union representative: Fascist nominees were given to them.
- Fascist representatives tended to side with the employers.
- Workers' interests regarding pay and conditions went unmet.

Nevertheless, there were some limited changes in the interest of workers: for example, sick pay and pay for national holidays was introduced in 1938. Overall, however, the system favoured the industrialists, who kept their non-Fascist organizations and could largely ignore the new corporations.

Read this source and answer the question that follows.

> In truth, the 'corporate revolution' never materialized. Conflict between the employer and employee was not solved, only suppressed, and the corporations never achieved the pivotal role in the state and the economy envisaged by the Duce. Although parliament itself was replaced by the Chamber of Fasces and Corporations in 1939, this meant nothing. Parliament had long since lost any power and the new Chamber was equally impotent.

Robson, M (2015). *Italy: The Rise of Fascism*. Hodder Education, p. 87.

According to this source, how had the Corporate State failed?

CHALLENGE YOURSELF

 Research and thinking skills

1. In pairs, research President Franklin D Roosevelt's 'New Deal' for the US.

2. Compare and contrast Mussolini's economic policies in response to the Great Depression with the 'New Deal'.

3. Discuss with the same partner the reasons that other capitalist democracies in Europe might have struggled to implement similar 'New Deal' programmes during the early years of the Depression.

The Corporate State was not immune to the impact of the global economic depression that took hold after the Wall Street Crash in the US in October 1929. Many Italian companies collapsed, and key industries such as car manufacturing reduced production by 50 per cent. Unemployment soared from half a million in 1928 to 2 million in 1933. In responding to the Depression, Mussolini's policies were not restrained by free market economics and 'laissez-faire' policies. He introduced massive public works programmes, such as the land reclamation programme or 'Battle for Land' (see page 109), that put people back to work. These programmes meant that people had money to spend, which kept demand going in the domestic market and therefore created more work. Mussolini also bailed out the Italian banks when business could not afford the debt repayments. The regime set up the Institute for Industrial Reconstruction (IRI) in January 1933, and took on the shares in companies held by the banks. This made the state the major shareholder in many key companies. The IRI also gave loans to industry. These policies meant that Italian society did not suffer the same degree of deprivations that many capitalist democracies did at this time, and some contemporaries even suggested that President Franklin D Roosevelt's 'New Deal' package in the US copied many of these ideas.

Mussolini's focus turned to preparing the economy for war in the 1930s and to this end he gave more support to the arms industries and attempted to create an autarky. The impetus for the drive for self-sufficiency was the League of Nations' attempt to curb Italian aggression and expansion in Abyssinia with sanctions in 1935. Mussolini understood that to fight a major war Italy had to be able to keep its people and military supplied. He gave generous government contracts to shipbuilders and the steel and chemical industries, and extended government control over these sectors. The regime encouraged the growth of near monopolies, believing that economies of scale would prove more efficient. However, this drive for autarky had limited success, and by 1940 Mussolini's Italy was not an autarky. Government debt continued to grow and the regime did not redress this by increasing taxation on big businesses. Workers suffered wage cuts throughout the 1930s. At first these cuts were manageable as the price of goods in shops was falling; however, as the drive for autarky continued and imports fell, so the price of everyday items increased.

Unemployment between 1928 and 1935, in France, Germany, Italy and the UK.

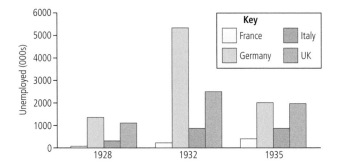

Real wages fell in the 1930s by 10 per cent, and there was a fall in the consumption of meat (an indicator for falling living standards). Mussolini's response was: *'We are probably moving toward a period when humanity will exist on a lower standard of living.'*

Policies for agriculture

When Mussolini came to power there were considerable underlying problems in Italian agriculture. There was a large class of rural poor and calls for the redistribution of land to the peasants. In addition, Italy's farming methods were backward and inefficient; Italy had to import grain to feed its people and this was a potential weakness should Italy become engaged in a war.

The *Duce*'s first main programme for agriculture was part of his drive for autarky: the Battle for Grain in 1925. The plan was political in that it aimed to increase Fascist power in rural areas, and economic as it aimed to increase grain production. The government gave grants to farmers to buy tractors and fertilizers, and offered them advice on modern farming methods. The regime also guaranteed a high price for the grain produced. These incentives had positive results; the harvest rose over 10 years from 5.5 million tons to 7 million tons, and in turn this enabled Italy to reduce its grain imports by 75 per cent in the same period. Mussolini, photographed getting 'his hands dirty' during the harvest, claimed personal success for this achievement and it certainly helped to strengthen his popular support. However, the real success of the Battle for Grain was limited. The land in the southern and central regions, forced to grow grain, was not suitable for this crop and should have been left to grow fruit, wine and olive oil, all of which went into sharp decline.

Mussolini helps with the harvest during the Battle for Grain.

Mussolini's next programme for agriculture was the land reclamation initiative. The regime funded the draining or irrigation of potential farmland. Malarial swamplands close to Rome were drained and small farms developed in what would be a 'showcase' of the initiative, the Pontine Marshes. Although the initiative was successful in that it provided thousands of jobs and improved public health, the amount of land reclaimed was relatively small.

Overall, the lives of agricultural workers, as for industrial workers, did not improve under Mussolini. Agricultural workers suffered significant wage cuts, and in the 1920s the US implemented tight restrictions on immigration that meant the traditional route of escape from rural poverty had closed. Despite Mussolini's attempt to prevent urban migration, half a million people migrated to the cities in search of work before the Second World War; in Rome the population doubled. Mussolini wanted to establish a class of pro-Fascist wealthy peasants. However, his policies only benefited the rich landowners and a proposed 1922 law to redistribute land was never implemented, as the regime did not want to alienate the landowners. It was this failure to break up the huge estates that arrested the development of agriculture in the south. In this situation, the gap between the industrial north and the poor agricultural south continued to grow.

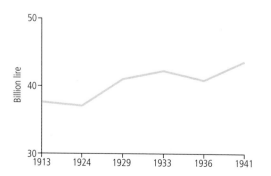

Value of sold agricultural produce 1913 to 1941.

109

Historians' perspectives

Did Mussolini's policies improve the Italian economy?

It has become a common conception that Mussolini did bring about some key improvements in the Italian economy, with foreign journalists praising his achievements at the time.

Nicholas Farrell, writing in *Mussolini: A New Life* (2004), and Spencer Di Scala writing in *Italy: From Revolution to Republic* (1995), emphasize the positive effects of Fascist policies, modernization of industry and the vast public works programmes and land reclamation initiatives that helped to make Italy a modern European state. Indeed, millions of hectares of land were developed into farmland and the country's infrastructure was improved – the Fascists had made *'the trains run on time'* and had built thousands of kilometres of roads. Overall, both historians argue that productivity increased.

However, Edward Tannenbaum, in *Fascism in Italy* (1973), argues that *'economically Fascism was a failure.'* He suggests that the near autarky in grain production was at the expense of other key products and that Italy's overall economic performance in the 1930s was worse than that of any other major industrialized country. John Whittam, in *Fascist Italy* (1995), also argues that businessmen were increasingly uneasy with the policies of autarky, and price and import controls. He highlights the fall in the standard of living for the working classes and the fact that many people joined the PNF merely to secure a job as unemployment rose.

Most historians agree that the Corporate State as a whole failed to transform the economy and trade relations. Martin Blinkhorn, in *Mussolini and Fascist Italy* (1984), argues that in practice it was merely a disguise for the exploitation and oppression of labour.

Activity 8 · **ATL** Self-management and thinking skills

Read Source A and Source B and answer the questions that follow.

Source A

> The manipulation of economic facts was an essential part of Mussolini's system. He gained much credit by promising that his annual budget would be of a 'crystalline simplicity' so that every citizen could know how his money was being spent; but in practice the figures became more obscure than ever. By the end of the 1920s, even the experts were baffled when they tried to find out about the balance of payments or how much was being spent on public works or the militia. The corte dei conti, whose job was to supervise expenditure, was artfully removed from parliamentary scrutiny and placed directly under the head of government. So was the Institute of Statistics, whose director was instructed to publish no figures without higher approval. Mussolini recognized the publicity value of statistics and thought it no sin to 'attenuate' [reduce the force of] those he objected to in the monthly statistical bulletin. Foreigners, as a result, learnt to pay little attention to official publications.

Mack Smith, D (2001). *Mussolini*. Orion, p. 142.

Source B

Graph of the Italian government's balance of payments between 1921 and 1940.

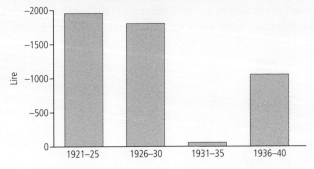

Balance of payments

The revenue a government receives minus the amount it spends.

1. According to Source A, how reliable were government statistics under Mussolini?

2. What does Source B suggest about the strengths of the Italian economy under Mussolini?

Your class will consider two major military commitments: Italian imperial expansion in the war with Abyssinia from 1935 and its intervention in the Spanish Civil War from 1936. Both of these wars put a considerable economic burden on Italy. Divide the class into two groups; Group A will research the Italian involvement in Abyssinia and Group B will investigate intervention in Spain.

Focus your research on the following key questions:

1. Why did Mussolini take military action in a) Abyssinia or b) Spain?

2. What military commitment was made by Italy in a) Abyssinia or b) Spain? (See Chapter 6 for more information on Italy's role.)

3. To what extent did Mussolini achieve his aims in a) Abyssinia or b) Spain?

4. What were the economic costs of involvement for Italy?

5. What impact did the war have on Italian foreign relations?

Group A should then present its research to Group B, and *vice versa*. This should be a brief ten-minute presentation. Make sure you support your main points with evidence. You must also cite your sources.

After both groups have presented, as a class discuss and reassess the impact of Mussolini's policies, both domestic and foreign, on the Italian economy.

Social policies

Mussolini's social policies were aimed at securing his own personal position as *Duce*, and ultimately the intention was that they would transform Italian society by moving it away from '*bourgeois mentalities*' and traditions that emphasized the Church, family and a comfortable standard of living towards a focus on fascism and '*the nation above all else*'. Mussolini wanted to create a society that was obedient to him, and physically and psychologically ready for war.

The Church

To achieve these aims Mussolini had to address the power and influence of the Catholic Church. As you have seen, he adopted a conciliatory approach towards the Church, as he believed that with its backing his personal control would be strengthened and the international credibility of his Fascist regime would improve. As he consolidated his control, Mussolini restored Catholic control of education and increased the state payments to priests in return for the Pope withdrawing his support for the *Popolari*. However, the key understanding with the Church did not come until 1929, with the Lateran Agreements. There had been resentment between the Church and the Italian state since the period of unification, when the Pope's territories of Rome and the Papal states had been seized. The terms of the treaty component of the Lateran Agreements set down terms to heal this rift; the Pope recognized the Italian state and its control of Rome and the Papal States, and in return the state recognized the Pope's control over the Vatican City (part of Rome) and its independence, and gave financial compensation for the lost territories of £30 million.

The other component of the agreement was the Concordat (papal agreement), and this established that:

• Catholicism was the state religion, which meant that the Pope could appoint all bishops and the state would pay the clergy;

• the clergy could not belong to political parties;

• religious education would be compulsory in schools;

• the Church had to give its consent to divorce, and a church ceremony was sufficient to have a legal marriage (removing the requirement for a civil registration).

Mussolini had achieved his aim of gaining the support of the Church for his regime. However, he had had to accept that the influence of the Catholic Church would remain in Italian society. In addition, as Mussolini moved to create a more fascist society in the 1930s, tensions re-emerged. When the regime tried to suppress Catholic Action (Catholic youth groups and potential rivals to the Fascist youth groups) in 1931, it had to find a compromise. The Church agreed to ban political activity by Catholic Action but kept the organizations that were important for maintaining its influence over the young; Radio Vatican continued to broadcast its own news and views during the 1930s. The Church also prevented Fascist interference in Catholic schools and the Catholic University of Milan, and even declared that the tenets set down by the Fascist youth movement, the ONB, were 'blasphemous'.

Activity 10

Source A

66 *Mussolini alone has a proper understanding of what is necessary for his country in order to rid it of the anarchy to which it has been reduced by an impotent [powerless] parliamentarianism and three years of war. You see that he has carried the nation with him. May he be able to regenerate Italy.*

Pope Pius XI to the French ambassador, Beyens. 1929. Quoted in Hite, J and Hinton, C (1998). *Fascist Italy*. John Murray, p. 75.

Source B

66 *The clear-cut, uncompromising views of Mussolini made an agreement easier…*

Peace of heart of the Italian people was the result of this agreement. An old problem was settled forever. Sons, educated to the love of new, forceful, active living, would not be in conflict with their fathers, who were attached to the traditions of the past. One could finally be both a good Italian, which is the same as being a Fascist, and a good Catholic. The Vatican itself found new dignity and new strength. The Lateran Treaty was, doubtlessly, one of the greatest achievements of the wise, realistic policies of Benito Mussolini.

Extract from Mussolini's memoirs, *Benito Mussolini, My Autobiography* (1939). Hutchinsons & Co.

Read Source A and Source B. With a partner discuss how Source A supports the views expressed in Source B.

Many leading clergy had supported Mussolini's wars in Spain and Abyssinia, as the campaigns were seen as crusades to preserve and spread Christianity. However, tension increased between the regime and the Church when the government passed anti-Jewish laws in 1938. By 1940 Pope Pius XI was distancing himself from Mussolini, and the alliance between Church and state was over.

Anti-Jewish laws

Mussolini had not pursued anti-Semitic policies such as those instituted by Hitler, but this changed in 1938. There were a number of reasons for this shift in policy. Firstly the relative ease of military success in Abyssinia was seen as proof that Italians were a confident, warlike and superior race; some leading Fascists began to view the Jews in Italy as an inferior group, and this view was heavily influenced by the policies of Nazi Germany. Indeed, as Italy's relationship with Nazi Germany developed in foreign policy so Nazi ideas gained ground in Italian society. Mussolini began to see the Jews as an obstacle to achieving fascist societies in Italy and Europe and, in July 1938, the regime backed the publication of the 'Manifesto of Racial Scientists', which declared that Jews were not part of the Italian race. In August 1938, Jews born outside Italy were banned from state schools, and this was extended to all Jews in September. Then, in October, Jews were banned from the Fascist Party and from owning larger companies. In November Jews were forbidden to marry non-Jews and they were excluded from banking and the military.

However, although life certainly deteriorated for Italian Jews, and there were many racist Fascists who wanted to pursue deportations, there was not a state policy of violence against Jews, as in Nazi Germany. There were also exemptions from the banning laws for Jews who had served in the Italian army in the First World War and those who had served the Fascist Party. Many Fascist officials did not impose the new anti-Jewish laws, sometimes because they agreed with the Church's position that persecution was wrong, or because they had personal or family connections with Jews.

Women

The Fascist perspective on the role of women was traditional and in many ways in line with the Church's views: women should primarily be wives and mothers, and birth control and abortion were unnatural. Women were discouraged from pursuing higher education and given incentives to have large families. Indeed, the *Duce* not only wanted women to play a purely domestic role in society, he also needed them to increase the size of the population in order to build the capacity of the Italian military. To this end, Mussolini launched the Battle for Births in 1927.

The Battle for Births aimed to increase the population from 40 million to 60 million by 1950, and set down a standard of 12 children per family. Mussolini encouraged women to have more children through financial incentives. Marriage loans were offered to couples and for each child born, part of the debt was cancelled. Married men with six or more children were exempt from taxation, and welfare clinics provided healthcare to poor families. However, persuasion went hand in hand with more coercive measures; single men had to pay higher tax rates and, in the 1930s, to get a job in the civil service you had to be married. Women were also coerced out of work as private companies were encouraged to employ only married men. The state railway

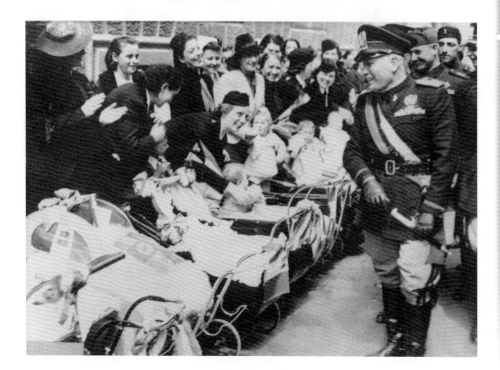

A photograph of mothers receiving awards during the Battle for Births.

sacked all women apart from war widows. In 1933, a quota system set down that a maximum of 10 per cent of the public sector workforce could be female, and this was extended to private businesses in 1938. Women were permitted to work in more traditional, domestic low-paid roles such as cleaners. These policies were in line with Fascist ideology, but they also helped reduce the growing unemployment figures.

However, despite the persuasion and coercion of the Battle for Births the initiative failed to achieve its key aim. The birth rate rose only slightly after 1936 and the number of marriages was unchanged by the policies. Some historians have pointed out that in 1911 the birth rate was 147 per 1,000 women of childbearing age, whereas in 1936 it was only 102 per 1,000. Furthermore, women still made up 33 per cent of the industrial workforce in the mid-1930s, and poorer women continued to need to work in order to feed their families.

The youth

Mussolini was very keen to shape the thinking of Italy's young, and ensure they supported his regime. He aimed to create a pro-Fascist, strong, disciplined and athletic youth. In 1923, the school reforms passed by the regime were more conservative than fascist in nature, and they focused on rigorous examinations for the children at elite schools and institutions.

However, radical Fascists demanded a more coherent fascist programme for education. To achieve his aims, Mussolini needed to ensure schools promoted fascism in their curriculum in order to achieve his aims. He focused on the teachers, many of whom were viewed as either openly anti-Fascist or unsympathetic to the regime. In 1925, all teachers who were deemed 'suspect' were dismissed from their jobs, and from 1929 teachers had to take an oath of loyalty to the *Duce*. The Fascist Teachers Association was established in 1931 and membership was made compulsory in 1937. To foster Mussolini's cult of personality among the young, biographies celebrating

A school textbook cover, (1941).

Mussolini's achievements were distributed to all schools and teachers were ordered to praise his genius in their lessons. The *Duce*'s portrait was hung next to that of the King. A textbook for eight-year-olds made it clear that children should have total loyalty to the great leader: '*The eyes of the Duce are on every one of you… You must obey because you must. What is the duty of a child? Obedience! The second? Obedience! The third? Obedience!*' To foster Fascist ideals students were taught about '*Italian greatness*' while nationalism was promoted in the curriculum, especially in history. Textbooks and works of literature that were deemed insufficiently patriotic were banned and by 1936 only one official textbook could be used.

Mussolini not only wanted to indoctrinate children in school, he also wanted to ensure their leisure time embraced Fascist ideals. In 1926 the *Opera Nazionale Balilla* (ONB) was set up. The ONB organized youth groups and activities. During the 1930s membership was made compulsory for children from eight years old and by 1937 it had 7 million members.

Activity 11 Thinking, research and social skills

Read through Sources A, B and C in small groups.

1. Discuss in your groups the content of each source and what it reveals about the impact of Fascist groups on young people in Italy.

2. In the same group, use all three sources, the material in this chapter, and some research of your own, to write a foreign correspondent's newspaper report on the ONB for a non-fascist newspaper in the 1930s.

Source A

Creed (statement of beliefs) of the Fascist Youth Movement, 1926.

> I believe in Rome the Eternal, the mother of my country, and in Italy her eldest daughter, who was born in her virginal bosom by the grace of God; who suffered through the barbarian invasions, was crucified and buried, who descended to the grave and was raised from the dead in the nineteenth century, who ascended into heaven in her glory in 1918 and 1922. I believe in the genius of Mussolini, in our Holy Father Fascism, in the communion of its martyrs, in the conversion of Italians, and in the resurrection of the Empire.

Quoted in Hite, J and Hinton, C (1998). *Fascist Italy*. John Murray, p. 153.

Source B

A photograph of some young members of the ONB, c. 1936.

Source C

❝ *The Fascist youth organizations had a powerful impact on youth growing up under the regime, although membership itself was by no means universal. An estimated 30 to 40 percent of the population between the ages of eight and eighteen never joined at all, the vast majority of whom were probably working-class youth and young women, especially those who left school before the age of fourteen. However, even before the enrolment was made compulsory, the overwhelming majority of middle-class children joined either out of conviction or because of the material advantages offered, or as a result of teacher pressure, parental fears, or a single desire not to be excluded from such a highly visible form of sociability. The generation born after World War I in Italy thus experienced Fascist regimentation as something entirely routine. Having had little or no contact with alternative organisations or cultural models, it was inevitably susceptible to propaganda that identified everything pre- or anti-fascist as decrepit or inept and the regime itself with dynamism and the energy of youth.*

De Gazia, V (1982). *Historical Dictionary of Fascist Italy*, P Cannistraro (ed). Westport: Greenwood Press, p. 572.

The activities run by the ONB were focused on Fascist ideology, preparing the youth for war through military training, sports training and parades. Young girls were also involved, but their activities prepared them for the domestic roles fascism dictated: sewing, cooking and childcare. There was also an organization for university students, the *Gruppi Universitari Fascisti* (GUF), that aimed to create a Fascist elite by ensuring that older students continued to engage with Fascist ideas and maintained their military training. The GUF organized the Littoriali Games, which encouraged university students to compete with each other in sports and other activities such as art and music.

Leisure time and the *Dopolavoro*

Mussolini also wanted to mould older Italians in order to transform society more quickly, and to this end the *Dopolavoro* was set up in 1925 to provide leisure activities that promoted Fascist ideas and values; its aim was to fill the gap left by the defunct trade union clubs. By the mid-1930s, the *Dopolavoro* controlled all football clubs, 8,000 libraries and 1,350 theatres. Membership of the *Dopolavoro* grew to a peak of 4 million in 1939, and there was little need to force people to join it as it gave subsidies to sports and entertainment, and for holidays. Its emphasis was on having fun rather than indoctrination or military training.

The arts

Artists in Nazi Germany and in Stalin's USSR were strictly controlled. However, in Italy there remained a degree of artistic freedom not enjoyed in these other regimes. Mussolini was drawn to two artistic movements: neoclassicism, which took classical Rome as its inspiration, and modernism, which experimented with abstract art. Most Fascists promoted the neoclassical style, and the regime attempted to control artists through government funds and commissions, and by forcing them to join the Syndicate of Professional Artists. However, private commissions continued and even those who joined the syndicate could pursue different artistic styles.

Political policies

As you have seen earlier in this chapter, Mussolini had, by 1926, achieved his political aim of becoming dictator. He also aimed to remove or deter any potential opposition. Parliament was subservient and no longer able to debate his decrees; it had become merely a forum for his Fascist supporters to applaud him. The armed forces had pledged loyalty to the King, who in turn was in thrall to Mussolini. His position seemed unassailable. He pursued personal power above all else and this disappointed radical Fascist Party members who wanted some movement towards a real 'Fascist revolution'.

The media

As a former newspaper editor Mussolini understood the power and influence of the press. In 1926 opposition newspapers were suppressed, and Mussolini's press office handed down the 'official version' of news events for publication. The regime also harnessed radio and the cinema for propaganda purposes. The state ensured radios were distributed to schools and even into more remote villages to enable the state to broadcast Mussolini's speeches and programmes praising his genius and achievements.

Cult of personality

> *I often would like to be wrong, but so far it has never happened and events have always turned out as I foresaw.*
> **Mussolini.**

Fascist propaganda poster, 1935.

Mussolini's promotion of a cult of the *Duce* aimed to gain widespread support for his personal dictatorship. The development of this cult was dependent on the media consistently depicting him as a new 'Caesar', a genius and a great international statesman. The Italian public were consistently fed headlines such as: '*Mussolini is always right*', '*he works 20 hour days*' and '*Mussolini is courageous and athletic*'. Mussolini controlled all images of himself in the media and those printed included him horse-riding, skiing and flying airplanes. All photographs were carefully selected to show a youthful and energetic man. There were no images of him wearing glasses and no press reports stated specifically how old he was.

Mussolini also promoted himself as a highly cultured man, a man who read literature and philosophy and was also a capable musician. He did not believe that the Italian masses were cultured or hard-working. Indeed, he believed that most Italians could not engage in political debate and preferred to be told what to do.

Propaganda focused on the great successes of the *Duce*, particularly in foreign policy. The Italian public was promised a glorious future that would fulfil the greatness of classical Rome and the Italy of the Renaissance. Mussolini's press office extended slowly and by the 1930s had become a ministry that controlled radio, film and all other cultural areas. It rolled out a vast propaganda campaign to support the war in Abyssinia (see research task on page 111) and in 1937 it was renamed the Ministry of Popular Culture.

The creation of a personal dictatorship

Mussolini achieved his political aims of achieving supreme power. After gaining power in 1922, he established unrivalled personal control over the National Fascist Party (PNF), and destroyed the power of the *Ras*. The Fascist *squadristi* were loyal to Mussolini, and when the Grand Council of Fascism was set up it reinforced his personal control. In the final Fascist Party congress Mussolini asserted that there should be no internal divisions. By 1928 all party posts were appointed from the party headquarters in Rome. Mussolini had total control over his party, and he had demonstrated great political skill in overcoming the deeply factional PNF.

As Mussolini promoted only obedient followers in the party, the Fascist Party shifted from being made up of the working classes and peasants to a party of state workers from the lower middle class. Members of the party that attained any fame or notoriety were moved from the centre of power to prevent them becoming a threat to Mussolini. High-profile Fascists such as Italo Balbo and Dino Grandi were given posts with no real power (a post in Libya and ambassador to London respectively). Mussolini's methods, coupled with the fact that the party needed him to hold it together, meant that no rivals emerged in the party before the Second World War.

Furthermore, the King was in awe of Mussolini and this enabled the *Duce* to deter him from any political involvement; he was never asked for his opinion. Mussolini did not share power with his government ministers and there was no cabinet or government team. In any case, Mussolini held the most important positions in foreign affairs, the interior, and the armed forces. Parliament, as discussed earlier, became irrelevant after 1926; it abolished itself completely in 1939 and was replaced with the Chamber of Fasces and Corporations. Mussolini gained control over the civil service and other institutions of state, without drawing a direct confrontation; many key posts in the civil service, judiciary, and armed forces were held by Conservatives sympathetic to fascism. Mussolini used a system of patronage to promote trustworthy Conservatives and to slowly remove those who were not actively pro-Fascist.

The party was given a key role in education, leisure and, of course, propaganda. When this led to disputes and disagreements between party organizations and government departments Mussolini's own power increased. For example, a rivalry developed between the party and the education ministry over control of the ONB, and the army argued with the Fascist militia over the distribution of weapons and supplies. In these disputes the groups involved looked to Mussolini to resolve the issue. The *Duce* used these divisions to strengthen his personal control: for example, he gave the control of the *Dopolavoro* to the party in 1927 but gave control of the ONB to the Ministry of National Education in 1929.

Activity 12

Read the source and answer the question that follows.

> *The effect of this diluting of the regime's supposed totalitarianism, ironically, was to enhance Mussolini's personal authority. In return for preserving some autonomy, his conservative allies effectively abandoned any idea of concerted action and surrendered to the Duce an awesome freedom to formulate and implement general ... policy.*

Blinkhorn, M (2006). *Mussolini and Fascist Italy*. Methuen & Co. Ltd, p. 52.

According to this source, what was the impact of 'diluting' the regime's 'totalitarianism'?

However, Mussolini adopted a different approach with the judiciary and here he implemented a purge. The *Duce* had to ensure the judiciary would enforce his laws and he sacked judges for being too independent or insufficiently pro-Fascist. The Italian judiciary was no longer impartial, and imprisonment without trial became common. Mussolini also occasionally intervened to offer a verdict on a specific trial himself. At the local government level, self-government was abolished and elected mayors and town councillors were now appointed from Rome.

Activity 13

Read the source and answer the question that follows.

> *Italy has never been so united as she is today... Fascismo has abolished the game of parliamentary chess; it has also simplified the taxation system and reduced the deficit to manageable proportions; it has vastly improved the public services, particularly the railways; it has reduced a superfluously large bureaucracy without any very bad results in the way of hardships or unemployment; it has pursued a vigorous and fairly successful colonial policy. All this represents hard and useful work, but the chief boons [achievements] it has conferred upon Italy are national security and national self-respect...*
>
> *Fascismo has had a great deal of courage [and] very considerable wisdom...*

An extract from the British newspaper, *The Times*, 31 October 1923.

In pairs identify the key points made in the source regarding Fascism's early achievements in Italy.

What were the limitations of Mussolini's domestic policies?

The main aims of Mussolini's domestic policies were to set up the Corporate State, drive the Italian economy into greater productivity and ultimately autarky, establish a Fascist society, and consolidate his personal control. The successes of his initiatives and programmes were emphasized, such as the infrastructure projects and sporting achievements (for example, Italian victories in the football world cups of 1934 and 1938), whereas the failures were not mentioned. However, in many areas he failed to achieve his aims. Indeed some historians view his only real achievement in domesitc policy as being the agreement with the Church. His failures can be seen in the following areas.

• The fact that Mussolini had to make the final decision on so many different issues led to serious delays in the system. It not only led to bad decisions, it also meant that the *Duce* could not make sure his decisions were being carried out. Ultimately, the regime suffered from '*confusion, delay and incompetence*' (Robson).

• Mussolini never really changed Italian attitudes, and there seems to have been a great deal of outward conformity to the Fascist state without much real conviction. He tried to break '*bourgeois thinking*' in Italian society and promote *fascisization* by, for example, making it compulsory in 1937 to replace the traditional greeting of a handshake with a Fascist salute; he even attempted to change the calendar, taking 1922 as the new 'Year 1'. However, these dictates were met with apathy and irritation, and directives on how women should dress and present themselves (they were not to wear trousers or make-up) were derided.

• There was resistance to the Battle for Births programme, and although the *Dopolavoro* was generally popular, Mussolini's other social initiatives were not. Most young people left school when they were 11 years old, many Catholic schools did not pursue the Fascist curriculum, and membership of the ONB was not enforced. It is also important to note that despite the best efforts of the Ministry of Popular Culture, often ridiculed and called '*Minculpop*', Fascist newspapers never achieved more than 10 per cent of total circulation. The Vatican's newspaper remained more popular and actually increased its readership from 20,000 to 250,000 in the late 1930s. Therefore, although Mussolini remained generally popular with the Italian public he was unable to enact a Fascist revolution in society.

• Some estimates have suggested that only 15 per cent of the civil service was Fascist in 1927. Although the number of Fascist Party members increased in the 1930s, as people became aware that this was the only way to get promoted, the reality was that there was no Fascist revolution in government.

Opposition to the regime

The weakness of the political opposition to the Fascist regime was not only due to repression by the state, but also because Mussolini ensured the support of political journalists who would have normally championed the opposition by offering them pay incentives and grants. He offered similar sweeteners to academics, including titles and generous pensions. Any criticism of the state would lead to the immediate removal of all benefits.

However, there was also a lack of cohesion, resulting in division, among the opponents of the regime. The Communists, for example, refused to work with any other group. Moreover, opposition to Mussolini was dangerous. Historians have estimated that by 1926 Fascist squads had killed around 2,000 people and the murder of Matteotti in 1924 had sent a clear warning that the Fascists were prepared to use violence to silence their opponents. The regime's secret police, the OVRA (*Organizzazione per la Vigilanza e la Repressione dell'Antifascismo*), tracked possible dissidents and had the support of thousands of informers. It also had its own court that had tried more than 4,000 defendants by the end of the 1930s, handing down more than 30 death sentences. In addition, 12,000 Italians were sentenced to house arrest, usually in isolated villages. Prison camps were set up on islands such as

Lampedusa and these camps held up to 5,000 political prisoners; however, although conditions were harsh and there was sometimes torture of inmates, the scale of these camps did not compare with that of the concentration camps in Nazi Germany.

Despite this intimidation the Communists maintained an underground resistance with 7,000 activists. They published their own newspaper, *L'Unita*, and distributed anti-fascist propaganda. As well as the Communists, another opposition party, Justice and Liberty, was founded by Carlo Rosselli, who aimed to form an alliance between the Socialists and Liberals. Based in Paris, he attempted to brief the international press about the real situation of oppression in Mussolini's Italy, and pamphlets were smuggled into Italy to spread anti-fascist ideas. Although the group had only a few thousand supporters, the *Duce*'s regime took Justice and Liberty seriously enough to have Rosselli murdered in 1937.

Essay writing

Review the essay writing template in the Introduction and plan the following essay.

To what extent were Mussolini's economic, social and political policies successful up to 1939?

Command term: To what extent.

Topic: Mussolini's economic, social and political policies up to 1939.

Concept: Change and consequence.

Essay plan

'To what extent' questions require you to develop arguments for and against the assumption/ assertion in the question.

For this essay you need to identify the aims and successes of Mussolini's economic, social and political policies up to 1939, and then counter-argue with the failings of these policies.

Introduction:	Set down your key themes: successes of Mussolini's economic, social and political policies up to 1939, but also include evidence that these policies failed.
Paragraph 1:	*Mussolini's economic policies were successful... he aimed to...* (evidence and explanations).
Paragraph 2:	*Mussolini's social policies were successful... he aimed to...* (evidence and explanations).
Paragraph 3:	*Mussolini's political policies were successful... he aimed to ...* (evidence and explanations).
Paragraph 4:	*However, his economic policies were also ineffective... and he failed to achieve his aims...* (evidence and explanations).
Paragraph 5:	*In addition, Mussolini's social policies failed to...* (evidence and explanations).
Paragraph 6:	*Finally, the limitations of Mussolini's political policies were...* (evidence and explanations).
Conclusion:	Based on the evidence presented, answer the question – overall were Mussolini's domestic policies successful?

What was the nature of the Fascist state?

Key concepts: *Change and continuity*

Mussolini claimed that the Fascist state was a new type of political system; it was a 'totalitarian state'. He explained this system as *'everything in the state, nothing outside the state, nothing against the state'*. His minister for justice, Alfredo Rocco, produced most of the laws that between 1925 and 1928 created this Fascist state. Rocco wanted to put all organizations under state control. Thus, as you have seen, only Fascist unions were allowed to exist; the authority of the state was also applied to the PNF itself, which became subordinate to it; the media was censored and extolled the glories of fascism; and even leisure time was directed by the state. However, Mussolini had had to compromise to consolidate his control. He found agreement with the Church that retained its influence in Italy; he allowed the industrialists their autonomy and profits; and Italy remained a monarchy where the King could dismiss Mussolini. Therefore, Mussolini did not establish a fully totalitarian state and in nature it was far less state-controlled than Nazi Germany under Hitler or the Soviet Union under Stalin.

An Italian historian, Renzo de Felice, claims that Mussolini enjoyed a broad base of 'consent' from the Italian people. However, the compromises Mussolini had found with the elites came under pressure in the 1930s. His wars put a strain on the economy, and those who had profited from the drive for autarky began to feel restricted by greater state interference in decision-making, while the Church became increasingly critical of the new race laws. As the regime became more Fascist in both domestic and foreign policy so Italian institutions became more nervous about the direction in which Mussolini was taking them.

In addition, although he was a capable politician, some historians have argued that Mussolini lacked many attributes of an effective leader. He maintained popular support by promoting a cult of personality, but again his critics believe that his regime lacked substance. The state took over the Fascist movement, and most historians assert that there was no Fascist revolution. The PNF was used as a tool for propaganda not as a party in power. Those traditionally involved in government institutions joined the Fascist Party to secure their careers and gain promotion. Indeed, the elites supported the regime while its interests were not threatened. Individual freedoms and liberties were suppressed, but there was not widespread terror and violence as was the case in other dictatorships.

CHALLENGE YOURSELF

 Thinking skills

In pairs discuss the viewpoint expressed by Kedward. To what extent do you agree with the idea that fascism had a 'wide appeal' in Italy?

Historians' perspectives

In 1969, the British historian Harry R Kedward argued that Mussolini's regime had been genuinely popular. Read the following extract from his book *Fascism in Western Europe*. Blackie, p. 43.

> Any account of European Fascism in the twentieth century must begin by saying that its strength lay in the willingness and enthusiasm with which large numbers of ordinary people welcomed it ideals, believed in its claims and endorsed its methods. In Italy in 1921 this was historical reality. In Germany in 1933 it was even more true. The wide appeal and attraction of Fascism is something which must first be admitted before any understanding of it can emerge.

The Italian historian Renzo de Felice, in *Interpretations of Fascism* (1977), also argued that Mussolini's regime was genuinely popular, particularly in the period between 1929 and 1936. He suggests that popular support for Mussolini continued until the invasion of Greece during the Second World War. Felice's book was controversial in Italy when it was published, but the historian Nicholas Farrell, writing in *Mussolini: A New Life* (2004), concurs with Felice's view that 'the truth is that a critical mass of people in Italy did actively support [...] Mussolini'.

However, the British historian RJB Bosworth, in *Mussolini's Italy* (2006), has suggested that support for the regime was far more limited and that pro-Fascist and pro-Mussolini public displays were essentially engineered by the oppressive state.

Deepen your understanding of the complexity of opinion towards Mussolini's regime by researching the following:

- different historians' views from the 1950s through to recent work on the regime;
- contemporary international newspaper reports on the regime in the 1920s and 1930s;
- contemporary Italian viewpoints on the regime from the 1920s and 1930s; attempt to find both pro-Fascist and anti-Fascist reports.

What challenges do historians face when attempting to assess the real extent and depth of the regime's popularity?

In pairs read the source below and then explain to your partner the points that Blinkhorn makes about the limitations of the *Duce's* regime.

> *The new system was a personal dictatorship under Mussolini, yet still legally a monarchy… The government ruled by decree… Local elections were eliminated… Yet the basic legal and administrative apparatus of the Italian government remained intact. There was no 'Fascist Revolution', save at the top… At one point [Mussolini] was nominally in charge of eight different ministries. In fact, he personally administered almost none, leaving them to be run by senior officials. State administration changed comparatively little; the provinces were still administered by state prefects, not the Fascist Ras, and on the local level affairs were still dominated more often than not by local notables and conservatives. Purging of civil servants was minimal, and there was little interference with the courts.*

An extract from the academic book, *History of Fascism*, by Stanley Payne (1995). Routledge, pp. 116–17.

Organize your class for a debate. You will need a team to argue for and a team to argue against the following resolution:

> *Nothing more graphically illustrates Fascism's limitations as a totalitarian regime than the endless yearnings of its own militants for a 'Fascist revolution' that never came.*

Quote from Blinkhorn, M (2006). *Mussolini and Fascist Italy*. Methuen & Co. Ltd, p. 55.

Essay planning

In pairs or small groups plan and draft detailed essay plans for the following questions:

1. **Examine the nature of the Fascist state established in Italy between 1922 and 1939.**
2. **Discuss the successes and failures of Mussolini's domestic policies.**
3. **To what extent did Mussolini achieve his economic aims between 1922 and 1939?**
4. **'Mussolini consolidated his control by intimidating his opponents.' To what extent do you agree with this statement?**

05

Spain: 1918–1936

The Spanish Civil War broke out in 1936 after more than a century of social, economic and political division. Half a million people died in this conflict between 1936 and 1939.

Its significance is highlighted by the Spanish historian Francisco J Romero Salvadó:

> *The Spanish Civil War was above all a domestic conflict, a brutal attempt to solve by military means a host of social and political issues that had divided Spain for generations. Questions such as land reform, centralism versus regional autonomy and the role of the Catholic Church and the armed forces in a modern society came to a head in the attempted military coup of July 1936 which precipitated the civil war. This cruel three years of fratricidal struggle was a traumatic experience which directly touched the lives of every family and even saw brothers fighting on opposite sides. The triumphant Nationalists then ensured that this climate of hatred and division lasted for 40 years.*
>
> *However, this was not just a domestic conflict but also one that transcended national barriers and aroused passions and acrimonious debate throughout Europe.*
>
> **Romero Salvadó, F (2005).** *The Spanish Civil War.* **Basingstoke: Palgrave Macmillan, p. ix.**

This chapter will cover the political, social and economic conditions in Spain that led to the outbreak of this civil war in July 1936. It will consider the role of the Primo de Rivera regime, the ensuing polarization and growth of different political parties under the Second Republic, and finally the personal roles of Manuel Azaña and Gil Robles.

Manuel Azaña addressing military personnel.

Key concepts: *Causation and consequence*

Essay questions:

- Discuss the role of political and economic conditions in causing tension and division in Spain up to 1923.
- To what extent was Primo de Rivera's regime effective in addressing the problems in Spain between 1923 and 1930?
- Examine the reasons for political polarization under the Second Republic.
- Compare and contrast the roles of Manuel Azaña and Gil Robles in the outbreak of the Spanish Civil War in 1936.
- To what extent were economic factors a key cause of the Spanish Civil War?

Activity 1  ATL Thinking skills

Study the timeline on the next page which lists events in Spain in the early 19th and 20th century. What evidence can you find in support of Preston's argument below?

> *The notion that political problems could more naturally be solved by violence than by debate was firmly entrenched in a country in which for a thousand years civil war has been if not exactly the norm then certainly no rarity.*
>
> **Preston, P (2006).** *The Spanish Civil War: Reaction, Revolution and Revenge.* **London: Harper Perennial, p. 17.**

Timeline of events – 1820–1931

1820	The Spanish army, supported by Liberals, overthrows the absolute monarchy and makes Spain a constitutional monarchy in a modernizing revolution
1821	Absolute monarchy is restored to Spain by French forces who want to reinstate the old order
1833–1839	In an attempt to prevent a female succession following the death of King Ferdinand, there is a revolt by 'Carlists'. The First Carlist War lasts until 1839. The army intervenes to defeat the Carlists, who nevertheless remain a strong conservative force in Spanish politics
1833–1869	The army's influence in national politics increases during the 'rule of the Queens'
1869–1870	Anarchist revolts take place against the state
1870–1873	Monarchy of King Amedeus of Savoy
1873–1874	The monarchy is overthrown and the First Republic is established
1874	The army restores a constitutional monarchy; Bourbon Restoration
1875–1918	During this period the constitutional monarchy allows for democratic elections. The system is corrupt, however. Power remains in the hands of the wealthy oligarchs or their local political agents the 'caciques'. Spanish Nationalism suffers when Spain is defeated in 1898 in a war with the US. Humiliation and loss of Cuba and Philippines
1914–1918	Spain remains neutral during the First World War and experiences economic growth
1918–1923	The economy falters and 12 different governments fail to redress the crisis. The regime reaches new lows in 1921 when the army, sent to crush a revolt led by Abd el-Krim in Spanish Morocco, is massacred
1923–1930	General Primo de Rivera takes control in a bloodless coup and rules for seven years, which is supported by the King. Its demise fatally undermines the legitimacy of the monarchy
1931	The Spanish King flees Spain and the Second Republic is established

King Alfonso XIII
▼

What were the political, social and economic conditions in Spain before 1923?

Political tensions

Weakness of central government

There had been much political instability in Spain throughout the 19th century: periods of absolute monarchy, military and foreign political intervention, and even the establishment of the First Republican regime. Spain had alternated between periods of conservatism and liberalism. In 1898 Spain was a constitutional monarchy and power was mainly held by the parliament, the Cortes. The king was head of state, and he appointed a prime minister who should have commanded a majority in the Cortes. Yet although the Cortes was in theory elected by the male population, actual power was held by the wealthy oligarchs; political control shifted between their different cliques. There were two main parties, the Conservatives and the Liberals, but in fact there was no real difference between them. Most governments were coalitions and elections were rigged or decided by corruption. The *Caciquismo* system meant that elections were controlled by local power brokers known as the *caciques*.

Although after 1900, socialist and republican organizations began to form in larger towns, most Spaniards did not believe that their interests were represented by the main political parties. King Alfonso XIII, monarch from 1886, was not a modernizer and he had no real aims to reform or change the institutions of state. He did concede limited self-government to Catalonia in 1913, but this did not appease the Catalan Nationalists.

> *There were no mass democratic political parties: the consequence was, at a very superficial level, political stability, but beneath it tremendous social instability, because nothing ever really changed… Elections changed virtually nothing. Only a relatively small proportion of the electorate had the right to vote, and since nothing changed… the population was forced into apathy or violent opposition to the system.*
> **Preston, P (1991). Modern History Review.**

Centralism and the Catalan and Basque regions

A map of Spain's autonomous communities.

A significant cause of political tension was the ongoing struggle between the centralist state and the Catalan and Basque regions, which wanted decentralization and independence. The Catalans and the Basques had their own separate languages and cultures, and by the early 20th century they had their own churches and industrialized economies. Indeed, most of Spain's industries were concentrated in these regions: for example, textiles, iron and coal industries in Catalonia, and shipbuilding in the Basque country. The Catalan Nationalist movement was the most active of the two, and its aims were initially promoted by the mainly conservative Lliga Party. Protests and strikes by workers led to brutal responses from the authorities. In 1909 the army was sent in to put down riots in Barcelona; in the so-called '*tragic week*' 200 people were killed. Indeed, between 1918 and 1921, 1,000 people were killed in protests in the city. The historian Hugh Thomas suggests that Barcelona was described at this time as the '*most turbulent city in Europe*'. A more radical Catalan party, Esquerra, led by Lluís Companys, was established in the 1920s.

Furthermore, there were a number of groups opposed to the political status quo in Spain, and each would play a part in the political divisions that led to violent conflict in 1936. The Liberal movement in Spain had achieved little during its opposition to Conservative forces in the 19th century, although it remained a political force and supported the revolution that ousted the King in 1931.

Working-class movements

The growth of industry led to working-class movements, generally divided between the Socialists and the Anarchists. The *Partido Socialista Obrero Español* (PSOE; Spanish Socialist Party) had been established in 1879 and had grown in urban areas in the late 19th century. In the 1920s the PSOE was led by Largo Caballero and Indalecio Prieto. However, although revolutionary in theory it worked through parliamentary methods and had minimal impact up to 1931. The Socialist trade union, the UGT was more visible in organizing strikes and protests in the urban areas and grew during the First World War. Following the Bolshevik Revolution of 1917 in Russia, the PSOE split over whether to support the Bolsheviks, and a small Spanish Communist Party emerged.

The Anarchists were also a major political force in Spain; this was mainly due to their demand for the redistribution of land, which was popular with the peasants, and it had become a strong movement after a visit to Spain by a leading Italian Anarchist and follower of Bakunin in 1868. The Anarchists argued for revolutionary methods and boycotted all democratic processes. They aimed to destroy the state through revolution or general strikes and set up self-governing communities. The Anarchist trade union, the CNT, set up in 1911, was the main competition to the Socialist UGT. It was popular with the workers in Catalonia and the peasants in Andalusia and active in organizing strikes and protests. In addition, there was a more extreme Anarchist faction called the *Federación Anarquista Ibérica* (FAI; Spanish Anarchist Federation), which carried out bombings and assassinations.

Activity 2 ATL Thinking skills

Read the source and answer the following questions:

> The rebellion of the Spanish masses was not a fight for better conditions inside a progressive capitalist system which they could admire; it was a fight against the first advances of capitalism…[and] against its very existence at any stage of its possible progress in Spain… the materialistic conception of history, based on the belief in progress, meant nothing to [Spaniards]; for the Spanish worker is little progressive. This is why the Barcelona engineer could feel one with the Andalusian peasant… The fight against oppression, the mentality of the [person] who leaves his village in order to be free, is still much stronger than the mentality of the trade unionist who accepts hard months of strike in order to become well-to-do. In consequence, violence is neither shunned in others nor rejected if proposed to the Spanish masses. But peaceful trade unionist action is suspect… And this, in my opinion, is the explanation of the preponderance of anarchism in Spain.
>
> Borkenau, F (1937). *The Spanish cockpit*. London: Faber and Faber, p. 20.

1. According to Borkenau, why was anarchism popular in Spain?

2. The founding leader of the Anarchist movement, Mikhail Bakunin, believed that the Spanish, even more than Russians, were a revolutionary people as they were not *'imbued with the capitalist spirit'*. In pairs discuss what Bakunin meant by this.

3. Borkenau commented, *'How could Spanish workers and peasants have refused the teaching of a man [Bakunin] who believed that the specific mentality of the Spanish lower classes ought to be the model for labour movements of the whole world?'* Why would Bakunin's ideas be seductive to the Spanish working classes?

4. With reference to its origin, purpose and content, analyse the values and limitations of this source for historians studying tensions in Spain in the 1920s.

The role of the army

The army had a powerful political position in Spain due to its role in Spain's imperial past. Its leadership believed that it was the protector of the nation, and this meant it had the right and duty to intervene in politics if a crisis occurred. It had intervened in this way several times, in 1820, 1871, 1874 and 1923, when the military had led coups or **'pronunciamientos'**. However the army was unpopular with the people. It had a reputation for brutality, it was expensive, and it required heavy taxes to maintain. The army was also in need of reform. It was too big, and had too many officers – one for every nine men. The upper and middle classes, however, defended their interests, as they dominated the officer corps.

The army was generally conservative, but the '*Africanistas*' – those who were experienced in the wars in Morocco – were the most nationalistic. The army had proved itself ineffective when it lost the Spanish Empire during the 19th century, and a war with the US in 1898. Spain lost most of its remaining colonies, including Cuba and the Philippines, which were ceded to the US in the Treaty of Paris. It also struggled to keep control of Morocco between 1906 and 1926. The Spanish had acquired part of Morocco through an agreement with France, but the Rif tribes – the native Moroccan people – were very difficult to pacify. In 1921 the credibility of the ruling regime was further undermined when Spanish forces were defeated by the Rif leader Abd el-Krim, and 10,000 Spanish troops were killed. When a parliamentary committee was set up to investigate the disaster, it seemed that the King and his government would be held responsible. Seemingly to prevent the downfall of the monarchy, the military governor of Barcelona, General Miguel Primo de Rivera, announced a *pronunciamiento* in September 1923. Alfonso supported this move, and asked Primo de Rivera to form a government of '*patriots rather than politicians*'.

Activity 3  ATL Thinking skills

Read the source and answer the following questions:

> In the years after the Moroccan war… the Moroccan officers, hardened in a difficult war, had no sympathy with the programme for peacetime soldiering, and were abused as 'drunks' devoid of civil conscience. The military disasters of 1921 in Morocco made the army feel at the same time insecure and indignant: indignant in that it sensed that the politicians had starved it of the material basis of glory, insecure in that it feared that the same politicians would once more turn the cry of 'responsibility' against an army to which their parsimony had denied the sinews of victory.
>
> **Carr, R (1982). *Spain, 1808–1975*. Oxford: Clarendon Press, p. 562.**

1. According to Carr, what impact did the Moroccan war have on Spain's military?

2. Discuss how the army having '*no sympathy with the programme for peacetime soldiering*' might cause tensions in Spain.

Economic tensions

Agriculture

The plight of the agricultural workers was a key factor in the discontent that led to the civil war. Spain was predominantly an agricultural economy, and agriculture was the chief source of employment. Unfortunately, there were fundamental problems that made it inefficient. It did not provide sufficient food, and work was only seasonal. Workers needed to migrate in search of work – most lived in abject poverty and the gap between the rich and poor was vast. In the centre and south of Spain, land was organized in huge estates, the *latifundia*, by the 'Grandees', who dominated the political system. In the north, peasants owned small plots of land, but often these were too small to allow them to make an adequate living. The **Civil Guard** was deployed to ruthlessly repress the rioting and disorder which often broke out in the countryside. For example, in January 1892, a makeshift army of landless day labourers, driven by hunger and desperation and armed only with scythes and sticks, invaded and briefly held the town of Jerez (Preston). The Civil Guard and police quickly moved in and drove the labourers out.

With no support from the Church, some looked to groups such as the Anarchists, who argued for the redistribution of land. Yet many of the Catholic small landholders were very conservative and resistant to socialist or anarchist ideas. This conservatism was used by the Catholic Agrarian Federation, which provided support for farmers in return for their rejection of socialist ideas; these same farmers would later support Franco and fight on his side during the war.

Industry

Industrially, there was a need for modernization and reform. Apart from in the north, there had been little Spanish industrialization in the 19th century. Expansion was limited by endemic poverty. Workers in the towns, meanwhile, faced low wages, long hours, unregulated working conditions, poor housing, and little in the way of welfare provision. This situation led to the growth of trade unionism. However, the trade unions competed with each other (for example the CNT and UGT) and they were unable to achieve anything substantial, as the employers could always find alternative labour sources from the countryside. The workers' political parties also lacked real political power. With no legal means of improving their situation, violent uprising appealed to many as the means to effect change.

Spain's neutrality during the First World War facilitated a short period of economic boom as the country benefited from a lack of competition. Spain's industrial sector prospered as it sold France textiles and other materials. With the increase of exports, however, there were also shortages of resources and inflation. Working-class living standards went down, and working-class militancy increased. However, this economic boom did not last and when the war ended in 1918 renewed competition led to a fall in exports and high unemployment. By the early 1920s, there were major economic problems, and this led to violent conflict between employers and employees, particularly in industrial cities such as Barcelona; here the industrialists attempted to overcome the post war recession by reducing wages and laying workers off. The workers responded by going on strike and the employers then hired gunmen and locked out strikers. The Anarchists responded with violence, and between 1919 and 1921 '*the streets of Barcelona witnessed a terrorist spiral of provocations and reprisals*' (Preston).

Social tensions

The Catholic Church was rich and powerful in Spain, and there had been disputes between the Church and state throughout the 19th century. In 1851 the Concordat (an agreement between the Vatican and a secular government) made Catholicism the state religion. The state had guaranteed the role of the Church in education and in elements of the economy, and the Church had used its wealth to gain considerable political and social influence. It used its power to support social, political, and economic conservatism and was opposed to modernizing and liberal forces.

There were 2,390 monasteries, nearly 60,000 monks and 33,400 nuns and 50,000 clergy in Spain at the beginning of the 19th century. The aristocracy was closely tied to the Church; they made up the vast majority of senior clergy, and provided much of the funding for the Church. This meant the Church was inclined to defend the rights and status of the upper classes, which led to resentment among the poor.

Although the Church was popular in the countryside, in urban areas many did not attend church services, seeing it as alien to urban working-class culture. The leader of the Radical Republican Party, Alejandro Lerroux, made aggressively anti-clerical speeches in Barcelona, tapping into the *profound anti-clericalism* of the migrant workers. Arson attacks on churches and convents were relatively frequent in these areas. On 27 and 28 July 1909, in Barcelona, 42 convents and churches were burned or vandalized, nuns were 'liberated' and the attackers paraded around in pillaged vestments (Carr). Some of the educated middle class were also anti-clerical and sought to limit the Church's power, particularly over education.

Spain's population grew from 18 million in 1900 to 24 million in 1930. Without a strong industrial base, emigration was key in alleviating the pressure of population growth and Spaniards would usually move to Spain's former colonies in South America or to France. However, after the First World War restrictions on immigration were imposed and this led to more of the rural poor migrating to the towns. This in turn led to housing shortages, poverty and increased tension.

Essay writing

Use the essay plan below to write a draft answer to this question:

> **Discuss the role of political and economic conditions in causing tension and division in Spain up to 1923.**

Command term:	Discuss.
Topic:	Political and economic conditions and tension up to 1923.
Concept:	Causation.
Intro:	Set down key themes and ideas regarding how political and economic conditions had caused tension and division in Spain. Also make your overall argument clear so that it is consistent throughout your essay.
Paragraph 1:	*Political conditions in Spain had led to tension and division due to the weakness of central government and the Caciquismo system...* (add evidence and explain). *There were also separatist movements in the Catalan and Basque regions...* (add evidence and explain).
Paragraph 2:	*In addition, political conditions in Spain led to an increasingly radicalized peasantry and working class...* (add evidence and explain).
Paragraph 3:	*Furthermore, the army in Spain had traditionally played a key role in politics...* (add evidence and explain).

Activity 4

Thinking, communication and self-management skills

1. Create a mind map or spider diagram of the key political, economic, and social issues in Spain up to 1923.

2. Discuss in pairs which factor was the main cause of division in Spain at this time: political divisions, economic problems, or social tensions.

Paragraph 4:	*However, there were also significant economic factors that led to tension and division in Spain up to 1923...*
	The plight of the agricultural workers was a key factor in causing the discontent... (add evidence and explain).
Paragraph 5:	*In addition, workers in the towns faced low wages, long hours, unregulated working conditions, poor housing, and little in the way of welfare provision...* (add evidence and explain).
Paragraph 6:	*Nevertheless, there were social factors that also divided Spanish society, and these were fostered by political and economic conditions. The role of the Catholic Church... Population growth...* (add evidence and explain).
Conclusion:	Based on the weight of evidence and analysis presented in the main body, draw a clear, well-reasoned and concise conclusion that answers the set question.

General Miguel Primo de Rivera
▼

What was the impact of the dictatorship of Primo de Rivera, 1923–1930, on Spain?

Political policies

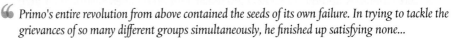

❝ *Primo's entire revolution from above contained the seeds of its own failure. In trying to tackle the grievances of so many different groups simultaneously, he finished up satisfying none...*
Ross, C (2000). *Spain, 1812–1996*. London: Arnold, p. 60.

General Primo de Rivera came to power in the political, social and economic turmoil that had been building to a crisis after the First World War. The impact of military defeat in Morocco and the post-war economic depression put pressure on the King, and after 12 unsuccessful governments during the period 1918–23, Alfonso did not resist the army's intervention in politics. In September 1923, General Primo de Rivera declared a *pronunciamiento* and overthrew the Liberal government of Garcia Prieto. Primo de Rivera ruled until January 1930 and his style of rule has been termed the *Dictadura*, or dictatorship. Despite this, Rivera himself has been seen as humane, and '*concerned to alleviate the grinding poverty in which most of Spain's population lived*' (Forrest). He also sent military delegates to root out corruption in the regions.

Politically, Primo de Rivera tried to establish an authoritarian right-wing regime to redress Spain's problems, similar to the Italian Fascist model. Indeed, the nature of his dictatorship can be determined from King Alfonso's description of him as '*My Mussolini*'. Although Primo de Rivera set up a military dictatorship, the King was retained and the monarchy supported the regime. Rivera was seen as a 'saviour' by many people in Spain, leading a crusade against social problems, political corruption, and imperial humiliation. Franz Borkenau summed up Rivera's programme as aiming to '*destroy the old political parties, and reorganize the state by modernizing the country.*'

Primo de Rivera has been called 'pragmatic' rather than ideologically driven. He believed that he intuitively understood the will of the people and was seen as a man of action. He began by closing down the Cortes, suspending the constitution and banning all political parties. He suspended elections and trial by jury, and he set up a Directory of Generals to run the government – claiming, however, that this was to be only a temporary suspension of the normal political process. He set up his own political party, the Patriotic Union, but this never achieved much popular support. The dictatorship was formally ended in 1925, but Primo remained prime minister.

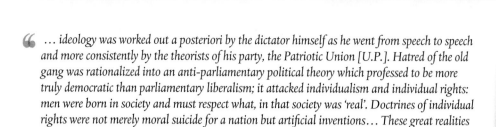

> *… ideology was worked out a posteriori by the dictator himself as he went from speech to speech and more consistently by the theorists of his party, the Patriotic Union [U.P.]. Hatred of the old gang was rationalized into an anti-parliamentary political theory which professed to be more truly democratic than parliamentary liberalism; it attacked individualism and individual rights: men were born in society and must respect what, in that society was 'real'. Doctrines of individual rights were not merely moral suicide for a nation but artificial inventions… These great realities were the triad of the U.P.'s programme: Nation, Church and King, in that order… Primo de Riverism was not fascism…*

Carr, R (1982). *Spain, 1808–1975*. Oxford: Clarendon Press, p. 566.

Activity 5

(ATL) **Thinking and self-management skills**

Review Chapter 3 for the main ideas of Italian Fascism. Read the following paragraphs on Primo de Rivera's regime and discuss the extent to which you agree with Carr's assertion that *'Primo de Riverism was not fascism'*.

Economic policies

Primo de Rivera's regime was relatively successful up to the Wall Street Crash in 1929, and the global Great Depression that followed. (For information on the Great Depression refer to Chapter 1, page 29.) He wanted to address Spain's problem of violent and militant industrial disputes and he was able to gain some tacit support from Socialists and the UGT by establishing a system of arbitration for labour disputes and some government subsidies for housing and healthcare. He was able to play on the divisions between the Socialists and the Anarchists by working with the former and persecuting the latter. (However, in 1927, three years after he banned the Anarchist trade union, the CNT, the Anarchists secretly established the extremist FAI.) Rivera was able to maintain some support from the Basques as, although he abandoned the idea of more autonomy for the region, he kept Conservative Basques in their posts. In addition, his tariffs on imported goods and state subsidies to local industries supported the Basque economy. More generally, Rivera also started various infrastructure programmes for railways, roads, and electrification, as well as irrigation schemes in Spain. He set up badly needed investment in the country's railways, and the first rail link between Spain and France was built. Industrial production developed at three times the rate of output prior to 1923 and the 1924 Municipal Statute gave local authorities the power to borrow money for urban development. Foreign trade increased as well. Primo de Rivera also ended the costly war in Morocco in 1925, with assistance from the French.

Social policies

Socially, although Primo de Rivera's regime recognized degrees awarded by Catholic universities, which enraged the Liberals, he also built 2,000 new schools and modernized 2,000 old ones. The education system became highly regulated. In addition, he built cheap housing for workers and increased maternity benefits for women.

Impact of policies

Nevertheless, Primo de Rivera's regime ran up massive debts that put Spain in a dreadful situation when the global downturn came. His finance minister, Calvo Sotelo, was unable to reform the tax system and his public works had to be financed using government deficits and loans. There was opposition to the monopolies the regime had granted for the sale of tobacco and petrol and, in 1928, wealthy landowners resisted the introduction of wage controls. Then, after a budget that required 'extraordinary' borrowing, the value of the peso fell, which wiped out the savings of Spain's small middle class. Primo de Rivera had also not addressed the burning issue of land reform in the countryside.

De Rivera's strict censorship of the press and restriction of freedom of speech led to widespread opposition, and his withdrawal of concessions to Catalonia (and the banning of the Catalan flag and language) also led to deep resentment. Catalan support for the anti-clerical and separatist party, Esquerra, grew. He also managed to alienate most of the powerful elements of society, including the landowners who had lost influence under his regime, and the army; he had changed the promotion system and closed down the artillery corps and he had not addressed the demands of the military for better wages and weapons. The cost of the war against the Riff and Jabala rebels in Morocco was another key issue for the regime.

Thus, when the Great Depression took hold, and despite the fact that Spain had a large self-employed agricultural sector and had high protective tariffs, food prices and exports fell and unemployment increased. When the army withdrew its support, de Rivera resigned in 1930, having not resolved Spain's economic problems, nor brought about long-term political stability. Indeed, it was his political failings that may have been more important in his regime's demise than the impact of the global economic crisis. However, Borkenau argues, *'During the last two years of the dictatorship the currency had been depreciated, the budget was unbalanced, the level of production began to fall; the world economic crisis did the rest. It hit Spain more severely than any other country.'* The middle classes were ruined. It seemed that dictatorship as a solution to Spain's problems had failed and Primo de Rivera lost the backing of the King.

It had been argued that de Rivera's regime was strangled by the powerful elites and interests that his policies had harmed. When de Rivera turned to the military for support on 26 January 1930, the same men that had backed his seizure of power in 1923, the armed forces, did not renew their vote of confidence. After that, de Rivera was humiliated and resigned the following day.

However, King Alfonso appointed another general to replace de Rivera, General Berenguer, who proved to be totally ineffectual. His successor, Admiral Aznar was also short lived. After promising and then delaying a general election, the credibility of the monarchy was further undermined. Some historians have suggested that if the King had restored the constitution in 1930 the monarchy may have survived. However, support for Republican movements had now grown and in August representatives of the Republican organizations signed the **Pact of San Sebastián**. After municipal elections in April showed support for the San Sebastián pact's coalition of parties (Republicans, Liberals, Socialists and Catalans), the King went into voluntary exile (although he did not formally abdicate, in order to leave his options open!). This time, neither the Church nor the army intervened to save him. A relatively peaceful revolution had occurred and the Second Republic was established.

When de Rivera's dictatorship fell, it left the monarchy isolated and unprotected. Some historians have argued that it was this destabilisation of the monarchy that unleashed revolutionary forces in Spain.

Pact of San Sebastián

An agreement by Republican parties to move towards the establishment of a Republic in Spain. A 'revolutionary committee' was set up to prepare for the overthrow of the monarchy.

Activity 6

Copy out and complete the following grid to summarize the successes and failures of Primo de Rivera's regime in dealing with the political, economic, and social problems faced by Spain.

Once you have added evidence of success and failure from this chapter, read the sources on the following pages and then add material from the sources to your grid.

	Successes	Failures
Political divisions		
Economic problems		
Social tensions		

Activity 7

Historians have suggested that Primo de Rivera's domestic policies were inconsistent:

- In Spanish Morocco, de Rivera moved from a policy of withdrawal to a strategy of war.
- He planned for a constituent Cortes but later abandoned this policy.
- De Rivera's state had political control and strict censorship, however it also attempted to build popular support.
- There were attempts to improve the lives of the poor, however the standard of living and working conditions got worse for many people.
- De Rivera had sympathy for the rights of women in Spanish society, but they were not given the vote.
- He had seemed open to Catalan and Basque regional autonomy, but moved away from this under pressure from military centralists.

With reference to his policies, evaluate the consistency of Primo de Rivera's regime between 1923 and 1930.

▶▶▶ Historians' perspectives

In pairs, discuss the following views of historians and decide whose views you mostly agree with. You should be able to support your viewpoint with evidence from this chapter.

Why did Primo de Rivera's regime fall?

- British historian, Hugh Thomas: Economic factors were the main problem for Primo de Rivera. The juxtaposition between people's high expectations in the new age of consumerism with the onset of the economic slump in the 1920s led to his demise.
- Tangiers-born Israeli historian, Shlomo Ben Ami (considered a leading authority on Primo de Rivera): Political factors were the main issue for Primo de Rivera. These political issues were caused by economic migration from the countryside to towns and cities, as people were drawn by potential employment in public works and expanded industries. This migrant population was more open to radical politics as they were now free of the *caciquismo*.
- The Spanish academic, A Ramos Oliveira: Primo de Rivera's regime was '*strangled*' by opposition from the groups whose interests it had damaged.

What was Primo de Rivera's legacy?

- The American historian, Gabriel Jackson: Primo de Rivera's legacy was positive, in that his public works programme was the basis for further modernization under the Second Republic.
- The British historian, Paul Preston: His legacy was the significant burden of excessive spending, borrowing, and government debt.

Activity 8

Source analysis

Source A

❝ *The Moroccan War was really to prove fatal to the dynasty, because it delivered the power in Spain into the hands of the military in the person of Primo de Rivera. Against this raw military dictatorship, there was a popular revolt. It was led by Spanish intellectuals… and its first cabinet was formed of rebels who were in jail. They issued from prison in 1931 to proclaim the Spanish Republic and set up a government of extreme liberalism, which glorified the things which the liberal intellectual most prizes: education, free speech, a free press and assembly, the divorce of Church and State, protection for all minorities, bountiful concessions to labor, while generously allowing the forces representing the Church, the army, the nobility and entrenched tradition to continue to exist, however curtailed. The first Republican cabinet … represented the intellectual élite of Spain, plus labor – the trade unions and the Socialists.*

An extract from an article by the respected American journalist and broadcaster, Dorothy Thompson (1939). *Let the record speak.* **Boston: Houghton Mifflin Co., p. 42.**

Source B

❝ *Primo de Rivera fell when his economic policies failed so dismally that even the timid Spanish industrialists abandoned him and joined their indignant protests to those of the intellectuals and the workers. The bourgeois elements began to fear that a further prolongation of the directorate might arouse a violent revolutionary movement of which they, too, would be the victims. Primo de Rivera protracted his term of office, and tried in vain to conceive of a dignified exit. With his customary lack of diplomacy he finally decided to poll the army generals and the admirals of the navy on whether he should remain in spite of the falling peseta and the rising discontent. Alfonso XIII, who by this time had come to realize his dictator's weakness and unpopularity, made an effort to extricate himself from the debris of the regime, censured the dictator for exceeding his authority, and demanded his resignation. Primo de Rivera, in disgrace, left for Paris in the last week of January, 1930, where he died a few months later.*

An extract from the academic book by Frank E Manuel, (1938). *The Politics of Modern Spain.* **McGraw-Hill, p. 56**

Source C

❝ *The Primo de Rivera dictatorship was to be regarded in later years as a golden age by the Spanish middle classes and became a central myth of the reactionary right. Paradoxically, however, its short-term effect was to discredit the very idea of authoritarianism in Spain. This fleeting phenomenon was born partly of Primo's failure to use the economic breathing space to construct a lasting political replacement for the decrepit constitutional monarchy, but more immediately it sprang from his alienation of the powerful interests which had originally supported him… he governed by a form of personal improvisation which ensured that he bore the blame for his regime's failures. Although by 1930 there was hardly a section of Spanish society that he had not offended, his most crucial errors led to the estrangement of industrialists, landowners and the army.*

Extract from the academic book by historian Paul Preston (2006). *The Spanish Civil War: Reaction, Revolution and Revenge.* **London: Harper Perennial, p. 36.**

1. According to Source A, which was the most important group to oppose Primo de Rivera?

2. According to Source B, what led to the demise of Primo de Rivera?

3. According to Source C, why was Primo de Rivera held responsible for his regime's failures?

4. In pairs, find comparisons and contrasts in the views expressed in Sources B and C.

Activity 9

 Self-management and communication skills

1. In small groups, draft a news report on the main events that led to the fall of King Alfonso of Spain in 1931. Consider who you might interview, the perspective of the reporter on events, and any conclusions or predictions that your news team will make regarding the situation for Spain. Present your news report to the rest of the class.

2. Add information about the regime of Primo de Rivera to your mind map or spider diagram of the key issues dividing Spain. Include key events and details up to 1931.

3. Organize a class debate on the following resolution:

   A civil war in Spain was inevitable after 1931, it was just a matter of time.

Essay writing

Use the essay plan below to draft an answer to following question:

> **To what extent was Primo de Rivera's regime effective in addressing the problems in Spain between 1923 and 1930?**

Command term: To what extent.

Topic: The regime of Primo de Rivera/problems in Spain.

Concept: Consequence.

Introduction: *There were political, social and economic problems facing Spain in 1923 and Primo de Rivera attempted to address these during his term as dictator. His regime implemented a number of programmes and initiatives that had some success, however there were also limitations and many of the key issues and divisions in Spanish society remained and perhaps had worsened by 1930.*

Paragraph 1: *Primo de Rivera attempted to address the political divisions in Spain...* (evidence and explanations). *These proved successful in...* (evidence and explanations).

Paragraph 2: *Primo de Rivera attempted to address the economic problems in Spain...* (evidence and explanations). *These proved successful in...* (evidence and explanations).

Paragraph 3: *Primo de Rivera attempted to address the social issues in Spain...* (evidence and explanations). *These proved successful in...* (evidence and explanations).

Paragraph 4: *However, Primo de Rivera failed to address the political divisions in Spain...* (evidence and explanations).

Paragraph 5: *In addition, Primo de Rivera failed to solve the economic problems in Spain...* (evidence and explanations). *Indeed his policies led to heavy government borrowing and debt...* (evidence and explanations).

Paragraph 6: *Furthermore, Primo de Rivera failed to resolve social tensions in Spain...* (evidence and explanations).

Conclusion: Based on the weight of the evidence and analysis presented in the main body, draw a clear, well reasoned and concise conclusion that answers the question.

Hints for success

The question refers to the 'problems in Spain' which is quite vague – it is up to you to identify clearly what these problems were in order to assess the effectiveness of the regime in addressing them.

How did the governments of the Second Republic lead to further division in Spanish society?

An image symbolizing the Second Republic.
▼

Key concepts: *Change and continuity*

Activity 10
 ATL Thinking skills

What is the message of this image of the Second Republic? Look carefully at the imagery being used – what do the various symbols indicate about the hopes for the Second Republic?

Activity 11
 ATL Thinking skills

In pairs, discuss how the following international circumstances might affect the new Spanish Republic:

- the Great Depression
- Hitler coming to power in January 1933
- growing belligerence of Mussolini's Italy and his corporate state
- Stalin's totalitarian Communist regime (Chapter 8).

Timeline of events – 1931–1936		
1931	Apr	Republicans win all major cities. King Alfonso abdicates to *'avoid civil war'*. Second Spanish Republic proclaimed
1931–32		More autonomy given to the regions. Church powers limited, the army reformed and land reform implemented. 7,000 new schools opened
1932		Catalonia given more autonomy. Land Reform Act
		General Sanjurjo rising
1933		CEDA established
		The Association Law prohibits priests and nuns teaching in schools
	Jan	Casas Viejas Anarchist Rising
		Socialists withdraw support from Azaña
	Nov	Spanish right wins general election
1934	Oct	Asturias uprising, also called the October Revolution
		Right Republic reverses reforms of the Left Republic
1936	Feb	Popular Front government elected
		Left Republic's reforms reinstated
	May	The CNT call a general strike
	July	Army rising

Between 1931 and 1936, Spain became politically polarized. You may have already decided, from what you have read thus far, that civil war in Spain was likely, given the long-term structural problems and clear divisions that already existed in the 19th century and early 20th century. Nevertheless, it is important to note the following:

   … in 1931 when the Second Republic was established, no one, except a tiny minority on the lunatic fringe on the extreme right or left, believed that Spain's problems could be solved only by war.
Preston, P (1991). *Modern History Review,* **p. 12.**

The Second Republic (April 1931–November 1933)

The Left Republic

… I have always and still do maintain that against tyranny everything is permissible and no law is binding. Just as I maintain that against the revolution that has now become the Republic by sanction of popular elections nothing is permissible that steps outside legal channels…

An extract from a speech by Manuel Azaña, then minister of war, July 1931.

Significant individual: Manuel Azaña Díaz

Manuel Azaña was minister of war in the first centre-left government of the Spanish Second Republic. When Prime Minister Alcalá-Zamora resigned in October, Azaña became prime minister of a coalition government of left-wing parties. Azaña implemented a major series of reforms, although he was a liberal Republican and not a Socialist. His reforms did not satisfy those that wanted more radical change, and at the same time they also alienated the right-wing groups. Azaña's anti-clerical speeches and reforms were particularly inflammatory to elements on the right. President Alcalá-Zamora asked for his resignation in September 1933 and new elections were held in November 1933. Azaña founded the Republican Left Party in 1934. When the October 1934 rebellion broke out in Asturias and Barcelona, the Right Republic, led by Lerroux and backed by the CEDA, arrested Azaña claiming he was complicit. The case against him was dropped, however it had given Azaña renewed public support. Azaña assisted in the organization of the Popular Front coalition of the left parties that won the elections of February 1936. He again became prime minister and immediately alarmed and enraged the right-wing groups by including PSOE and Communists in his government and releasing political prisoners, including those involved in the October Revolution. He renewed his programme of reforms and legalized land seizures by peasants in the countryside. In May 1936 Azaña was elected president and Casares Quiroga became prime minister. There was increasing political violence and social disorder throughout Spain and in July the military moved to overthrow Azaña's regime in a coup.

Manuel Azaña

In the elections that followed King Alfonso's departure, the centre-left won, with the objective of modernizing Spain. The Cortes had 473 seats and the right won only 57. The government declared a new constitution, stating that Spain was a '*democratic republic of workers of all classes*'. The constitution established that:

- the Cortes would be elected every four years
- there would be universal suffrage, including for women
- there would be a president as head of state
- there would be freedom of worship for all religions.

At first, the government was led by Prime Minister Niceto Alcalá-Zamora, a wealthy liberal Catholic who wanted limited reform. Manuel Azaña, a leader of the Republican Action Party, was minister for war. When Alcalá-Zamora resigned after reforms of the Church were passed, Azaña became prime minister, and Alcalá-Zamora took on the role of president. Azaña thus became the leading figure in the new regime. However, the key issues causing tension in Spain before the revolution of 1931 continued to dominate the political, economic, and social atmosphere under the new left-wing government.

- One of Azaña's key aims was to address the issue of the Church's power. His speeches were anti-clerical, and an attempt was made to separate the Church and state, and to limit Church powers. The Church was no longer in control of education, and the state payment of the clergy was to be stopped gradually over a two-year period. Divorce was legalized and civil marriages were introduced. The Associations Law 1933 prohibited priests and nuns from teaching in schools and nationalized Church property. According to Andrew Forrest, CEDA (see page 140) described the '*atheistic*' Republic as a '*communist class dictatorship*' hostile to the family, private property and the free market.

The Socialists and the Liberals played a significant role in the revolution of 1931, but each party divided over what reforms should take place. The more moderate Socialists were then led by Indalecio Prieto, and the Radicals were led by Francisco Largo Caballero.

General Franco led the Nationalists to victory in the Spanish Civil War between 1936 and 1939. The regime he established after the war was characterized by authoritarianism, nationalism, promotion of National Catholicism, militarism, anti-liberalism, anti-communism, and anti-socialism. The historian Stanley Payne argues that despite some similar features to Fascist Italy and Nazi Germany, Franco was not *a core fascist*.

- The government, which saw education as key to modernizing Spain, also invested heavily in building new schools and training teachers, as the Church was no longer responsible for education. Over 7,000 new schools were opened between 1931 and 1932. This was more than ten times the number built in the preceding 20 years. A People's University was established in Madrid. Although impressive, this programme was expensive. There were also 'cultural' missionaries who took theatre, art, and cinema to the rural poor communities. Important Spanish artists – like the painter, Miro, and the playwright and poet, Lorca – flourished. More women entered politics.

- The power of the army was also attacked. The government attempted to reduce numbers by offering early retirement on full pay, an offer taken up by 50 per cent of officers, and the military academy of Saragossa was closed (**Franco** had been its director). Yet this policy backfired to a certain extent, as not only was it expensive for the government, but it meant that the army was radicalized; those who remained in the army were the conservative and nationalist core, including the *Africanistas*.

- The desperate economic problems that existed in Spain had been exacerbated by the Great Depression: agricultural prices were tumbling, wine and olive exports fell, and land had gone out of cultivation. Peasant unemployment was rising. The effects were also being felt industrially; iron production fell by a third and steel by almost a half. However Azaña's government did not reform the taxation system to raise urgently needed government funding from the wealthy. It also tended to support the powerful industrialists against the strikers, particularly the Anarchist unionists, CNT.

- Largo Caballero, minister of labour, initiated an extensive land redistribution programme, with compensation for landowners. In 1932, a law enabled the state to take over estates and to redistribute land to the peasants. Yet the government did not have the money for this reform, and by 1933 fewer than 7,000 families had benefited from the programme. The Socialists had wanted state-funded collective farms set up, but this was not included in the act. The right saw land reform as a major threat to its interests and an attempt to copy the Soviet system.

- Civil unrest and violence continued under the Left Republic and it dealt with its perpetrators brutally. The government introduced the **Assault Guard** in an attempt to create a paramilitary force loyal to the Republic. There were risings by both the right (General José Sanjurjo in 1932) against the reforms, and by the left (a significant example was the Casas Viejas Anarchist Rising in 1933 – see the next page) against the slow pace of change. These risings were suppressed, as the majority of the army remained loyal.

- As for the regional issues, Catalonia was given its own parliament in 1932, as well as some powers, including law and order and dual control over education. Right-wing groups were angered by this change, as they saw it as a move towards independence for the regions and the break-up of Spain.

Each reform was perceived as an attack on one or more right-wing groups – the Church, army, landowners, or industrialists. In response, a new right-wing party, the *Confederación Española de Derechas Autónomas* (**CEDA**; Spanish Confederation of the Autonomous Right), was formed from more than forty right-wing groups to defend the Church and landlords. CEDA was led by José María Gil Robles; he admired the Austrian authoritarian leader Engelbert Dollfuss of the Christian Social Party as CEDA was not just a party of the 'right', but was also based on traditional Catholic movements. In his closing speech at its founding congress in Madrid in February 1933, Gil Robles declared:

CEDA was a right-wing party, led by Gil Robles. It was established during the Second Republic to protect the interests of the elites, the Church and 'Christian civilization' from the threat posed by the left and by Marxists.

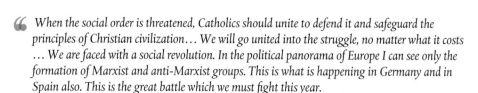

> When the social order is threatened, Catholics should unite to defend it and safeguard the principles of Christian civilization… We will go united into the struggle, no matter what it costs … We are faced with a social revolution. In the political panorama of Europe I can see only the formation of Marxist and anti-Marxist groups. This is what is happening in Germany and in Spain also. This is the great battle which we must fight this year.

Quoted in Preston, P (2006). *The Spanish Civil War: Reaction, Revolution and Revenge.* **London: Harper Perennial, p. 62.**

Indeed, political divisions within Spain increased under the Second Republic. The right wing opposed the reforms, sometimes with violence. Although some historians see the failure of land reform as central to the failure of the government during this period, historian Paul Preston has argued that the right wing was in any case never going to give the regime a chance. A key incident in January 1933 lost the government more support; government guards set fire to houses in the village of Casas Viejas near Cadiz in an attempt to 'smoke out' a group of Anarchists. Twenty-five people were killed. This was hugely damaging to the government. It lost the left-wing Republic a lot of working-class support as many were outraged by these events and it even led the Socialists to withdraw support from Azaña, who resigned in 1933.

Gil Robles

Significant individual: José María Gil Robles

Gil Robles had been the secretary of the Catholic-Agrarian National Confederation and involved with the Catholic daily paper *El Debate* during Primo de Rivera's rule. When the Second Republic was founded, he led the Popular Action Party. He pursued the ideas of 'accidentalism' claiming that it did not matter whether Spain was governed by a monarchy or a republic as long as its laws were in line with Catholic principles. Later, Gil Robles founded the Spanish Confederation of the Autonomous Right (CEDA), which won the largest proportion of the vote in the November 1933 general election. CEDA managed to gain the support of both Catholic republicans and monarchist groups. However, the president, Alcalá-Zamora, did not trust the CEDA leader and made Alejandro Lerroux prime minister. Gil Robles was able to use the power of the CEDA in the Cortes to pressure the prime minister for more influence and in 1935 he was made minister of war. In the final elections before the civil war CEDA was the largest group in the National Front coalition that opposed the Popular Front coalition. When the National Front lost the election, support for the CEDA rapidly declined, and many of its youth movement joined the Falange. Although he later denied direct involvement in the military coup of July 1936, Gil Robles had been informed about the plot and CEDA members were involved in its organization and funding.

Activity 12

(ATL) Thinking and self-management skills

Review questions

1. How did the actions of the Second Republic create more tension? In what ways did they, in Paul Preston's words, *'ensure that Spain's underlying conflicts were transmitted into national politics'*?

2. The historian Frances Lannon suggests that the Catholic Church was already deeply insecure before 1931. How would Azaña's reforms have increased this sense of insecurity?

3. Look at the list below and explain which reforms caused discontent for each group and how this opposition undermined Azaña's reforms:

   - the army
   - landowners and the elites
   - Anarchists who sought revolution rather than reform
   - groups on the left that did not agree about the nature and extent of reform
   - agricultural labourers
   - urban workers
   - the Church.

The Right Republic (November 1933–February 1936)

  ❝ *Nazism was much admired on the Spanish right because of its emphasis on authority, the fatherland and hierarchy – all three central preoccupations of CEDA propaganda. More worrying still was that… El Debate [the CEDA newspaper] pointed out that Hitler had attained power legally. The paper frequently commented on Spain's need for an organization similar to those which had destroyed the left in Germany and Italy, and hinted that… CEDA could fulfil that role.*

Preston, P (2006). *The Spanish Civil War: Reaction, Revolution and Revenge.* **London: Harper Perennial, p. 63.**

In the elections of 1933, the Republic swung to the right, with the right-wing and centrist parties benefiting from the disunity of the left. Although CEDA was the largest party, the president resisted giving Gil Robles power, and Alejandro Lerroux, leader of the second largest party, the Radicals, became prime minister. However, CEDA forced the government's hand in October 1934 by withdrawing support. Gil Robles was made war minister and two other CEDA party members were given cabinet posts. The new government ruled for two years in what became known as the '*Biennio negro*', or 'two black years', because it embarked on systematically reversing the Left Republic's reforms. Church control over education was restored and the clergy were again to be paid by the state. Public spending was cut, particularly on education. Azaña's key economic reform – the land programme – was halted. In Estremadura alone there were 19,000 peasant evictions.

In response, there was an Anarchist uprising in Barcelona in December 1933 and this was put down in ten days of violence. Catalonia attempted to resist interference and declared itself independent after CEDA joined the government. Catalonia's autonomy was then suspended after the Asturian miners' uprising in 1934. This rebellion was significant and known as the 'October Revolution' and was only put down by sending in troops, including Moroccan forces. After this the government censored the press, and even suggested Azaña had been involved in the uprising. Threats of a 'general strike' from the left increased. Historians have argued that the violent suppression of the Asturian uprising increased the likelihood of a civil war in Spain. In addition, the right lost the support of the Basques, who now backed the left.

This tense and polarized political climate could also be seen on the right, as the fascist Falange Party was formed under the leadership of the son of Primo de Rivera in September 1934. The CEDA lost ground, particularly among the young, to this more radical party. Violence was widespread and the political response to the Right Republic was divided. Caballero was more extreme in his speeches than the more moderate Prieto. He suggested that CEDA was the Spanish Nazi Party and that the left should seek a Soviet-style solution for Spain. Thus, he articulated the parallels between Spanish politics and the broader European political landscape. In response, Gil Robles demanded a shift to a more authoritarian approach to control the Communists in Spain. Gil Robles' response led to more cooperation between the left's factions: Socialists, Anarchists, Syndicalists, and now Communists. Indeed, Prieto attempted to find some common ground between the left and centre groups to enable them to fight the right wing more effectively.

Read the source and answer the questions that follow.

> When a combination of Gil Robles' tactic of erosion of successive cabinets and the revelation of two massive scandals involving followers of Lerroux led to the collapse of the Radicals, the CEDA leader assumed that he would be asked to form a government. [President] Alcalá-Zamora, however, had no faith in the CEDA leader's democratic convictions… It is indicative of Alcalá-Zamora's suspicion of Gil Robles that throughout the political crisis, he had the Ministry of War surrounded by Civil Guards and the principal garrisons and airports placed under special vigilance. Gil Robles was outraged and in desperation he investigated the possibilities of staging a coup d'etat. The generals whom he approached, Fanjul, Goded, Verla and Franco, felt that, in the light of the strength of working-class resistance during the Asturias events, the army was not yet ready for a coup…
>
> Elections were announced for February… Already in late October, Gil Robles had requested a range of Nazi anti-Marxist propaganda pamphlets and posters to be used as a model for CEDA publicity material… Ten thousand posters and fifty million leaflets were printed for the CEDA. They presented the elections in terms of a life-or-death struggle between good and evil, survival and destruction.

Paul Preston (2006). *The Spanish Civil War: Reaction, Revolution and Revenge.* **London: Harper Perennial, p. 83.**

1. From the information you have from this chapter, why might Gil Robles assume 'that he would be asked to form a government' by President Alcalá-Zamora after the collapse of the Radicals?

2. According to the source, what evidence was there of Alcalá-Zamora's suspicion of Gil Robles?

3. What does the source reveal about Gil Robles' response to Alcalá-Zamora's actions towards him?

The Popular Front (February–July 1936)

The right wing disintegrated as the economic and the political situation deteriorated, and in September 1935 the prime minister, Alejandro Lerroux, resigned after being embroiled in financial scandals. In the elections that followed in February 1936, the Popular Front, which was an anti-Fascist pact made up of various left-wing groups, including Socialists and Communists, was victorious. This idea of forming anti-Fascist, or Popular Front, coalitions was supported by Stalin and pursued by the **Comintern**; a Popular Front government subsequently took power in France. In Spain it was not only a coalition of the left-wing groups, but also included Liberals like Azaña.

The Popular Front was for many in Spain a final attempt to uphold democracy and peace, but others associated it with Stalin and the more extreme Communist supporters. The manifesto promoted by Azaña, who was now returned to power initially as the prime minister and then as president, was liberal and not radical. Nevertheless, the government wanted to restore the reforms of the 1931–1933 regime, and political prisoners were released. However, there was still no political consensus; Caballero's Socialists did not join the government and the right would not accept the restoration of reforms.

The Anarchists encouraged peasants to seize land, which led to an increase in violence in the countryside. Azaña responded by legitimizing the land seizures. The Anarchists also openly recruited for their militias and organized bombings and assassinations. Open conflict between the anarchist FAI and the right-wing CEDA and the Falange increased. The government again faced increasing disorder. In May, the CNT called a general strike, and there were several strikes throughout June. Thousands of peasants began to occupy estates in the countryside. Gil Robles declared that a country could

CHALLENGE YOURSELF

 ATL Research skills

In small groups, investigate further into the different political groups and factions that developed in Spain during the Second Republic. Attempt to find examples of propaganda and newspapers from different parties in Spain during this period. Discuss the extent to which Spanish society was fracturing and polarizing during this period.

survive as a monarchy or a republic, but *'cannot live in anarchy'*. The right wing believed that Spain was in the early throes of a left-wing revolution.

The victory of the left in the 1936 elections threw the right-wing CEDA into turmoil. Gil Robles began to use his funds to support military plans for a coup. In fact, military officers began planning for a coup as soon as the Popular Front gained power. An extreme nationalist group of junior officers joined with senior *Africanista* officers, including Mola and Franco (although Franco's role in the plot remained unclear). The catalyst for the coup was the murder of a popular right-wing leader, José Calvo Sotelo, on 13 July 1936.

Azaña knew that there were plans for a coup, and attempted to prevent it by moving key military figures to remote posts. However, the conspirators had already made their plans and set a date for the coup – 18 July 1936. They had the support of the Falange, the CEDA, and the monarchist 'Carlist' and 'Alfonsist' groups. Spain was clearly polarized between two groups: those who were anti-Fascist, and those on the right who were anti-Communists. When the details of the coup were discovered, it was initiated earlier, on 17 July, from Morocco. It spread to the mainland, and was successful in taking Cantabria and parts of Andalusia. Yet the rising failed in the main industrial areas, and the rebels did not take Madrid. Half the army had remained loyal to the Republic. Thus the coup was unsuccessful overall, and, had it remained a Spanish affair, it is quite possible that the Republicans would have won.

Activity 14 **Thinking, communication and self-management skills**

Review the material on the governments of the Second Republic and answer the questions that follow.

1. To what extent did economic issues lead to a civil war?
2. Divide your class into three groups. Organize a class debate where each group argues one of the following:
   - The right wing was responsible for the Spanish Civil War.
   - The left wing was responsible for the Spanish Civil War.
   - Both left and right were equally responsible for the Spanish Civil War.
3. As a class, discuss the impact of international events on the growing divisions in Spain.
4. Andrew Forrest writes that in the period 1931–36, *'legislation [and the dread of it] reacted with privilege and deprivation, exacerbating pre-existing tensions and leading ultimately to civil war... the Republic had defined itself as the engine of change but... was derailed. Governments seemed at times less interested in building political bridges than in blowing them up.'* Discuss the extent to which you agree with his assessment.

What was the role of Manuel Azaña in causing tension and division in Spanish society?

Key concept: *Significance*

As you have already read, Azaña had led two of the three republican governments between 1931 and the outbreak of civil war in July 1936. He had attempted to implement a programme of reforms, but was not a Socialist nor a radical reformer. His policies had led to opposition from both the left and the right, and had arguably led to further radicalization and polarization of Spanish society. As prime minister and then president of the Popular Front government in 1936, he had released political prisoners, included Socialists and Communists in government and appointed them to leading positions in the Assault and Civil Guards, and legitimized peasant land seizures. He was opposed to monarchists, clericalism and the CEDA. Azaña did not effectively address the violence of radical left-wing groups, claiming that the real threat to society came from the radical right-wing groups. To this end, he attempted to suppress the Falange. Azaña was unable to prevent the escalation in violence after he became president of the Republic in May 1936, and there were more than 200 political assassinations prior to the military coup in July. When Calvo Sotelo was killed Azaña's government did not act quickly to punish the perpetrators. Ultimately, he failed to unify the left behind his regime and was unable to defuse the right-wing plot to overthrow it, despite knowing that the coup was imminent. When the rebels failed to take Madrid, Azaña replaced Casares Quiroga with Martinez Barrio as prime minister and attempted to find a compromise with the rebels. However, General Mola refused to compromise.

Activity 15
 Thinking and self-management skills

Source analysis

Read the source below and answer the questions that follow.

> Three days [after Azaña became prime minister in 1936] Franco was relieved of his position as Chief of Staff and sent to the Canary Islands as Military Governor, a virtual exile. General Goded was sent to govern the Balearic Islands. On Febuary 20 the new Prime Minister announced his commitment to wide changes. …
>
> Azaña then appealed to the working classes for unity in the work of reform and reconstruction. Above all, he said, there should be no disturbances. But prison riots forced him to bring forward a proposed amnesty without first submitting it for parliamentary approval… some land on the large estates in Extremadura was occupied by farm laborers… They wanted to be in possession of the soil in time to plant their grain. The only way to achieve this was to seize land without delay. The government accepted the seizures by special decree.
>
> Churches were also burnt, and property belonging to the rich destroyed. In reaction to the activities of the Left… Fascist vigilante groups, the Falanaga Espagnola, took up arms and went on a rampage of their own. On April 3… Azaña appealed for an end to all extra-parliamentary activity by whatever extreme group. This, he said, was the last chance for Spain to make progress by parliamentary methods. …
>
> The political crisis came to a head on April 10, when… the President was dismissed. For a month there was political as well as social chaos. Fascists and Socialists fought on the streets. On April 17 a government decree made all Fascist groupings illegal. On April 20 an emergency Bill was passed forbidding anti-Republican activity in the army.
>
> On May 10 the Prime Minister Azaña accepted the Presidency… from the Right the call grew for the army to take over, restore social discipline and 'save Spain'… But on July [13] the police went to the home of a leading Rightist, Calvo Sotelo, intending to arrest him. In the struggle, Sotelo was shot dead. As public anger mounted on both sides of the political divide, Parliament was suspended for a week to prevent violence in the chamber. The army decided that the time had come to act.

**Gilbert, M (1999). *Descent into barbarism: a history of the 20th century, 1933–1951.*
London: HarperCollins, pp. 91–92.**

1. What evidence is there in the source that Azaña understood the possible threat posed by the army and the military generals?

2. What reforms and policies, according to the source, did Azaña implement that led to further discontent and hostility in Spanish society?

3. Discuss in pairs what Azaña meant when he said on 3 April 1936, this was the '*last chance for Spain to make progress by parliamentary methods*'.

4. In pairs, discuss and answer the following question: 'Azaña's policies provoked the military into taking action in July 1936.' To what extent do you agree with this statement?

What was the role of Gil Robles in causing tension and division in Spanish society?

> **Key concepts:** *Significance and consequence*

As you have already seen, Gil Robles was a significant figure on the right of Spanish politics. He was a key critic of the Azaña regime and he was able to rally support from very different factions, including Catholic republicans and monarchists. However, his political theories were often seen as inconsistent; he followed an 'accidentalist' approach that viewed the nature of the ruling regime as irrelevant as long as it abided with religious principles. The historian Paul Preston argues that Gil Robles was essentially a Fascist and that his 'accidentalism' would have been replaced by a Fascist dictatorship had he had the opportunity to gain power. Yet other historians have suggested he was more a traditional politician who attempted to unite the right behind a legal framework and in line with Catholic values.

Gil Robles had founded the CEDA, a party backed by the Catholic daily paper *El Debate*, which became the largest party on the right before the 1933 elections. Indeed the CEDA won that election. However, Gil Robles had been thwarted by the president's reluctance to give him the premiership and served as minister of war in the Lerroux government. He attempted to use his CEDA powerbase to influence the government. Later he led the National Front coalition that opposed the Popular Front government in the February 1936 election.

Gil Robles used examples from Nazi propaganda in his campaign to whip up fear of a '*Marxist revolution*'. *El Debate* ran an article exclaiming in January 1936, '*Between the ruin and the salvation there is no middle way*'. The youth wing of the CEDA, the JAP, rallied again behind the slogan: '*all power to the Jefe!*' Gil Robles was re-elected to the Cortes, however, the National Front lost the election. After this defeat, support for the CEDA rapidly declined and many members of its youth movement joined the Falange. Gil Robles tried to prevent the formation of the Popular Front government by going to see Prime Minister Portelo directly and he urged him to declare martial law. He warned that a Popular Front government would mean violence and anarchy. Gil Robles also sent a message to General Franco suggesting that he should lead the army against the formation of a government. Franco and General Goded did attempt to respond to his requests, but when Goded tried to raise troops from the barracks in Madrid the men refused. Subsequently, Gil Robles was kept informed of the military plot that would attempt to seize power in July 1936. Although he later denied involvement, there is evidence that he gave 500,000 pesetas to General Mola's rebel funds, and CEDA members were involved in assisting the organization of the coup.

*'**Jefe**'* or *'Chief'* was similar to *'Duce'* or *'Führer'*

José María Gil Robles, standing next to General Franco, speaks in Parliament in 1936.

1. What is the message of the source?

2. The historian Paul Preston wrote in his book, *The Coming of the Spanish Civil War*, of Gil Robles:

 … he played an active and indeed crucial role in parliament and the press, in creating an atmosphere which made a military rising appear to the middle classes as the only alternative to catastrophe.

   In pairs, discuss the extent to which you agree with Preston's assessment of Gil Robles' role.

3. Review the material in this chapter and draft an essay plan for the following question:

   Discuss the significance of Gil Robles in the polarization of Spanish society up to 1936.

Andrew Forrest has highlighted the key role of the Spanish press in fermenting an environment ripe for civil war by creating an *'intoxicating aura of confrontation while contributing to the making of revolution and reaction more directly'*.

Research the headlines, editorials and articles published by the right-wing and left-wing media from 1931 to July 1936. Present these to the class, and then assess the extent to which you agree with Forrest that they *'contributed to the making of revolution and reaction'*.

Activity 18 Social and self-management skills

Prepare thematic arguments and evidence for the following essay question:

Compare and contrast the roles of Manuel Azaña and Gil Robles in the outbreak of the Spanish Civil War in 1936.

Get into groups of four or five students. Your group will write a 5–10 minute documentary comparing and contrasting the roles of Manuel Azaña and Gil Robles in causing the divisions in Spanish society that would lead to the outbreak of civil war in 1936. You should include interviews with key figures, including Azaña and Gil Robles. Remember you are attempting to find similarities and differences in their policies, actions and impact.

Historians' perspectives

Paul Preston has consistently argued in his books on the Spanish Civil War that it was the right that would not accept the reforms of the left-wing governments and its response to reform led to political polarization and violence. In the short term it was again the actions of the right – the attempted military coup – that caused the civil war. This perspective on the causes of the war is generally supported by Julián Casanova writing in *The Spanish Republic and Civil War* in 2010. Casanova agrees that the military coup of July 1936 *'undermined the ability of the State and the Republican government to maintain order'* and unleashed the civil war.

In contrast, the historian Stanley G Payne argues that the left failed to create a stable government by excluding right-wing or even more centrist views and representatives. He also highlights the failings of Manuel Azaña's policies and actions, and finds them key to the political polarization in the build up to war, to the breakdown in law and order, and to the descent into civil conflict.

In pairs, discuss which of these two perspectives – Paul Preston's or Stanley G Payne's – you think is more persuasive.

Activity 19 Thinking skills

Read Sources A through to D and answer the questions that follow.

Source A

 All the right-wing political groups were aware of preparations for the coup and contributed their contacts, finances and manpower to its successful accomplishment.

In July 1936 everybody in the country… seemed to be conscious of the military threat. With a confidence stretching sometimes to the borders of insanity, the prime minister kept dismissing the worrying news as 'unfounded rumours'… the monarchist leader Calvo Sotelo was arrested and murdered [on 13 July]… Gil Robles noted that the government, although not to blame for Calvo's execution, was responsible for creating the circumstances which made it possible… Calvo Sotelo's death… persuaded dithering officers to participate in the plans for a coup that had been underway since the right had lost the political argument in a democratic ballot.

Francisco J Romero Salvadó (2005). *The Spanish Civil War*. Basingstoke: Palgrave Macmillan, p. 59.

Source B

Republican propaganda during the civil war always emphasised that its government was the legally appointed one after the elections of February 1936. This is true, but one also has to pose an important question. If the coalition of the right had won those elections, would the left have accepted the legitimate result? One strongly suspects not. The socialist leader Largo Caballero threatened openly before the elections if the right had won, it would be open civil war. The nationalists tried from the very beginning to pretend that they had risen in revolt purely to forestall a communist putsch. This was a complete fabrication to provide retrospective justification for their acts… Both sides, of course, justified their actions on the grounds that if they did not act first, their opponents would seize power and crush them.

Antony Beevor (2006). *The Battle for Spain*. Penguin, p. xxvii.

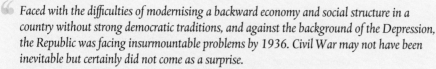

Source C

" Faced with the difficulties of modernising a backward economy and social structure in a country without strong democratic traditions, and against the background of the Depression, the Republic was facing insurmountable problems by 1936. Civil War may not have been inevitable but certainly did not come as a surprise.

Patricia Knight (1998). *The Spanish Civil War.* **Hodder & Stoughton, p. 25.**

Source D

" The Spanish Civil War… was a class war, and a culture war. Competing visions of Spanish identity were superimposed on a bitter struggle over material resources, as the defenders of property and tradition took up arms against a Republican government committed to social reform, devolution and secularization.

Frances Lannon (2002). *The Spanish Civil War.* **Osprey, p. 7.**

1. What are the key causes of the civil war identified by each of these historians:
   a. Francisco J Romero Salvadó in Source A?
   b. Antony Beevor in Source B?
   c. Patricia Knight in Source C?
   d. Frances Lannon in Source D?
2. Discuss the comparisons and contrasts between the views expressed in these sources.
3. With reference to Sources A, B, C and D, and the view of Preston and Payne, discuss in small groups which historians' views you agree with. You should support your view with evidence from this chapter.

Essay writing

Choose one of the essay questions below and then plan and write a response to it.

1. **To what extent were economic factors a key cause of the Spanish Civil War?**
2. **Discuss the role of ideology as a cause of the Spanish Civil War.**
3. **'The right would never accept the reforms of the left.' To what extent do you agree with this statement?**
4. **Examine the role of the different political parties in the outbreak of the Spanish Civil War.**

Example essay plan

To what extent were economic factors a key cause of the Spanish Civil War?

You need to address the theme of the question fully in the first half of your essay.

- Economic factors in the long term that caused tension and division.
- Economic factors in the short term under the Left Republic.
- Economic factors in the short term under the Right Republic and Popular Front governments.

As the command terms are 'to what extent', you should also develop counter arguments.

However, perhaps political and ideological divisions were more significant causes of the Spanish Civil War…

- Political / ideological factors in the long term.
- Political / ideological factors under the Left Republic.
- Political / ideological factors in the short term under the Right Republic and Popular Front governments.

Before you start writing, make sure you are clear as to which factors you consider to be most important so that you can be consistent in your argument from your introduction through to your conclusion.

The following bullet points give you some suggestions for what to include in each paragraph. You would not be expected to include everything set down here in a timed essay, and you could rationalize the number of paragraphs by considering the short-term economic and political/ideological factors in one paragraph. In pairs, discuss the essay frame and attempt to find historians' viewpoints from this chapter to include as evidence for the main arguments.

Paragraph 1:   Economic factors in the long term

- lack of industrialization and modernization
- Catalonia, Bilbao and Asturias
- trade unions, CNT and UGT
- *Latifundia* and seasonal work
- economic failings of Primo de Rivera
- impact of Great Depression.

Paragraph 2: **Economic factors in the short-term Left Republic**
- impact of Great Depression on exports and prices
- unemployment rising
- Land Reform Act 1932 – only 7,000 benefit by 1933
- cost of educational reforms
- cost of military reforms.

Paragraph 3: **Economic factors in the short-term Right Republic and Popular Front governments**
- impact of Great Depression ongoing
- public spending cut
- Land Reform Act was halted
- trade unions threaten a general strike
- prime minister forced to resign in September 1935 due to financial scandal
- economic situation deteriorating.
- restoration of reforms of Left Republic under Azaña
- government lack funds for effective reform
- land seizures in countryside
- CNT call general strike in May – cities increasingly paralysed.

Paragraph 4: **Political/ideological factors in the long term**
- weakness of government
- absolute monarchy/constitutional monarchy/First Republic
- role of military
- regionalism – Basques and Catalans
- General Primo de Rivera, 1923
- Anarchist movement/extremist FAI
- Liberals
- Socialists and Communists.

Paragraph 5: **Political/ideological factors under the Left Republic**
- anti-clerical speeches
- separation of Church and state – pay/education
- reduction in power of army – officers pensioned off
- General Sanjurjo rising, 1932
- Casas Viejas Anarchist Rising, 1933
- Catalonia given own parliament, 1932
- new right-wing party established, the CEDA – defend Church and landlords.

Paragraph 6:   **Political/ideological factors in the short term: Right Republic and Popular Front governments**

- two black years
- power of Church returned – pay/education
- Anarchist Rising in Barcelona, December 1933
- Catalonia declared itself independent after CEDA joined government
- government suspends Catalan autonomy after Asturias miners' uprising in 1934
- government imposes press censorship
- the right lost support of the Basques
- Falange Party formed, September 1934
- restoration of reforms of Left Republic under Azaña
- released political prisoners
- Socialists did not join government
- Anarchists encourage land seizures in countryside/bombings/assassinations
- FAI fought Falange and CEDA militias
- CNT call general strike in May
- military and CEDA plan coup
- Azaña unable to prevent coup plot.

06

The Spanish Civil War: 1936–1939

In July 1936 a failed military coup led to a catastrophic civil war in Spain that lasted until February 1939. The war was made more deadly, and was potentially protracted, by the intervention of foreign powers including Nazi Germany, Fascist Italy and Communist USSR. Ultimately the Nationalist forces won the brutal conflict and the reasons for victory may be found in the strengths of Franco's forces, the limitations of the Republicans and the relative impact of foreign assistance.

Dead horses used as a barricade for fighters in the Spanish Civil War, Barcelona, 1936.

Key concepts: *Significance and consequence*

Essay questions:

- Examine the role of foreign intervention in the course of the Spanish Civil War.
- Evaluate the role of foreign intervention in determining the outcome of the Spanish Civil War.
- To what extent did Franco's Nationalists win the civil war in Spain due to their military strengths?
- Discuss the reasons for the defeat of Republican forces in the Spanish Civil War.

Timeline of Spanish Civil War

1936	July	Franco's forces airlifted from Morocco to southern Spain
	Aug	Britain and France begin policy of non-intervention
	4 Sep	Largo Caballero forms new Republican government
	13 Sep	San Sebastián taken by Nationalists
	Oct	Republic incorporates militias into new Popular Army
	1 Oct	Franco becomes head of Nationalist government and supreme military commander
	29 Oct	Soviet intervention begins; German and Italian planes bomb Madrid
	6 Nov	Republican government leaves Madrid for Valencia
	23 Nov	Nationalists abandon attempt to take Madrid
1937	Feb	Nationalist offensive to cut the links between Madrid and Valencia fails at the Battle of Jarama; Russian tanks and planes play a crucial role in the battle
	8 Feb	Fall of Málaga to the Nationalists
	March	Nationalist offensive to tighten the pressure on Madrid from the north fails at the battle of Guadalajara; this was a major defeat for the Italian army, and again Soviet equipment was vital to Republican success
	April	Franco unites Carlists, Fascists and monarchists into one movement
	26 Apr	German Condor Legion bombs and destroys Guernica
	15 May	Fall of Largo Caballero
	17 May	Juan Negrín forms new government
	19 June	Fall of Bilbao to the Nationalists; end of Basque independence
	July	Republican offensive to break the siege of Madrid to the west fails at Brunete
	Aug	Republican offensive to break out from Madrid to the north-east fails at Belchite
	Sep–Oct	Nationalists capture rest of northern Spain
	Dec	Newly organized Republican Popular Army captures Teruel in central Spain.

1938	Feb	Nationalists retake Teruel and launch the strategically crucial advance to the Mediterranean to cut Catalonia off from the rest of Republican Spain
	Apr	Nationalists reach the Mediterranean and Republican zone is split in two
	July	Republican offensive on the River Ebro fails
	Nov	Nationalists drive Republicans back across River Ebro. Nationalists march on Barcelona
1939	Feb	Barcelona falls to Nationalists
	28 Mar	Nationalists enter Madrid
	1 Apr	Franco announces end of war

What was the role of foreign involvement in the Spanish Civil War?

Key concepts: *Significance and consequence*

As you have read thus far, the origins of the Spanish Civil War lay in Spain's domestic tensions and divisions; however, it became a broader European war fought on Spanish soil. In general, the decision by foreign governments to get involved, or to pursue a policy of non-intervention, was a result of both ideology and self-interest. The main interventionist powers were Nazi Germany, Fascist Italy, Portugal and the USSR. In addition, the role of Britain and France and the Non-Intervention Committee (NIC) must also be considered as a factor in the ultimate victory of the Nationalists.

A photograph of the devastated Basque town, Guernica. It had been bombed by the German Condor Legion and the Italian Aviazione Legionaria in April 1937.

In order to analyse the role of foreign involvement in the Spanish Civil War, we should begin by considering an overview of the course of the war itself. Read the following summary, and make a note of when foreign involvement played a role in Nationalist gains or Republican resistance.

Francisco Franco Bahamonde

Significant individual: Francisco Franco Bahamonde

Franco became the leader of the Nationalist forces during the Spanish Civil War. He was a Conservative and supporter of the monarchy, and he opposed the establishment of the Second Republic. When the conspiracy to overthrow the Popular Front government in the final months of the Republic was executed Franco played a pivotal role. When the coup failed and the civil war developed, other leading Nationalist generals were killed in the fighting. Franco assumed the role of 'Caudillo' or 'Chief'. After the Nationalist victory in 1939, Franco remained Caudillo of Spain until his death in November 1975.

An overview of the course of the Spanish Civil War

With the assistance of Nazi Germany, General Franco airlifted 24,000 experienced troops of the Army of Africa to Spain. Franco's efforts were kept alive by the fact that Hitler responded to his pleas for help. The uprisings in the north were under way when Franco's forces landed from Morocco. Once on the Spanish mainland, he used a policy of terror as his forces moved towards Madrid in August. Franco's success was complemented by the achievements of General Emilio Mola, who took territory in the north (see map on page 156, showing the situation in July 1936).

The army coup had aimed to crush the 'left revolution', but had instead politicized it and radicalized many Spaniards towards the left. The supporters of the Republican regime of 1936 became known as the 'Loyalists', and those that supported the rebels called themselves 'Nationalists'. Divisions could generally be drawn by class: the workers supported the Republic and the upper class backed the Nationalists, but the middle class included some Republicans and some Nationalists. The Nationalists also had the overwhelming support of the Church. However, alliances could also be accidental, depending on where people were when the war developed; the peasants of north and central Spain tended to be Nationalists, while the landless labourers of the south followed the Republicans. The Basques and Catalans supported the Republic, as it had backed their aspirations for autonomy.

Although the Nationalists made gains in the first weeks of the war, the Republic retained some advantages. It remained in control of most major cities and key industrial areas, it had Spain's gold reserves, and important elements of the military – most of the air force and navy – remained loyal. Yet, as you can see from the timeline and the maps on the following pages, the Nationalists were able to make steady progress in pushing back the Republic.

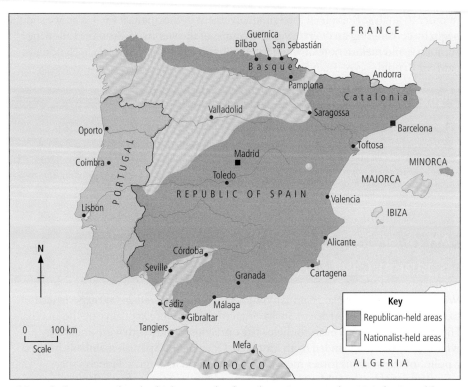

Spanish Civil War July 1936

Although the Nationalists had taken much of northern Spain in July 1936, the Republicans had defeated them in Barcelona and in the capital, Madrid, and held most of the coastline. Franco's forces had advanced from the south northwards and had taken the city of Badajoz with great ferocity, killing over 2,000 people. However, atrocities were committed on both sides with Republicans massacring around 4,000 priests, nuns and monks. Franco's strategy was to systematically occupy territory and then purge all republicans and their sympathizers before moving on. Overall, 50,000 were killed on the Republican side.

Spanish Civil War October 1936

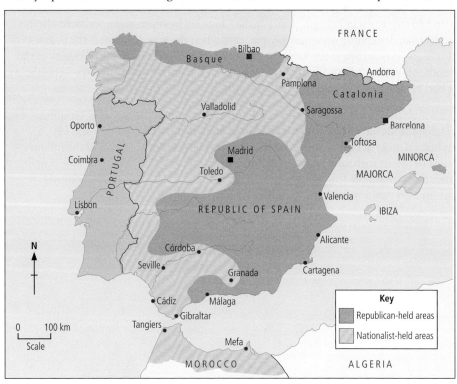

By the beginning of November, Madrid was holding out against Nationalist forces to the west and south. Nationalist forces were strengthened by support from the German Condor Legion. However, Soviet military aid, support from the International Brigades, and the determination of the civilian population of the city who were ably led by the Communist Party meant there was committed defence of the capital. Madrid did not fall in November.

The Nationalists continued to consolidate their position in Andalusia with considerable support from Italian forces. Indeed, Italian forces were key to taking several cities in February 1937. However, in March 1937, Italian forces were held back by Republican forces at Guadalajara. In addition, Republican forces had managed to capture Nationalist territory around the town of Teruel.

Franco focused on capturing northern Spain in the spring of 1937 in order to take the key industrial areas, which would cut off supplies coming into the north from the sea. The Republicans in the north were politically divided. The Basque Nationalist Party fought the Nationalists, who were led by General Mola. It was during this phase of the war that the bombing of Guernica was perpetrated by the Condor Legion. In June 1937 Bilbao fell after intense bombing. In October the Nationalists had captured the Asturias coalfields. Their forces had superior tanks and control of the air. The Republican air force was based centrally and the north was out of range. The Nationalist campaign in the north, through aerial bombardment, was completed in the autumn of 1937.

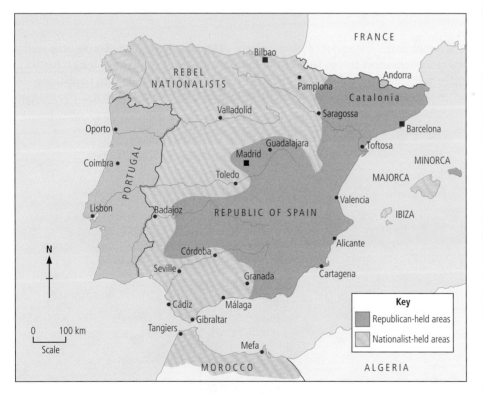

Spanish Civil War October 1937

The loss of the northern territories was a huge blow to the Republic as it lost valuable resources, coal, iron and armaments industries. The three Republican offensives – Brunete in July 1937, Belchite in August 1937 and Teruel in December 1937 – all ultimately failed. The Nationalist navy now could focus on attempting to blockade the Republic via the Mediterranean. By the end of April 1938 the Nationalists had reached the Mediterranean coast, and this split Republican Spain in two (see map on the next page, showing the situation in May 1938).

Spanish Civil War May 1938

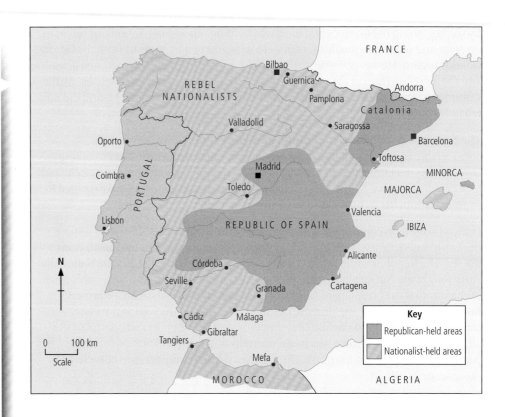

The Republicans' last major offensive in July 1938 – the Battle of the Ebro – collapsed as Franco sent more troops to the front lines. It was one of the hardest-fought battles of the war. The Nationalists' air superiority forced the Republicans into retreat, and when the battle ended in October 1938 the Republic was on its knees.

Spanish Civil War February 1939

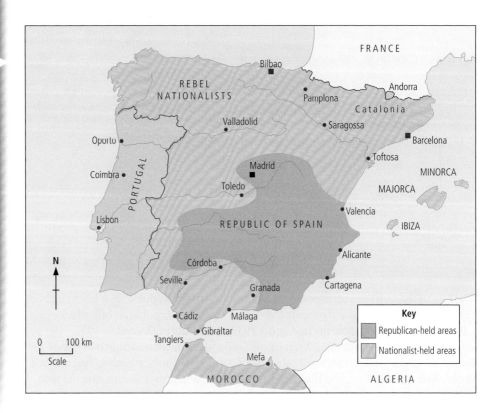

Stalin ended support for the Republic after the Munich Conference, signalling an end to the prospect of an anti-Fascist alliance in Europe and the defeat of the Republic seemed inevitable.

As the Nationalists now advanced against Catalonia, hundreds of thousands of Republican soldiers and civilian refugees fled across the French border. At the end of January 1939, the starving city of Barcelona fell. On 27 February, Britain and France recognized Franco's government and President Azaña resigned. After a struggle in Madrid between Communists, trade unionists and anti-Communists, a negotiated settlement was attempted with Franco. Franco would not accept the terms and Nationalist forces took Madrid on 27 March. On 1 April Franco declared that the war was over.

Foreign intervention had two main effects: it lengthened and intensified the war, and it meant that the Spanish issues that had caused the war were overtaken by the wider ideological battles taking place in Europe.

What was the role of foreign intervention in support of the Nationalists?

> ❝ Nazi and Italian fascist presence did not so much start the conflict as play a major role in sustaining it, manipulating and redefining it, and in determining its outcome.
> **Forrest, A (2000). *The Spanish Civil War*. Routledge, p. 73.**

The role of Germany

As commander of the Army of Africa, General Franco had sought assistance from Italy and Germany. The Republic had control of the navy and Franco needed to get his *Africanista* force across the Strait of Gibraltar to the mainland. Hitler's Germany was initially cautious when the appeal for help came from the rebels, as Hitler was not yet ready for a general European war. Hermann Göring was key in the decision to support the rebels; he shared Hitler's desire to stop the spread of communism, but, most importantly, he also wanted to test out his *Luftwaffe* (air force) in live conditions. There were economic benefits for Germany too as it could gain raw materials such as iron ore and other minerals. It could also make strategic gains: by militarily committing to Spain, Germany hoped to hamper Anglo-French maritime communications through acquiring the use of naval bases in the area and through limiting their correspondence via Gibraltar, where the British had a communications base.

The Germans decided to aid Franco and then facilitated the first airlift in military history by transporting the *Africanistas* to the mainland. During the course of the war, the Germans sent between 10,000 and 16,000 advisors, instructors, troops, pilots and communications experts in the Condor Legion (a mixed air and tank unit). Some historians have seen this as a pivotal event in the war, as without Franco's troops the Republic may have been able to isolate rebel forces and crush the rebellion.

Nevertheless, Hitler did not think the war would last long, and only wanted to commit to limited aid. He supplied the Nationalists through Portugal and ultimately, according to the historian Hugh Thomas, committed 540 million Reichsmarks to the war. Although initially a member of the NIC (see page 162), Germany left in May 1937.

As well as its support of Franco in the initial stages of the war, the Condor Legion played an important role as the war developed. It perpetrated the now infamous bombing of Guernica, a Basque market town, in April 1937. This attack was perpetrated by over 50 Condor Legion aircraft and by the Italian Aviazione Legionaria.

Activity 1 Thinking skills

1. At the beginning of the war the Republicans had control of half the army, and the air force, the navy, the capital city, key industrial areas and Spain's gold reserves. In pairs discuss what advantages the Nationalists had as they launched their attack on the Republic.

2. From the summary of the course of the war above identify when foreign interventionist powers played an important role in events.

Condor Legionnaires on the cover of the Nazi air ministry magazine, June 1939.

159

The justification for Guernica was that, as a communications base and escape route for retreating Basque forces, it was a military target. General Mola also wanted to target the town as part of a plan to wipe out Basque resistance.

With the support of the Condor Legion, the defences of Bilbao collapsed on 7 June 1937. This gave Franco control of naval shipyards and strengthened the Nationalists' advantage in terms of communications. The Basque army finally surrendered in August 1937. Preston suggests that elements of the campaign against the Basque territory were actually masterminded by the Germans. In addition, the Condor Legion played a pivotal role in the fall of Catalonia, as it reinforced Nationalist forces and kept the rebels supplied with German equipment. Furthermore, the introduction of Messerschmitt 109s in 1937 gave the Nationalists superiority in the air. Indeed, the Germans played a key role in the Nationalists' campaigns of 1937 and 1938.

Overall, the involvement of Germany was important to the outcome of the war, not only as it played crucial military roles at critical times during the fighting, but also because other governments were deterred from getting involved due to its presence.

The role of Italy

Italy gave the most assistance of all the foreign powers in the Spanish Civil War, and its aid to the Nationalists was significant. Italy agreed to intervene after Franco's calls for support for a number of reasons. Firstly, Mussolini wanted to be involved as support for the Nationalist cause would have been in line with his anti-communist/ socialist/democratic outlook and his pro-Fascist stance. Secondly, he wished to challenge Britain's position as the dominant power in the Mediterranean, and thereby demonstrate Italy's might. Thirdly, a Fascist victory would weaken France and prevent its left-wing influence in Spain. Another Fascist power (Spain under Franco) would encircle France and put pressure on French colonies in North Africa.

The Italians not only sent 70,000–75,000 troops, they contributed many planes, tanks and weapons. Italian bombers of the Italian Aviazione Legionaria attacked Spanish cities, and their submarines were a constant threat to supplies. Italy, like Germany, ignored its membership of the Non-Intervention Committee set up by Britain and France. Historians suggest that although Italy sent many troops, the significant element of its intervention was its air and naval support, which included participation in the bombardment of Madrid and, in particular, the Italian navy's blockade of Republican supplies. These interventions helped the Nationalists to secure victory.

The relationship between Italy and Germany was enhanced by their interventions in Spain.

The role of Portugal

Portugal was an important part of the foreign contribution to Franco's victory. Not only did Portugal send 20,000 troops, it was also fundamental in supplying the rebels along the Spanish–Portuguese border, and provided a base for communications. Portugal's long-term alliance with Britain led to the British being reluctant to counter its support for the Nationalists. This was, of course, an important benefit for Franco's troops.

The impact of foreign interventionist support for the Nationalists

As suggested above, some historians have argued that foreign aid was a crucial factor in the Nationalists' victory over the Republic. Hugh Thomas writes that the conflict '*became an international crisis whose solution was decided by external circumstances*'. Indeed, the rebels benefited from more aid, which was of a better quality than that given to the Republicans, and its supply was continuous throughout the war as they could utilize the border between Portugal and Spain. This assistance was significant in several ways. It allowed the Nationalists to fight in the first place, owing to the German airlift, but German planes also gave the Nationalists control of the air from 1937. Franco's command was not compromised, and after an Italian defeat at Guadalajara, Italy's forces were taken under Spanish command. The key benefit for the Nationalists, however, was not the manpower, as most of their armies were Spanish, it was the modern equipment they received.

What was the role of foreign intervention in support of the Republicans?

The role of the USSR

By the middle of September 1936 the Republic was under serious threat as the Fascist-backed rebel forces advanced on Madrid. In September, Stalin approved Operation X to send secret military assistance to the Republicans, although until mid-October Soviet aid consisted mainly of food. Nevertheless, the arrival of Soviet military assistance subsequently meant there would be no quick Nationalist victory and Madrid was held. By November 1936 there were approximately 500 Soviet advisors in Spain.

The USSR's reasons for supporting the Republic were not simply ideological. The Spanish conflict in fact presented Stalin with a dilemma. The emergence of another fascist state in Europe would strengthen Hitler's position in Europe. On the other hand, a Republican victory could panic Britain and France into an alliance with Hitler against the threat of communism. Such an outcome would ruin Stalin's policy of bringing Britain and France into an alliance with the USSR to contain Hitler. Stalin was divided between these two concerns. Initially he welcomed the NIC but, seeing that Germany and Italy were able to ignore its rules, he then went on to organize the transport of international volunteers to Spain and also sent weapons from the Soviet Union, declaring that the USSR was not bound by the NIC as long as Germany and Italy broke the agreement. Historian Denis Smyth suggests that the USSR's actions were aimed at encouraging British and French intervention to defend the Republic and at fostering an anti-Fascist alliance with the USSR.

Soviet assistance not only helped to save Madrid at the beginning of the war, but also aided the Republic's war in the air. In addition the Soviets took the lead in the creation of the International Brigades, which grew to a force of 35,000 and drew on the resources of 54 countries. Andrew Forrest writes, 'The USSR intervened in Spain with vitally timed material and military advisers who... were attached to the staffs of Republican generals and played a significant part in the field, for example, at Guadalajara'.

However, on 15 September 1936, shortly after the Soviets entered the war, the entire gold reserves from the Bank of Madrid, the fourth largest in the world, were shipped for 'safety' to the USSR. The Republic would have to pay for Soviet assistance.

Once intervention had begun, Stalin also had a motive for dragging out the fighting. The war would drain the resources of Germany, and the longer it went on the more likely it was for the war to develop into a general war. This general war would then be waged on the other side of Europe, far from the borders of the USSR.

Stalin began to reduce Soviet forces from June 1938; Soviet resources were stretched as it was engaged in border conflicts with Japan in Manchuria and Mongolia in 1938 and 1939, and was also attempting to send military aid to China. Not only did the Republic seem to be losing, but it now seemed that the Western democracies were set on appeasing the Fascist dictators. Stalin's aim of creating a bloc to resist Hitler ended when Czechoslovakia was abandoned by Britain and France in the Munich Agreement in September 1938. The USSR's withdrawal fatally undermined the Republic's ability to wage war.

The role of the International Brigades

The other key allies of the Republicans were the **International Brigades**, which were organized by the Comintern. Some 35,000 foreign volunteers went to fight in Spain. They were formally integrated into the Republican People's Army from 1937. The left-wing French historians Pierre Broué and Émile Temime argued that the International Brigades formed an elite force and were involved in the most significant fighting until the end of October 1938.

Although their role does seem to have been significant in the defence of Madrid in November 1936, where they made up 15 per cent of the Republican forces, at Brunete in July 1937 and in the Ebro offensive in 1938, overall their impact was limited. In 1938, the Soviets withdrew their support and the International Brigades went home in October 1938; a final blow for the Republic.

The impact of foreign interventionist support for the Republicans

Foreign aid has been seen as a critical factor in determining the outcome of the Spanish Civil War. Some historians have suggested its role has been exaggerated; nevertheless, there is no doubt that the foreign assistance given to the Republic was far more limited than that afforded to the Nationalists. The main ally of the Republic was the USSR, and it was the Soviets who initially saved the Republic and enabled it to fight a civil war in 1938 to 1939. In addition, Soviet aircraft and tanks were better early on in the war than their German and Italian counterparts. However, this aid had to be paid for by the Republic, which sent, as we have seen, all of its gold reserves to Moscow. No Soviet troops were sent to fight and the USSR only committed 1,000 aircraft and 750 tanks.

Activity 2   **(ATL) Communication, self-management and social skills**

Get into groups of four students. Two students will design a recruitment poster for German, Italian and Portuguese forces to go to Spain to support the Nationalists, and two students will design a recruitment poster for Communist and Socialist Party members around the world to join the fight to save the Republic (you can include ideas that might have been promoted by the USSR at the time). Each pair will present their poster to your group.

Discuss in your group the similarities and differences between the motivations for intervention on both sides. Consider in your discussion the role of ideological, political, economic or social factors.

What was the role of Britain, France and the NIC in the war in Spain?

> 66 *[The NIC] was never more than a sham which actually worked in favour of the insurgents. A legal government was equated to a group of seditious generals. The Republic was hindered by an arms embargo from mounting an effective defence and a perfect cloak was provided for the Axis powers to continue their activities. Under British auspices, the committee would remain until the end of the war an empty talking shop. It was a perfect weapon to prevent France from making a more direct commitment, preserve consensus at home and avoid confrontation with Germany and Italy.*
>
> **Extract from the article 'The Spanish Civil War: The International Dimension' by Francisco J Romero Salvadó, *Modern History Review*, February 1995.**

Britain and France were concerned that the conflict in Spain could develop into a broader European war. In August the two governments drafted a policy for a non-

The Abraham Lincoln Brigade

The Abraham Lincoln Brigade was formed of just over 3,000 US volunteers who travelled to fight and serve in the Spanish Civil War. The volunteers arrived in Spain in February 1937, were in the 15th **International Brigade** and fought as soldiers and pilots in the war. They also assisted the Republicans as technicians and medical personnel. They sustained high casualty rates, and 681 were killed.

intervention committee which would prevent foreign intervention and contain the war in Spain. The first meeting of the NIC was held in September 1936, and members declared a policy of non-intervention in Spain. Britain, France, the Soviet Union, Germany and Italy were all members of the NIC. Although France sent aid initially, Prime Minister Léon Blum promoted the policy of non-intervention that was supported by the British. This policy was primarily driven by anti-communist sentiments in Britain and domestic issues, as well as Blum's pacifism in France. Non-intervention also meant that Hitler and Mussolini had no direct opposition from the Western democracies.

The role of France

French support for the Republic was inconsistent, and this reflected the complexity of its domestic political response to the civil war. Events in Spain mattered more to France than any other European state. However, the issue had divided the Popular Front government of Léon Blum. It was not in French interests to have a right-wing regime on its border that could join with Italy and Germany to encircle France. But French politics was also polarized, and the government feared a revolt in France should it fully commit in Spain. France was also reliant on Britain, which was more anti-Republic, for its foreign policy options. After initially supporting the Republic, France proposed the establishment of the NIC. This initiative was supported by the British (British Foreign Secretary Anthony Eden had cautioned Blum to 'be careful' when considering interventionist options). In August 1936, Britain and France persuaded the rest of Europe to sign the Non-Intervention Agreement to prevent the escalation of war and to contain it in Spain. However, 94 French aircraft had been sent to Spain by mid-October. Although France reopened the border occasionally, in the end, the French restricted themselves mainly to humanitarian assistance. The impact of the French pursuing non-intervention dealt a fatal blow to the Republic, which could have benefited greatly from support from this large country on its border. The resulting reliance of the Republic on the Soviets polarized the politics of the Spanish Civil War, and associated the Republic with 'Soviet communism'. Nevertheless, the French did not stop citizens from joining the International Brigades; 10,000 joined up and constituted 26 per cent of the brigades (the largest contingent), and the International Brigades were mainly organized in France. In addition, France was the main centre for the coordination of Soviet aid.

Refugees from Spain flee to France, 1936.

The role of Britain

> *... the British let their class interests overcome their strategic interests.*
>
> **Paul Preston, 'In Our Time: the Spanish Civil War', quoted from BBC Radio 4's 'In Our Time' programme (3 April 2003).**

Public opinion in Britain favoured supporting the Republicans. However, the British government were more concerned about the revolutionary left than the authoritarian right and were actually hoping for a swift Nationalist victory. Richard Robinson argues that British officials believed Spain had been on the brink of anarchy under the Popular Front government and that the Nationalist rebels would restore order. Many in the British establishment and elites with investments in Spain believed Franco would bring public order to Spain and safeguard its interests. Paul Preston suggests that the government made the mistake of interpreting events in Spain as a '*class war*' rather than as a struggle for democracy; this was exactly the line that had been presented in the right-wing press in Spain.

Britain took a leading role in the setting up of the NIC in August 1936 and at its first meeting in London in September 1936. Britain's fear was that the war would spread and become a general European conflict. However, three of the key members of the NIC – Germany, Italy and the USSR – ignored the NIC completely and became the main foreign forces in Spain. In addition, Britain's non-intervention policies were limited and tended to favour the Nationalists. They focused on preventing aid going to the Republic and allowed the Nationalists, but not the Republicans, to use Gibraltar as a communications base. In December 1936, they signed a trading agreement with the Nationalists that permitted British companies to trade with the rebel forces.

It would seem that Spain was sacrificed to the policy of **appeasement** (see Chapter 2) in the same vein as Czechoslovakia; Britain wanted to avoid a general war at all costs, and did not want the civil war to damage its relations with Italy or Portugal.

Activity 3   (ATL) **Thinking skills**

A cartoon by David Low published in the *Evening Standard*, 5 August 1936. The speech bubble reads: '*Hear, I say, fair play! You shouldn't encourage the aggressor you know. After all, my friend and I aren't trying to help his victim.*' The title of the cartoon is '"Correct attitudes" in Spain'. The man on the floor is labelled 'democracy', the two men holding him down are labelled 'army fascism' and 'fascist international'. The two men observers are British officials.

1. What does the source reveal about the British policy towards the conflict in Spain?
2. Read through the quote by Francisco J Romero Salvadó on page 162. Discuss with a partner the ways in which Salvadó supports the message of the cartoonist in the source.

The role of the US

The US generally supported the NIC, but did not sign up due to its neutrality policy and pursuit of **isolationism**. The Neutrality Act, which banned arms sales to belligerents in a war, was extended to include civil wars in 1937. This new American neutrality act, passed in May 1937, is said to have indirectly strengthened Franco's position and his eventual victory in the Ebro Valley in November 1938. This victory was militarily decisive.

Furthermore, despite the neutrality acts, US companies continued to provide the Nationalists with war supplies, including oil on credit from the Texaco oil company and trucks supplied to Franco by Ford, Studebaker and General Motors. It has been estimated that the Nationalists obtained $700 million of supplies on credit during the war.

Activity 4	Communication and social skills

As effective communicators you should be able to express ideas and information confidently and creatively in a variety of ways, not just in your written work. Organize your class into different characters for a class role-play activity. Each student should take on one of the roles listed below. Prepare a short speech, approximately one or two minutes long, rallying people to join your forces and fight for the 'freedom of Spain!' You must include examples, events and details of why you believe your perspective to be right, and why people should either fight or remain neutral in the war. Present your speeches to the class.

- a Spanish Socialist from Barcelona
- a Spanish Nationalist from Madrid
- an Anarchist landless peasant from the South of Spain
- a member of Franco's forces
- a Spanish Catholic priest
- a French supporter of the Republicans
- a German supporter of the Nationalists
- an Italian supporter of the Nationalists
- a Soviet supporter of Stalin's intervention in Spain
- a British non-interventionist
- a French non-interventionist
- an American supporter of the Abraham Lincoln Brigade.

Activity 5	Self-management skills

Using the information in this section, copy and complete the following grid:

	Actions	Motivations for involvement or non-intervention	Impact
Germany			
Italy			
France			
Britain			
USSR			
US			

For top markbands for Paper 3 essays:

Introduction and main body paragraphs

Responses are clearly focused.

The question is fully addressed and implications are considered.

The essay is well structured and the material effectively organized.

Supporting knowledge is detailed, accurate, relevant to the question and used to support arguments.

Arguments are clear, well developed and consistently supported with evidence.

There is evaluation of different perspectives.

Conclusion

The conclusion is clearly stated and it is consistent with the evidence presented.

Essay Planning

In small groups plan the following essay question:

Examine the significance of foreign intervention in the course and outcome of the Spanish Civil War.

Review the essay writing template in the Introduction. Remember to structure your essay to address the command terms in the question.

Examine: Consider an argument or concept in a way that uncovers the assumptions and interrelationships of the issue.

Introduction: You will need to set out in your introduction the main arguments you will develop in order to 'examine' the significance of foreign intervention. You will address the command term by considering its significance in a number of different ways.

Foreign intervention was significant in the course and outcome of the Spanish Civil War as it strengthened the Nationalist forces militarily and economically, and did not undermine its political unity, whereas foreign interventionist forces gave the Republicans only limited military and economic support, and undermined its political unity.

Main body paragraphs:

Begin each paragraph with an analytical point that uses the words of the question.

You could use the following as themes for each of your main body paragraphs:

- military support for Nationalists
- limited military support for Republicans
- economic support for Nationalists
- lack of economic support for Republicans
- did not undermine Nationalist political unity
- undermined Republican political unity.

For each paragraph you need to go on to explain how foreign intervention assisted or undermined each side and support your analysis with detailed evidence.

Conclusion: Based on the weight of evidence you have given in the main body, answer the question by explaining the significance of foreign intervention in the Spanish Civil War.

Activity 6

ATL Thinking and research skills

A cartoon by David Low, published in the British *Evening Standard* newspaper, 14 December 1936. The title is: 'SPAIN – League Discussion'. The soldiers are saying: *'The League! Pah! Fancy suggesting nations could unite for peace'.*

1. What does the source suggest about the response of the League of Nations to the conflict in Spain?

2. In small groups, research the response of the League of Nations to the civil war in Spain. You should make sure you include:
   - the Republic's appeal to the League of Nations
   - the League's mandate regarding civil wars
   - the official response of the Council
   - the response of other member states in the Assembly.

3. Give feedback on your research findings to the class. Explain why the League did not intervene in the Spanish Civil War.

Why did the Nationalists win the Spanish Civil War?

Key concepts: *Causation and consequence*

We have considered the ways in which foreign intervention may have determined the outcome of the Spanish Civil War; we should now consider Spanish factors in the ultimate victory of Franco. Indeed, to what extent did the Nationalists win the war because of their own strengths? Or was the war lost by the Republicans due to their inherent weaknesses?

Nationalist strengths

Political unity

The major strength of the Nationalists was unity. In July 1936, however, the Nationalists were almost as divided as the Republicans. Their only common aim was to overthrow the government. Initially, Generals Mola, Goded and Sanjurjo seemed more important than Franco, but after the first few weeks Franco had emerged as the leader. In September 1936, the generals decided that they needed a unified command and it was agreed that Franco would assume political and military control. Thus he became head of government and head of state. This rise to power was due not only to other leaders dying (General Mola was killed in a plane crash in June 1937) or doing badly in the war, but also to his position in command of the Army of Africa and because important German aid came through him.

To achieve political unity, Franco needed to control both the Carlists and the Falange. In 1937 their numbers were impressive: 70,000 and 1 million respectively. In April, Franco merged the two parties. This new party, *Falange Española Tradicionalista* (FET; Spanish Traditionalist Phalanx), was under his control.

Franco was also assisted by support from the Church, which opposed the left and its secular ideologies. From the pulpit, church leaders would denounce atheist communism and call for a crusade to protect Christian civilization. Indeed, Franco used a mixture of propaganda and terror in the areas under his command.

Although some historians argue that the Soviet involvement in the war led to its protraction (which may have been Stalin's deliberate policy), others have suggested that Franco gained power and authority from his victories on the battlefield, and that it was

CHALLENGE YOURSELF

Social and research skills

Independently, or in small groups, investigate the international response to the Spanish Civil War and foreign intervention. Attempt to find examples from across Europe, including newspaper and other media reports, government statements and evidence of public opinion. Try to gather examples and material from European countries whose governments were sympathetic to either the Republicans or the Nationalists. Also attempt to find news reports from the Americas regions, Asia, Africa and the Middle East.

Give feedback on your research to your class, and discuss the similarities and differences within and between regions, in terms of the public's attitude to and sympathy for each side in the conflict in Spain.

Activity 7

 Self-management skills

In pairs discuss the extent to which you agree with Andrew Forrest's assertion that *'Nazi and Italian fascist presence did not so much start the conflict as play a major role in sustaining it, manipulating and redefining it, and in determining its outcome'.*

167

A Nationalist propaganda poster.

he who extended the war to enhance his own dictatorial power. The nationalistic politics of Franco were not undermined by the foreign support given by Germany and Italy.

Military unity

Militarily the Nationalists initially had similar problems to the Republicans – 'columns' of Carlist and Falangist militias attempted to operate alongside regular army units. In contrast, however, these militias were effectively drawn into the regular army. The Army of Africa played a significant role. It contained the best troops in the country, and it could cover for other forces while they were being trained and equipped. In open and mobile offensive operations, the *Africanistas* proved themselves the most effective force in the entire civil war.

The unified command was key to the Nationalists' success. Franco's leadership was accepted by the other generals and right-wing parties. Ultimately, the Italian forces were under his command too. They were successful in pushing on and winning offensives, and were also able to adopt effective defensive tactics during the Republican offensive campaigns of 1937.

The Nationalists had sound communications, and managed to equip their growing army throughout the civil war. They could also rely on their large number of junior officers.

Franco was an able military and political leader. He would often not pursue the more radical advice given to him by his German and Italian advisors. His concern for his troops ensured that the majority were obedient.

> 66 *Franco's army was better organized than that of his enemies. Political unity gave him unity of command. Nationalist forces were more disciplined than their opponents and their logistical arrangements were excellent, as seen in the ease with which reserves were moved from one front to another. German technical training, particularly in signals, played a considerable part. But equally important was the availability of so many middle-class young men… whose education made them more effective than the junior Republican officers.*
> **Thomas, H (1990). *The Spanish Civil War*. Penguin, p. 910.**

Economic advantage

The business community backed the Nationalists, which meant they could get credit to buy war supplies. Also, by September 1936 they were in control of the main food-producing areas. After their successes in 1937 in the north, they added the main industrial areas to their control.

The Nationalists also benefited from international trade and credit, which was not restricted. It has been estimated that the US gave $700 million in credit during the course of the war. This meant that Franco's forces could buy all the rubber and oil they needed, which was acquired from US companies.

> 66 *The financial management of the war was a success for the nationalists, a disaster for the republic. The former paid for their war effort by delaying the interest both on national debt and on most of the debt due on the war; by ruthlessly reducing unnecessary spending; by new taxes; by the establishment of a new bank of Spain, which lent to the nationalist authorities 9,000 million pesetas; and of course, by foreign aid, which was not paid for until afterwards. The republic had recourse to similar financial methods but they undertook a formidable expansion of the currency, vast governmental spending, with substantial inflation, as well as severe rationing which did not prevent scarcity of food from late 1937 onwards.*
> **Thomas, H (1990). *The Spanish Civil War*. Penguin, p. 912.**

A Spanish Republican propaganda poster, 1937. The title is 'The General'. The figures holding the cloak are a general, a capitalist and a priest.

1. What is the message of the Republican propaganda poster?
2. Read the two excerpts from Hugh Thomas's book *The Spanish Civil War* (page 168). What does Thomas highlight about the military and economic strengths of the Nationalists during the war?
3. In pairs discuss the extent to which you agree with the following statement: 'Franco's key strength was that the Nationalists were an effective military force'.

Republican weaknesses

Political disunity

Largo Caballero became head of a coalition government in September 1936. His rule was weakened by the fact that the Republicans were politically divided. Indeed, Republicans subscribed to widely different ideologies. The key divisions were between the Communists and Socialists, who believed that the 'revolution' should now be postponed until the war was won, and the Anarchists, who argued that the war could only be won through revolutionary policies. The Anarchists, dominant in Catalonia, Aragon and Andalusia, encouraged 'revolution from below' in the areas they controlled, and some historians suggest that this added a crucial hurdle for the Republic, as it had to try to regain its centralized control. The Communists and Socialists had more influence in Madrid and Valencia. The Basque region and the regions of Catalonia and Asturias became virtually independent.

The war generally increased the popularity of the Communists. For example, in July 1936 the Spanish Communist Party numbered around 40,000 members, but by October 1937 it had 400,000 members. The Communist Party exploited the fact that it was the only Republican group with clear foreign support – from the USSR. However, to retain control the Communists often used 'terror' tactics, which led to some resistance even in sympathetic territories (for example, the 'May Days' in Barcelona in 1937 – see below). In addition, the Communists and Socialists wanted victory in the war to strengthen the Second Republic, whereas the Anarchists wanted a new revolutionary regime.

The lack of unity between the forces of the Republic is exemplified in the four days of street fighting in Barcelona in May 1937 – Communists and Socialists on one side and the Anarchists and **POUM** on the other, though this description is a simplification of a more complex struggle between the forces of central authority and the revolutionaries. This fighting became known as the 'May Days'. As a result of this turmoil, Caballero was replaced by Socialist Juan Negrín, the Communists' favoured choice as leader. Negrín

A Republican propaganda poster. '*No pasaran*' means '*They shall not pass*': it was the rallying cry used in the defence of Madrid.

 POUM The *Partido Obrero de Unificación Marxista* (Workers' Party of Marxist Unification) was a small influential Catalan Marxist party that was critical of the Soviet system and often opposed the Communists and Socialists, siding with the Anarchists.

attacked the POUM and Anarchist leaders, who were imprisoned or executed. His more authoritarian regime lasted until March 1939, when there was a military coup in Madrid.

Activity 9 ATL Thinking skills

Read the source below and answer the questions that follow:

An extract from *Adelante*, a PSOE newspaper. Valencia, 1 May 1937

> At the outbreak of the Fascist revolt the labour organisations and the democratic elements in the country were in agreement that the so-called Nationalist Revolution, which threatened to plunge our people into an abyss of deepest misery, could be halted only by a Social Revolution. The Communist Party, however, opposed this view with all its might. It had apparently completely forgotten its old theories of a 'workers' and 'peasants' republic and a 'dictatorship of the proletariat'. From its constant repetition of its new slogan of the parliamentary democratic republic it is clear that it has lost all sense of reality. When the Catholic and conservative sections of the Spanish bourgeoisie saw their old system smashed and could find no way out, the Communist Party instilled new hope into them. It assured them that the democratic bourgeois republic for which it was pleading put no obstacles in the way of Catholic propaganda and, above all, that it stood ready to defend the class interests of the bourgeoisie.

1. What criticisms are made by the PSOE of the Communist Party in this source?
2. With reference to its origin, purpose and content, analyse the value and limitations of this source for historians studying the political divisions within the Republic during the Spanish Civil War.

Military limitations

Despite some excellent commanders, such as Rojo, the Republic lacked strong military leadership. There was no unified command, and the Communists and Anarchists would not work together. Indeed, the Anarchist militias and the Basques refused to be led by a central command structure. The Basques would not permit their forces to defend areas outside their own territory. In addition, loyal army officers, with potentially valuable experience, were not trusted by the Republic.

In the first vital weeks of the war, the Republic was dependent on ineffective militia units that formed haphazardly. This meant that they fought a series of local conflicts rather than one clear overall campaign. Different fronts operated separately, although to some extent this situation was due to the territory held by the Republicans. Many battlefields were not within range of their air force, and they failed to sustain offensive campaigns in 1937 at Brunete, Belchite and Teruel. Indeed, it was not until the end of 1936 that the Republicans started to replace militias with a coherent 'Popular Army'.

Paul Preston argues that had the Republic armed the working classes in the early stages of the revolt the rebels could have been defeated.

Economic problems

In areas under Anarchist control, industries, public utilities and transport were taken over by workers' committees; in the countryside, collective farms were set up. However, neither of these systems could supply the needs of the Republic to fight the war. Some historians have argued that this situation was due more to the impact of the war than to a badly run government, but most believe that the collectives impaired the Republic's war effort. Production in the key area of Catalan fell by two-thirds between 1936 and 1939, and the Republic was increasingly affected by food and raw material shortages. Inflation was also a problem, reaching 300 per cent during the war. At the same time wages only increased by 15 per cent.

> The republican zone lived in a spiral of hyperinflation. The cost of living has tripled in less than two years of war… the rate of pay, however, was not raised… As well as the huge cost of

importing arms, the Republic had to buy oil, supplies of all sorts and now food after the loss of Aragon's agricultural regions. Chickpeas and lentils bought from Mexico became the staple of the republican zone diet… Food queues were worse than ever and women were killed and maimed during bombing raids because they would not give up their places. The daily ration of 150 grammes of rice, beans or, more usually, lentils [known as Dr Negrin's little pills] could not prevent vitamin and protein deficiency among those unable to afford black market prices… In 1938 the death rate for children and the old doubled.

Beevor, A (2006). *The Battle for Spain*. Orion publishing, p. 332.

The NIC, established by Britain and France in 1936 for the purpose of preventing the foreign influx of support to the warring parties in Spain, also had an economic impact on the Republic. Its unintended impact was to compound the starvation of the Republic of all credit; the USSR was the only country willing to trade with it and even this trade had to be paid for using the entire gold reserves of Spain. Paul Preston has argued that Communist domination ultimately improved the situation by centralizing control, but this happened too late in the war to save the Republic.

Activity 10  Thinking and self-management skills

Read Source A and Source B and answer the questions that follow.

Source A

> *After Catalonia fell, a huge area amounting to about 30 per cent of Spain remained in the hands of the Republic. Nergin still cherished hope of fighting on until a European war started and the democracies at last realized that the anti-fascist battle of the Republic had been theirs too. Franco was in no hurry to go into battle since the repression was a higher priority. In any case, he had reason to believe that the Republic was about to face major divisions that might save him the trouble of fighting in central Spain. … On 4 March, Colonel Segismundo Casado, commander of the Republican Army of the Centre, formed an anti-Negrin National Defence Junta, in the hope of negotiating with Franco. He thereby sparked off what was effectively a second civil war within the Republican zone. Although he defeated the pro-Communist forces, there was no prospect of a deal with Franco. Troops along the line were surrendering or just going home. On 26 March, a gigantic and virtually unopposed advance was launched along a wide front. The next day, Franco's forces simply occupied deserted positions and entered an eerily silent Madrid. … The war was over.*

> **Paul Preston (2012). *The Spanish Holocaust: Inquisition and Extermination in Twentieth-Century Spain*. Harper Press, p. 468.**

Source B

> *On 12 March [attempts were made by Casado's Council]… to initiate negotiations with the Nationalist headquarters. It was not long before its euphoria evaporated. In fact, during the next two weeks the bankruptcy of Casado's plans was brutally exposed. All demands for time to organize the evacuation and for assurances on no reprisals… were dismissed. Franco simply reiterated what had always been his goal: unconditional surrender. The Caudillo was bent on humiliating the enemy… In a few days Casado had ruined the possibility of further resistance and had rendered pointless the bloodshed and sacrifices of the previous three years.*

> *On 26 March the Nationalists resumed the offensive virtually unopposed. Republican troops deserted en masse, while many others escaped towards the coast in a final – and in most cases futile – attempt to escape abroad. When the capital was occupied two days later, Ciano [the Italian foreign minister] noted that Fascism had won its more formidable victory to date. On 1 April 1939 the Caudillo announced the end of the war.*

> **Francisco J Romero Salvadó (2005). *The Spanish Civil War*. Palgrave, p. 179.**

1. Compare and contrast what Source A and Source B reveal about the final weeks of the Spanish Civil War.

2. Read the quotation from Anthony Beevor on page 170. What were the key economic weaknesses of the Republicans identified by Beevor?

3. The historian Paul Heywood suggests that political division was key to the Republic's defeat. Writing in *History Today*, March 1989, his article, 'Why the Republic lost', suggests, '*The Republic was at war... with most of the world. Most importantly and tragically, however, they were often at war with themselves.*' In pairs find evidence in this chapter to support this view.

4. In large groups or as a class debate the following resolution: **'If political unity helped the nationalist victory, division among the republicans was a prime cause of their defeat.'** Hugh Thomas (1990). The Spanish Civil War. Penguin Books, p. 906.

> ### Historians' perspectives

Preston argues that had the Republic armed the working classes as the rebellion began, the revolt could have been put down. He then highlights the failure of France and Britain to defend the Republic. G Hills also suggests that the Republic could have won the war in the first few months if it had executed the plan to isolate Franco and his forces in Morocco and Mola in Navarre.

Mary Vincent argues that the defeat of the Republic was inevitable given the scale of foreign support for the Nationalists, and it was extraordinary that the Republicans were able to resist for so long.

Thomas suggests that the inherent military strengths, and later the economic competence of the Nationalist side, and the military and economic limitations of the Republicans determined the outcome of the war.

Denis Mack Smith argues that the Nationalists would have been isolated and would have faced '*piecemeal defeat*' had Germany not airlifted Franco's Army of Africa to the mainland. However, during the course of the war the German impact may have been more limited than some historians have claimed. The American historian Robert Whealey suggests that there were only around 5,500 Condor Legion personnel in Spain at a time.

Francisco J Romero Salvadó highlights the role of the NIC in both seriously hampering the Republic's ability to wage war and to gain foreign support and in its failure to stem the assistance given to the Nationalists.

Activity 11   Thinking and self-management skills

Discuss the different perspectives presented above in small groups. Whose view do you agree with? Explain your perspective, with supporting examples, to your group. Does your group share the same perspective on the reasons for the defeat of the Republican forces?

Activity 12   Communication and self-management skills

Create two mind maps/spider diagrams. One should summarize the strengths of the Nationalists and the other should show the weaknesses of the Republicans. On your diagram, organize your information under the following headings: political, economic, military, foreign intervention.

What was the impact of the Spanish Civil War?

Key concept: *Significance*

The impact on Spain

The civil war had brought great human and material destruction to Spain. Around 100,000 Republicans were killed during the war, and about 70,000 Nationalists. Moreover, the killing continued after the war, as Franco launched a terror campaign to eradicate opposition. It is estimated that a further 40,000–200,000 were killed during this period, known as the 'White Terror'. Another 250,000 escaped into exile, many ending up in refugee camps in France.

Thousands of Republicans and their sympathizers were held for years in concentration camps and prisons. Often Republican children were taken from their parents to be 're-educated'. Some were placed with reliable Nationalist/Catholic families, while others were sent to orphanages where they were indoctrinated against the views and actions of their own parents. Divisions and hatred remained in Spanish society for decades.

Spain's economy was devastated by the war. Some 10–15 per cent of its wealth was destroyed, and per capita income was 28 per cent lower in 1939 than in 1935. Seventy per cent of Madrid's factory machinery needed to be replaced, and its communications systems, including the city's tram network, had to be rebuilt. Around a third of its merchant shipping was out of action. There was high inflation due to the cost of fighting the war and because of the method used to attempt to pay for it: printing money. The Republican land reform was reversed by Franco, and Spain's agricultural economy remained inefficient and ineffective. Labourers had to tolerate periodic unemployment, and landowners were not interested in modernization. In addition, Spain had massive debts to pay. Due to the human cost of the war, there was a corresponding lack of skilled workers, and an overriding general labour shortage. Spain attempted to find foreign loans for investment, but the British demanded that debt was paid back first, and the Germans also wanted the Spanish to repay the cost of the aid sent to them before further investment was made.

The economy may have improved due to the outbreak of the Second World War. Franco seems to have attempted to gain leverage over Spain's debt to Britain and France in August 1939, by offering to remain neutral and not ally Spain with Nazi Germany. He also had discussions with the Germans, presumably offering a similar exchange, in November and December. Once war broke out, Britain and France relented, and signed trade agreements with Spain (France in January 1940, and then Britain in March 1940). But the German exploitation of Spain's resources during the Second World War may also have weakened the economy. The original debt remained after the war, and this gave Britain, France and the US influence in Franco's Spain. Spain was in isolation after the Second World War, and suffered famine in 1946. With industrial output at a level below that of 1918, Spain's economy may have been saved by aid from the right-wing Argentine dictator, Perón.

Nevertheless, in the longer term, as the Cold War took hold, Spain became less isolated, and with some reforms in the 1950s and 1960s it developed a powerful capitalist economy. Spain industrialized and also developed a strong service industry.

Franco emerged from the war as Spain's dictator. He remained in power until his death in 1975, ruling, as Preston writes, '*as if it were a country occupied by a victorious foreign army*'. Franco's regime declared that they had to save the country from communism. The White Terror that ensued led to the killing of thousands of Republicans and the exodus of half a million Spaniards, who fled to neighbouring countries. They included many of the intellectuals of Spain – teachers, lawyers, researchers, doctors and famous writers, poets, artists and musicians. Those that remained had to conform to Franco's authoritarian, Catholic and conservative views.

In 1939, the Law of Political Responsibility had made supporters of the Republicans (either before or during the war) liable to punishment, including confiscation of land, large fines or even the death sentence. The law allowed for the transfer of vast amounts of land from Republicans to the state.

The key objectives of the new regime were to restore the power of the privileged class and to control the working class. Wages were cut and all industrial political activism was outlawed. The CNT and the UGT were destroyed. Employment for those Republicans who had escaped imprisonment was almost impossible. In rural areas, the inequalities and iniquities of the social and working system, described earlier in this chapter, were preserved and maintained by the Civil Guard.

All of the Republic's reforms concerning the Church were repealed, and indeed the 1950s have been termed the 'era of the national church'. The historian Frances Lannon writes, *'The Catholic Church enjoyed a degree of state support that was much greater than at any time since the 18th century. Government and church combined to preach order, hierarchy and discipline. The counter-revolution had triumphed.'* The Church took up the cause of the workers, and created links with their movements; Patricia Knight argues this was an attempt to infiltrate and prevent any resurgent communist groups. The aspirations of the Basques and Catalans for autonomy were also ended. Use of Catalan, Basque and Galician languages was forbidden and all power was centralized in Madrid. As Preston writes: *'Behind the rhetoric of national and social unity, until the death of Franco every effort was made to maintain the division between the victors and the vanquished'.*

The suppression and removal of all political opposition led to a period of political stability in Spain. Fear of state repression meant that Spain appeared more unified than it had been for decades. Nevertheless, the defeat of the Fascist powers in the Second World War made Franco more vulnerable. Under pressure from the monarchists, Franco agreed to restore the monarchy, but kept himself as head of state. The army also lost its pre-eminence in society after Spain's last colony, Morocco, gained its independence in 1956. Without an empire to run, and with no real external or internal threat, the old-style Spanish army became defunct.

Franco increasingly delegated control from the 1960s and, following his death, a democracy was restored in 1977. But the results of the war and the Nationalist victory for Spain meant that in some ways it was a country 'frozen in time'. Spain also had a difficult relationship with the rest of Europe and did not join **NATO** or the EU .

Was the Spanish Civil War a causal factor in the outbreak of the Second World War?

Key concepts: *Causation*

A number of key factors suggest that the Spanish Civil War played a significant part in the causes of the Second World War:

- It emboldened Hitler by increasing his popularity at home and abroad.
- Hitler drew closer to his former enemy, Italy.
- Hitler gained practical military lessons that he would later apply in the campaigns of 1940.
- It was a distraction for Britain and France and pushed the US further into isolation.
- It fostered a new direction for Soviet foreign policy, meaning that there could be no broad alliance in Europe to contain Hitler.
- It strengthened the support for a policy of appeasement in the democracies.

Historians' perspectives

Preston suggests that the policies of the British during the Spanish Civil War were a key factor in the outbreak of the Second World War. He argues that German intervention was primarily aimed at strategically weakening the British and the French. He points to a meeting in Rome in the first week of January 1937 where Göring told Mussolini that they had just three weeks to secure victory for Franco before the British *'woke up'* and intervened to stop them. But the British did not change their policy. Preston suggests that the whole course of events in Europe from 1937, including *Anschluss* and the Munich Conference, would not have happened had Britain acted decisively in Spain. The subsequent Nazi-Soviet Pact may also not have been agreed had there been a firmer stance for democracy in Spain. However, this is 'counter-factual' history and merely speculation. The historian AJP Taylor concludes that the Spanish Civil War was *'without significant effect'* in the outbreak of the Second World War.

Discuss in small groups the evidence that supports Preston's view that the Spanish Civil War was a key causal factor in the outbreak of the Second World War. Using the material you have studied in this book about Nazi Germany and Stalin's USSR now discuss the evidence that supports Taylor's view that the civil war was *'without significant effect'* in the outbreak of the Second World War.

Essay planning

In small groups plan the following essay question:

Discuss the reasons for the Nationalist victory in the Spanish Civil War.

Remember to structure your essay to address the command terms in the question:

Discuss: Offer a considered and balanced review that includes a range of arguments, factors or hypotheses. Opinions or conclusions should be presented clearly and supported by appropriate evidence.

Introduction:

You will need to set out in your introduction the main arguments you will develop to address the command term and topic of the question.

In order to offer a 'balanced view' you should set down clear lines of argument. For this essay you could consider the strengths of the Nationalists as the main reasons for their victory in the Spanish Civil War, and then counter-argue that the weaknesses of the Republicans were the main factor in the Nationalists' victory.

Main body paragraphs:

Begin each paragraph with an analytical point that uses the words of the question.

You could use your mind maps as a basis for your essay: i.e. organize the paragraphs of the main body of your essay thematically.

Strengths of the Nationalists:

- political
- economic
- military
- role of foreign intervention.

Weaknesses of the Republicans:

- political
- economic
- military
- role of foreign intervention.

For each paragraph you need to go on to explain how foreign intervention assisted or undermined each side and support your analysis with detailed evidence.

Conclusion:

Based on the weight of evidence you have given in the main body, answer the question by concluding it was either the strengths of the Nationalists or the weaknesses of the Republicans that led to the Nationalist victory in the Spanish Civil War.

Essay planning

In the same groups now plan the following questions. Make sure you address the command terms, have clear and focused themes for each paragraph, include supporting detailed evidence (events, battles and campaigns during the course of war) and select the views of one or two historians to support your arguments:

Examine the role of foreign intervention in the course of the Spanish Civil War.

Evaluate the role of foreign intervention in determining the outcome of the Spanish Civil War.

To what extent did the Nationalists win the civil war in Spain because of their military strengths?

Discuss the reasons for the defeat of Republican forces in the Spanish Civil War.

07

The Soviet Union: 1918–1929

> *In less than a year… the Revolution [of October 1917]… revealed its true colours. Not a soviet democracy but a dictatorship, and – since the Communist Party claimed to be the vanguard of the proletariat – a dictatorship of the Communist Party.*
> **McCauley, M (1996). *The Soviet Union 1917–1991*. Longman, p. 12.**

The inter-war years saw a radical political and economic transformation within Russia. In 1918, a fledgling Communist government led by Vladimir Lenin was fighting for survival against a wide range of opposing forces; by 1939 the Communist government had become a powerful dictatorship under the control of Stalin. The economy had also changed from one that was backward and ravaged by war to one that was highly centralized and in a position to take on Nazi Germany in the Second World War. The reasons for this transformation lie in the events of the Russian Civil War and actions of Lenin in the early 1920s, and in the personality and rule of Joseph Stalin in the 1930s.

Essay questions:

- Discuss the impact of the First World War on one European country (other than Germany, Italy or Spain) in the inter-war years.

- Examine political and economic developments in one European country (other than Germany, Italy or Spain) during the 1920s.

- To what extent was there economic and social change in one European country (other than Germany, Italy or Spain) in the 1920s?

Timeline of events – 1917–1929

1917	Feb	Revolution overthrows Tsar
	Mar	Provisional government formed
	Apr	Lenin returns to Russia
	25 Oct	Bolsheviks seize power
	26 Oct	Bolsheviks establish *Sovnarkom*
	Nov	Decrees on Land and Workers' control
		Elections for Constituent Assembly
	Dec	Armistice signed to end fighting in the First World War
		Cheka created
1918		Civil war starts
	Jan	Constituent Assembly closed by Bolsheviks
		Red Army created
		The Russian Soviet Federative Socialist Republic (RSFSR) created
	Mar	Treaty of Brest-Litovsk
	June	Decree on Nationalization
	July	Forced grain requisitions start
		Tsar and his family are murdered by the Bolsheviks
	Sept	Red Terror officially starts
1919	Mar	Comintern established
		Bolshevik Party renamed as Communist Party
1920		Red Army driven out of Poland
1921		Civil war ends: White defeated or driven out of Russia
	Mar	Sailors at Kronstadt rise up against Bolsheviks
		NEP introduced

1924	Jan	Lenin dies
1924–29		Leadership race to see who will succeed Lenin

Russia in 1918

The Russian people: Russia was a huge empire consisting of many different nationalities. The Russians made up half of the population, most of whom lived to the west of the Ural Mountains in what was known as European Russia. The tsars had followed a policy of Russification to try and ensure that non-Russians followed the Russian language and customs; many of the national minorities therefore wanted to have independence from Russian control.

Agriculture: Most of the population, almost 80 per cent, were peasants. Agriculture was inefficient and backward; there was much overcrowding and competition for land. At the time of the revolution, the nobility made up 1 per cent of the population but owned 25 per cent of the land.

Industry: This was growing rapidly but working conditions in the cities were poor and wages were low. Living conditions in towns were also appalling.

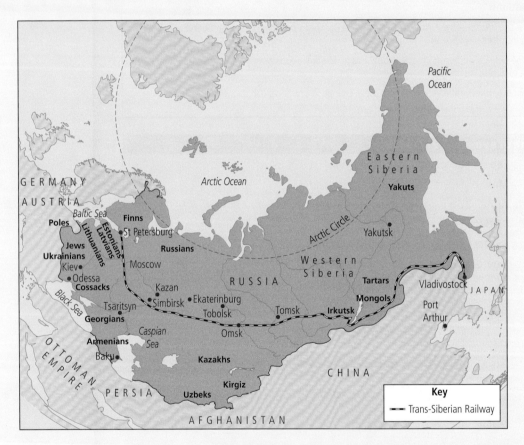

Impact of war: Russia suffered military defeats in the First World War and terrible losses of men, which meant that morale in the army was extremely low. The disruption of supplies also meant that civilians suffered terribly; by 1917 there were extreme food and fuel shortages in the major cities and inflation was rampant. It was this intolerable situation that had caused the spontaneous revolution leading to the overthrow of the Tsar. Shortages of food and supplies continued throughout 1917 and 1918.

Political parties: By the time of the first revolution in Russia in February 1917 there were several key political groups. The Liberals, which included the group called the *Kadets*, wanted a parliamentary democracy, civil rights and free elections. The Socialist Revolutionaries had their main support from the peasantry and supported land reform. The Social Democrats were a Marxist party and had split into the Bolshevik and the Menshevik parties. The Bolsheviks were the dominant group by 1917. They were led by Lenin and believed that the leadership should be a tight-knit disciplined group, which had the job of bringing socialist consciousness to the workers though revolution. The Mensheviks believed in a more broad-based party in which members could have a say in policymaking. (See Chapter 1, page 17, for an explanation of the ideas of Karl Marx)

Nicholas II was the last of the tsars to rule Russia. His government had been an autocratic one: as with all previous tsars, he was an absolute ruler. Despite promises to give the people more of a role in government through a *Duma* (parliament), following a revolution in 1905, he had never really shown any commitment to this idea of sharing political power and historians such as Martin McCauley argue that revolution would have happened even without the impact of war due to the growing frustrations of the Russian people. Although war had united the population in support of the Tsar, his decision to take over as the commander of the Russian troops meant that he was also blamed for the military failures; by February 1917 he had lost the support of his army, his ministers and the people of Russia, and was forced to abdicate. The Tsar and his family were taken prisoner after the Bolsheviks took power in October 1917, and were executed during the Civil War.

What was the situation in Russia in 1918?

 Key concepts: *Causation*

Russia in 1918 was a country that had just undergone tremendous political turmoil against a backdrop of economic and social dislocation caused by the impact of four years of war. In 1917, a spontaneous revolution in Petrograd had led to the abdication of the Tsar (see Significant individual box) and the establishment of a new provisional government. This government consisted mainly of the leading figures of various liberal parties and was dominated by the *Kadets*. However, it had to work alongside the Petrograd Soviet (council) of Workers' and Soldiers' Deputies, which was intended to ensure that the provisional government protected the interests of the working class.

The Provisional government planned to hold elections in November of the same year in order to establish Russia's first parliamentary-style democracy. However, it was undermined by continuing military failure in the war (in which it had continued to participate in order to maintain the support of Britain and France) and the inability to meet the raised expectations of the population. Russia's peasants, for example, wanted a redistribution of land and were unwilling to wait for this until the elections for a Constituent Assembly took place. It was also undermined by the leader of the Communist Bolshevik Party, Vladimir Lenin, who returned from exile in April 1917 with his 'April Theses', which demanded '*Peace, bread, land*' and '*All power to the Soviets*'. He was determined to push for a second Marxist revolution of the proletariat, which would put power in the hands of his Bolshevik Party. He succeeded in achieving this by a bloodless coup in Petrograd in November 1917. Although some Bolsheviks were prepared to support the idea of a socialist coalition that would include members of other socialist parties, such as the Socialist Revolutionaries (SR), it soon became clear that Lenin was not prepared to share power with other left-wing parties.

How did the Bolsheviks secure power following the revolution of November 1917?

The new government established by the Bolsheviks was the Soviet of People's Commissars or *Sovnarkom*. Lenin was chief minister and all of the first commissars (or ministers) were Bolsheviks. However, outside of Petrograd, the Bolsheviks were not in a strong position in November 1917. In the countryside they had virtually no influence and they faced strikes and protests from other socialists who objected to being excluded. The actions of the Bolsheviks in the first few months were thus key; these involved the following:

1. Initial decrees

The Bolsheviks passed several decrees that were a clear attempt to win popular support:

Land Decree, October 1917: This gave peasants the right to take over land from the gentry and divide it up among themselves.

Decree on Workers' Control, November 1917: This put the running of factories in the hands of the workers. Factory committees were to control production and finance, and 'supervise' management.

Declaration on the Rights of the People of Russia, November 1917: This gave the right of self-determination to the national minorities within the Russian Empire.

2. Control of the army

A real danger for the Bolsheviks was the army; the generals and officer class were unlikely to be sympathetic to the new government. However the high command was already weakened by the politicization of the army that had taken place after the abdication of the Tsar, and the ordinary troops were quickly won over when Lenin moved swiftly to end the fighting. An armistice was signed with the Germans, which was followed by the humiliating Treaty of Brest-Litovsk; the treaty gave Germany one-third of Russia's land (see map on page 181). The army disintegrated quickly after this and although the generals themselves were anti-Bolshevik, they could not rely on the loyalty of their troops to fight against the Bolsheviks.

3. Establishment of the Cheka

Lenin was determined to suppress all political opposition and so, in December 1917, *Sovnarkom* established its own secret police, Cheka, which had as its aim the destruction of '*counter-revolution and sabotage*'. This meant that anyone who might be considered an opposer of the new government could be arrested: this included class enemies such as the '**bourgeoisie**' but also opponents on the left. In addition a decree was passed in October to ban opposition press.

4. Ending the Constituent Assembly

When the Bolsheviks took power in Ocober 1917, they claimed that they were doing it on behalf of the Congress of Russian Soviets and with the support of other socialist, revolutionary parties such as the Socialist Revolutionary Party (SR). Lenin's 'April Theses' had included the demand of '*All power to the Soviets*' and so it was believed that this was exactly what would happen. However, when the Constituent Assembly met in November 1917 it was clear that Lenin had no intention of sharing power with other socialists.

The results of the elections to the Constituent Assembly were as follows:

	% of the votes
Socialist Revolutionaries	40.4
Bolsheviks	23.2
Mensheviks	2.9
Other socialists	15.0
Kadets	4.6
National parties	7.7
Cossacks	2.2

This was not a result that could be tolerated by Lenin: they had gained only 24 per cent of the vote and had been outvoted by nearly two to one by the Socialist Revolutionaries. Lenin's reaction was fast and ruthless. After only one day, the Constituent Assembly was shut down at gunpoint by the Red Guards. Lenin argued that the will of the people had already been expressed through the October Revolution and thus the Constituent Assembly was no longer needed as it was '*an expression of the old regime when the authority belonged to the bourgeoisie*'. Thus it was clear from the start that the Bolsheviks intended to rule as a one-party dictatorship.

Map showing the Treaty of Brest-Litovsk

Russia lost one-sixth of its population; 27% of farmland, including the 'bread basket' of Ukraine; 26% of railway lines; and 74% of iron ore and coal reserves. Finland, Estonia, Latvia and Lithuania now became independent republics.

Other decrees passed by Lenin

In addition to the decrees mentioned on page 180, the *Sovnarkom* passed a range of other decrees in the first months of power which introduced the following:

October 1917

• maximum eight-hour day for workers;
• social insurance to cover old age, unemployment and sickness benefits.

November 1917

• abolition of titles and class distinctions;
• abolition of justice system;
• equality for women with the right to own property.

December 1917

• nationalization of banks and industry;
• democratization of the army meaning abolition of ranks and election of officers;
• nationalization of Church land;
• separation of Church and state; marriages and divorces now handled by the state.

Activity 1

ATL **Thinking and social skills**

From what you have read so far about the actions of the Bolsheviks in the first months of power, discuss in pairs the groups that you think would have been supportive of the Bolsheviks and those that would have been opposed to the Bolsheviks.

Consider the following in your discussion: workers, peasants, civil servants such as lawyers, army officers, members of other political parties, soldiers, women, factory owners.

Lenin delivering a speech in Moscow.

The impact of civil war

Why did a civil war develop?

Key concepts: *Causation*

Although the Bolsheviks initially secured their position, particularly in the cities, opposition forces, collectively known as the Whites, started to emerge almost immediately. This was due to several reasons:

The disintegration of the Russian Empire

As you read on page 180, Lenin had decreed in November 1917 that non-Russian territories were free to leave Russia; this resulted in many nationalities such as the Fins, Latvians, Ukrainians declaring themselves independent of the Russian Soviet Federative Socialist Republic (RSFSR) – the name given to the Russian state after the October Revolution.

Throughout Russia, soviets took over large areas and often pursued their own policies. By June 1918, there were 33 sovereign governments in Russia. Many Russians were appalled by this break-up of the Russian Empire and were prepared to fight to maintain it. Those who had declared independence, however, were determined to fight to keep their newly found self-government.

The impact of the Treaty of Brest-Litovsk

Patriotic Russians were horrified by the terms of the treaty (see map and information box on pages 181 and 182), which had given away so much Russian land, and this encouraged many to join anti-Bolshevik forces.

Political opposition

Because of Bolshevik policies towards other political parties, opposition groups quickly emerged and the Bolsheviks faced challenges from both left and right. The Socialist Revolutionaries, who were in total opposition to the Treaty of Brest-Litovsk and who felt that their rightful place in a Socialist government had been usurped, organized an anti-Bolshevik coup in Moscow. It failed, but Lenin was the subject of two assassination attempts by the Socialist Revolutionaries in July and August. The second one, carried out by Dora Kaplan, came close to succeeding.

Foreign intervention

The Treaty of Brest-Litovsk was a severe blow to the Allies who were still fighting the war against Germany. German troops were now no longer tied up on the Eastern Front fighting the Russians; they were free to join the German army in the west and this put increased pressure on the Allies. Thus Britain and France were willing to send help to any enemies of the Bolsheviks who would be prepared to reopen the war against the Germans.

When the war ended in November 1918, foreign interest in the outcome of the civil war continued. The British continued to send aid, viewing the Whites as defenders against the dreaded Bolshevism which, it was feared, could spread to the rest of Europe if it was not destroyed. The French also remained because they had invested millions of francs into Russia and the Bolsheviks had nationalized foreign-owned industry without providing any compensation. The Japanese sent troops to the area around Vladivostok in the hope of gaining territory, while the US sent troops to try to prevent this from happening.

The economic crisis

The failure of the new regime to end hunger was an important factor in creating opposition to Lenin's government. By the summer of 1918 the food situation in the cities was desperate; the loss of the wheat-growing Ukraine, known as 'the bread basket', to Germany in the Treaty of Brest-Litovsk meant that the situation was exacerbated and hunger forced many workers out of the industrial cities. With no products to buy in the shops and continued inflation, the peasants were reluctant to sell their produce. In response, Lenin sent out requisition squads to look for grain, while poor peasants were encouraged to seize food from their more wealthy neighbours. Such strategies also increased opposition to the Bolsheviks.

The range of factors creating opposition towards the Bolsheviks meant that the Whites ended up consisting of a wide range of interest groups: liberals, former tsarists, Nationalists, Socialist Revolutionaries, foreigners and moderate socialists. Fighting for their survival, the Reds consisted of the Bolshevik army (known as the Red Army), the Kronstadt sailors, who had been strong supporters of the Bolshevik cause from the start, along with volunteer workers and soldiers from the collapsed Imperial Army. However, it was more complex than just the Reds versus the Whites, with the Greens also playing a role in the fighting. These were peasant armies whose main concerns were often to protect only their own areas. Thus this was not simply a class conflict, as the Bolsheviks liked to portray it. Local issues often dominated when the peasants decided which side to join; sometimes they fought just to protect their own areas.

The course of the civil war

Armed resistance to the Bolsheviks took place sporadically from October 1917. However, hostilities started in earnest in the spring of 1918 due to the actions of a foreign army, the Czech Legion. This legion had been created by Czech nationalists who had volunteered to fight on the side of the Russians and against the Austrians in the First World War, in the hope of strengthening their case for having independence from the Austro-Hungarian Empire. Following the signing of the Treaty of Brest-Litovsk, they decided to join the Allies on the Western Front; this involved travelling to Vladivostock where they would go by sea to Western Europe. However, there were tensions between the Bolsheviks and the Czechs; when the Bolsheviks tried to disarm them, the Czechs resisted and took control of large sections of the Trans-Siberian Railway. The Czechs travelled along the railway towards Moscow but the Red Army that was sent out to stop them collapsed and fled, which encouraged other groups to come out openly against the regime. Thus a full-scale war was underway by the summer of 1918 in several key regions:

- The SR set up a government in Samara based on the members who had been elected to the Constituent Assembly. They also organized a number of uprisings in central Russia.
- In the south, on the River Don, a White 'volunteer army' was led by General Denikin, who was an old-fashioned Nationalist determined to maintain a united Russia. His army included thousands of army officers as well as *Kadets* and other liberals. He failed to take the city of Tsaritsyn (later Stalingrad) in 1918, but an offensive in 1919 got his army 320 km from Moscow.

- In Siberia, Admiral Kolchak, who proclaimed himself the '*Supreme Ruler of Russia*', headed an army of around 140,000. He hated socialism but had no clear political plan. Initially this army was very successful and they had got as far as Kazan and Samara by June 1919.
- In Estonia General Yudenich led an army of around 15,000 men; it attacked Petrograd in 1919.
- In the Ukraine, the Green Army of Makhno fought a guerilla war against both Reds and Whites, supported by the Ukrainian peasant population.

The key areas of fighting and the extent of their advances are shown on the map below. The Bolsheviks were fighting for their very survival and the Red Army had to deal with all of the different invading forces as well as quell several uprisings. At one point they had lost control of 75 per cent of Russia. The fighting was bitter and resulted in terrible atrocities and huge loss of life. However, by the end of 1920, the Bolsheviks had resisted the attacks and driven the armies back.

Activity 2

ATL   **Thinking and communication skills**

Work in pairs. Review the information thus far on the civil war, including the map below. What conclusions can you draw as to the advantages and disadvantages that each side had in the fighting?

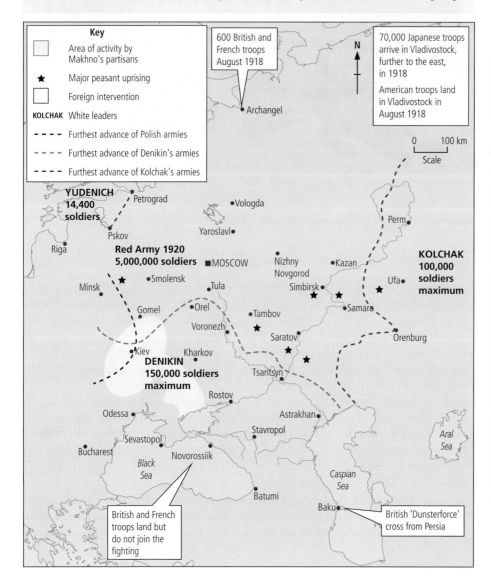

Why did the Bolsheviks win the civil war?

Key concepts: *Consequence*

As the map and description of events will have indicated, there were several fundamental reasons as to why the Bolsheviks were successful in ultimately defeating all of the attacks by the Whites. These can be divided into the weaknesses of the Whites versus the advantages of the Reds.

Activity 3 — ATL Thinking skills

Bolshievk propaganda poster showing the three White generals, Denikin, Kolchak and Yudenich, as three vicious dogs.

What is the message of this Bolshevik propaganda poster?

The weaknesses and errors of the Whites

• As the map indicates, the various White armies were geographically split up around the central area, which was controlled by the Bolsheviks; they were also separated by large distances. This made communications difficult and it was almost impossible to coordinate the attacks of the different White armies.

• Even if they had been able to physically work together, the different groups had entirely dissimilar beliefs and aims. Some were fighting for the Constituent Assembly and others to restore tsarism, some for the rights of minority groups and others to keep the Russian Empire together. For example, Admiral Kolchak ultimately had hundreds of Socialist Revolutionaries, who had joined forces with him, arrested and many were executed. Socialist Revolutionaries then launched several attacks against him which contributed to the failure of his campaign.

• The foreign interventions also lacked any unity of purpose. Each country had a different aim and there was little cooperation between the occupiers.

• In terms of leadership, the White generals were of a second-rate calibre. Their harsh treatment of the troops, which was reminiscent of tsarist times, alienated the peasant conscripts, many of whom deserted. Furthermore, the White generals distrusted each other, which also contributed to the difficulties of cooperation. In addition, there was much indiscipline and corruption in the White armies.

- The land policy of the Whites ensured that peasant support was more likely to go to the Reds; the Whites made it clear that they wished to return land to their former owners and thus reverse the land reforms that had been carried out by Lenin. Indeed, Denikein helped landowners recover their lands.

- The brutality of the White armies further antagonized the peasants. For example, the Cossacks in the southern army drove many Russians and Ukrainians from their lands and carried out pogroms (organized massacres) against Jewish communities.

- Nationalist groups were also antagonized by the Whites who supported the maintenance of the Russian Empire. Thus groups such as the Ukrainians and Georgians would not support the Whites when they were in these areas.

- Although foreign intervention meant more money and supplies for the White armies, their association with foreigners handed a propaganda opportunity to the Bolsheviks, who were now able to pose as defenders of the motherland (see propaganda poster on page 186).

The strengths of the Reds

- The Bolsheviks controlled the central area of Russia, which included Moscow and Petrograd. This had several advantages: it meant that they controlled the hub of the railway network, which was essential for moving around men and supplies; it contained the main armament factories; it was heavily populated, allowing them to conscript large numbers of soldiers.

- There was one overall commander of the Red Army, Leon Trotsky (see Information box on page 188), who was an excellent leader; he organized the conscripts into an effective fighting force, established discipline and maintained morale.

- The Bolsheviks did not have widespread popular support. However, the peasants were more likely to support the Bolsheviks due to the land reforms. Although much of this active support was lost due to the grain requisitioning, nevertheless the fear of a loss of land stopped the peasants from supporting the Whites. Urban workers also wanted to protect the gains of 1917.

- In general the Reds were much more effective with regard to propaganda. Not only did they capitalize on the fact that the Whites were getting foreign support to make themselves appear as the true patriots, they were also able to present the vision of a new future under a new government as opposed to a return to the old ways under the Tsar.

- The Bolsheviks were ruthless in using terror to silence 'counter-revolutionary' opposition during the war. The most famous victims of this terror were the Tsar and his family (see page 179). Following the assassination attempts on Lenin, the terror was intensified under the Cheka. Execution now became the most common punishment and some estimates for deaths at the hands of the Cheka between 1918 and 1920 are as high as 300,000. However, as McCauley writes, each provincial section of the Cheka had its own way of killing people:

> In Kharkov Chekists scalped their prisoners and took the skin, like 'gloves', off their hands. In Voronezh they placed the naked prisoner in a barrel punctured with nails and then set it in motion. They burnt a five-pointed star into the forehead and placed a crown of barbed wire around the neck of priests. In Tsaritsyn and Kamyshin they severed bones with a saw. In Poltava they impaled eighteen monks and burnt at the stake peasants who had rebelled. In Ekaterinoslav they crucified priests and stoned them. In Odessa they boiled officers and ripped them in half. In Kiev they placed them in a coffin with a decomposing corpse, buried them alive and then after half an hour dug them out.

McCauley, M (1996). *The Soviet Union 1917–1991.* Longman, p. 25.

Concentration and labour camps were also established. Victims included those who were actively opposing the regime such as Socialist Revolutionaries and Anarchists, but also middle-class professionals, traders, priests and prostitutes – anyone who was accused of 'counter-revolution' – though in most cases such accusations were random and unfounded.

Trotsky's role in the civil war

As commander of the Red Guards, Trotsky had already played a key role in the Bolshevik takeover of power in October 1917. He was then made commissar for war in 1918 and became pivotal to the success of the newly formed Red Army. He reintroduced ranks into the army and recruited former tsarist officers to train and command the army units, introducing political commissars to supervise the officers. He also re-established harsh military discipline – including the death penalty for a range of offences. Perhaps most significant though was his energy and passion, which could be seen in his leadership of the army; for three years he lived largely on his armoured train which travelled up and down the front helping to maintain morale and enforce discipline.

Activity 4

1. What does the following extract from the novel *Doctor Zhivago* by Boris Pasternak reveal about the nature of the fighting in the civil war?

2. With reference to its origin, purpose and content, analyse the value and limitations of this source for a historian studying the Russian Civil War.

In this extract the key character, Dr Zhivago, describes coming across a man who has crawled into a partisan camp that has been surrounded by a White army.

> *His right arm and left leg had been chopped off. It was inconceivable how, with his remaining arm and leg, he had crawled to the camp. The chopped-off arm and leg were tied in terrible bleeding chunks onto his back with a small wooden board attached to them; a long inscription on it said, with many words of abuse, that the atrocity was in reprisal for similar atrocities perpetrated by such and such a Red unit—a unit that had no connection with the Forest Brotherhood. It also said that the same treatment would be meted out to all the partisans unless, by a given date, they submitted and gave up their arms to the representatives of General Vitsyn's army corps.*

Pasternak, B (1958). *Doctor Zhivago*. Translated by Hayward, M and Harari, M. Pantheon Books.

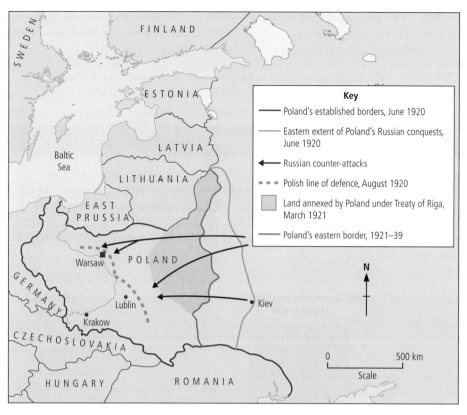

Key
— Poland's established borders, June 1920
— Eastern extent of Poland's Russian conquests, June 1920
← Russian counter-attacks
▪▪▪ Polish line of defence, August 1920
▨ Land annexed by Poland under Treaty of Riga, March 1921
— Poland's eastern border, 1921–39

Map showing the movements of the Polish and Russian troops in the 1920–21 war.

Activity 5

ATL   Communication and self-management skills

Using the information on pages 186–88, create a mind map to show the reasons for the victory of the Reds. Use these headings: geographical factors, organization, unity, leadership, popular support, propaganda, foreign intervention.

Political policies of the Bolsheviks 1918–21

Key concepts: *Consequence*

Centralized control over party structure

The failure of the Whites and the continued attacks on Socialist Revolutionaries by the Cheka consolidated the hold of the Bolshevik Party on Russia and the development of a one-party state. It also meant that the Central Committee of the Bolshevik Party, which was the key decision-making body of the party up until 1919, increased its grip over the party's structure and its members.

This move towards centralized power was partly due to the civil war. Two new committees were set up to run the war more effectively after 1919: the Politburo to control overall strategy and the Orgburo to oversee internal administration. Each body

The Russo-Polish War
Hoping to take advantage of the chaotic situation within Russia and push their eastern border further than the so-called Curzon Line, which had been agreed after the First World War, Polish troops captured Kiev in May 1920. Having defeated the Whites by 1920, the Bolsheviks now attacked the Poles, pushing them back to Warsaw. It was hoped by many Bolsheviks that Polish workers would rise in support of the Bolsheviks and indeed that they could even spread revolution to Germany. However, the Russians had now overstretched their supply lines. The Poles regarded the invasion as traditional Russian aggression and the Russian army was defeated, with French help, at the Battle of Vistula. In 1921 the war was ended with the Treaty of Riga, which established a new eastern border to Poland.

was elected by groups within the party; however, although this seems to imply an element of democracy within the party, in fact the leadership began to exercise control over the membership and the appointment of local officials.

The control of the party leadership was backed up by the Cheka, which attacked not only Bolshevik enemies but also critics within the Bolshevik Party itself.

Party control over the state

Following the revolution of October 1917, the Bolsheviks set up new state organizations in 1917, the most important of which was *Sovnarkom*. However, it was the party itself that controlled the decision-making; over time the meetings of the government bodies – the Congress of the Soviets, All Russian Central Committee and the *Sovnarkom* – became less frequent and they became little more than administrative bodies.

The political structure of the Soviet Union in the mid-1920s.

The Communist Party of the Soviet Union

The Soviet Government

Politburo
Political bureau of the Central Committee that formulated policy.

Council of People's Commissars (*Sovnarkom*)
Cabinet of ministers, chosen by leading members of the Party. Each commissar was responsible for a government department.

Orgburo
Responsible for the organisation of policy. Ran the Politburo when it was not in session.

Central Committee
Main administrative body of the Party. Ran Communist Party when Party Congress was not in session. Controlled all key party officials, government ministers, leading army and navy personnel and key ambassadors.

Secretariat
Civil service responsible for implementation of Party decisions and undertaking administrative tasks for the Politburo and *Sovnarkom*.

All-Russian Central Committee
Senior government administrators selected from All-Russian Congress.

Party Congress
Composed of representatives selected from regional and district branches. Elected members of Central Committee.

All-Russian Congress
Fulfilled role of parliament. Deputies elected from regional soviets. All were members of the Communist Party.

The economic policies of the Bolsheviks, 1918–21

Every aspect of life during these early years had to be directed towards winning the civil war. The initial economic measures introduced by Lenin in 1917, which gave workers control of the factories and allowed peasants to have their own land, had created economic chaos. In order to ensure that the Red Army was supplied with munitions and had enough to eat, it was essential for the government to get control over production and distribution of food in the areas under their control. This involved introducing a set of harshly restrictive economic measures known as War Communism, which involved the following:

Nationalization of industry: All industry was brought under state control. The workers' committees that had been given control of the factories in 1917 had failed to get them producing goods and there were acute shortages. Now industry was geared to war production and workers were forced to labour for excessive hours without wages. Discipline was re-established in the workplace with fines for lateness and absenteeism. Internal passports were introduced to prevent workers escaping to the countryside.

Grain requisitioning: The Bolsheviks were desperate to force the peasants to produce more food and had already been sending soldiers out into the countryside to take grain from them. In 1918, a Food Supplies Dictatorship was set up and forcible requisitioning of grain became official policy. Requisition squads terrorized the countryside between 1918 and 1921; those who resisted were arrested by the Cheka. This was to seriously damage the relationship between the Bolsheviks and the peasants.

Ban on private trade and rationing: A ban on private trade and rationing was introduced. This was class based so that those who were part of the bourgeoisie or middle classes (now called 'former people') were given the smallest rations, while the largest rations during this period went to the Red Army.

What were the effects of War Communism?

Activity 6   ATL Thinking skills

What is the message of this table concerning the effects of War Communism?

Industrial output in 1913 and 1921		
	1913	1921
Index of gross industrial output	100	31
Index of large-scale industrial output	100	21
Electricity (million kilowatt hours)	2039	520
Coal (million tons)	29	8.9
Oil (million tons)	9.2	3.8
Steel (million tons)	4.3	0.18
Imports (millions at 1913 rouble value)	1374	208
Exports (millions at 1913 rouble value)	1520	20

The overall result of War Communism was economic chaos and famine. Knowing that surplus food would be taken by the requisition squads, the peasants decided that it was not worth producing more than they needed for themselves. This resulted in acute food shortages in 1920 and, combined with drought and the disruption of war, led to a terrible famine in 1921. The situation was so desperate that the Bolsheviks even accepted foreign aid and the US in particular sent substantial amounts of food to feed starving Russians. Nevertheless, it is estimated that over half of the 10 million casualties of the civil war died as a result of starvation.

In the cities, nationalization failed to increase production. The situation was made worse by the drain of people from the cities and thus the factories. This was a result of **conscription** into the Red Army along with the terrible conditions in the cities, which drove people into the countryside to search for food or to flee disease and the ravages of war. The populations of Moscow and Petrograd fell by a half between 1918 and 1921.

The scarcity of consumer goods led to the existence of a flourishing black market. Inflation also took hold due to the government's continued policy of printing money. By the end of 1920, the rouble had fallen to 1 per cent of its worth in 1917. Workers were paid in goods rather than in the worthless money.

Despite the economic chaos caused by War Communism, many in the party believed that this type of system was true revolutionary communism. They hated the market system and believed that centralized control and the ending of private ownership was key to establishing true socialism. Thus, many were reluctant to abandon it when the civil war ended. However, the need for change was made clear by the widespread anti-Bolshevik uprisings that took place between 1920 and 1921. There were hundreds of peasant risings in these years due to the impact of requisitioning. At the same time there was a wave of strikes in the cities. However, the most serious threat to the regime came from the Kronstadt Rising of 1921.

The Kronstadt Rising, 1921

The sailors on the Kronstadt naval base near to Petrograd were dedicated supporters of the revolution and had played a key role in supporting the Bolsheviks in both the 1917 October Revolution and in the civil war. However, many were of peasant origin and by 1921 they had become disillusioned with Bolshevism; they heard from their villages the impact of grain requisitioning and they were sympathetic to the workers of Petrograd who were suffering from food shortages and poor conditions in the factories. Thus, when demonstrations began in Petrograd in 1921 unrest quickly spread to Kronstadt.

Activity 7 Thinking and communication skills

In pairs, read the demands from the Kronstadt sailors. What do these demands reveal about life under Bolshevik rule? What do they reveal about the concerns of the Kronstadt sailors? Why could such demands not be tolerated by Lenin?

Resolution of political demands passed by the crew of the *Petropavlovsk* on 8 February 1921:

(1) Immediate new elections to the Soviets. The present Soviets no longer express the wishes of the workers and the peasants. The new elections should be by secret ballot, and should be preceded by free electoral propaganda.

(2) Freedom of speech and of the press for workers and peasants, for the Anarchists, and the Left Socialist parties.

(4) The organization, at the latest on 10th March 1921, of a Conference of non-Party workers, soldiers and sailors of Petrograd, Kronstadt and the Petrograd District.

(5) The liberation of all political prisoners of the Socialist parties, and for all imprisoned workers and peasants, soldiers and sailors belonging to workers and peasant organizations.

(6) The election of a commission to look into the dossiers of all those detained in prisons and concentration camps.

(7) The abolition of all political sections in the armed forces. No political party should have privileges for the propagation of its ideas, or receive State subsidies to this end. In the place of the political sections, various cultural groups should be set up, deriving resources from the State.

(8) The immediate abolition of the militia detachments set up between towns and countryside.

(9) The equalization of rations for all workers, except those engaged in dangerous or unhealthy jobs.

(10) The abolition of Party combat detachments in all military groups. The abolition of Party guards in factories and enterprises. If guards are required, they should be nominated, taking into account the views of the workers.

(11) The granting to the peasants of freedom of action on their own soil, and of the right to own cattle, provided they look after them themselves and do not employ hired labour.

(12) We request that all military units and officer trainee groups associate themselves with this resolution.

Lenin acted swiftly to end the rebellion. Although the first attack on the Kronstadt base failed, eventually 50,000 Red Army troops crossed the frozen ice towards the base. The sailors resisted fiercely; however, in the end the base was recaptured. Any ringleaders who had survived were shot and any who had escaped were hunted down by the Cheka and killed or sent to a concentration camp.

The Red Army attacking across the ice to capture the Kronstadt base.

Nevertheless, Lenin realized that the Kronstadt Rising needed to be taken seriously. At the Tenth Conference of the Communist Party, in March 1921, he announced that the Kronstadt Rising had *'lit up reality like a lightning flash'*. He now moved to tackle the economic chaos by introducing the New Economic Policy (NEP). This was not, however, to be accompanied by any lessening of Bolshevik control over society such as had been demanded by the Kronstadt sailors; indeed it would become even tighter.

Economic policy, 1921–24

The New Economic Policy

Key concepts: *Change and continuity*

At the 1921 Party Conference, Lenin told the delegates:

> *We must try to satisfy the demands of the peasants who are dissatisfied, discontented, and cannot be otherwise. In essence, the small farmer can be satisfied with two things. First of all, there must be a certain amount of freedom for the small proprietor; and, secondly, commodities and products must be provided.*

This change in thinking led to the following measures, which became known as the New Economic Policy or NEP:

- There was to be an end to grain requisitioning. Instead peasants were to pay a tax in kind (i.e. grain) to the government; this was much less than the amounts taken by requisitioning. They would then be able to sell the remainder, their surplus crops, for profit on the open market.
- Small businessmen were to be allowed to own and run medium-sized firms and factories and to make a profit. This included businesses that sold goods such as shoes, nails and clothes. It was essential to have such goods available to purchase – otherwise the peasants would still have been unwilling to sell their goods for money.
- Private traders were to be allowed to buy and sell goods for profit on the open market.
- Rationing was abolished. A new revalued currency was to be reinstated for use in trading.

State industries such as coal, steel and iron, which Lenin called 'the commanding heights of the economy', were to remain in government hands. Nevertheless the NEP was a significant move away from state control of the economy. Russia now had a 'mixed' economy where elements of **capitalism** existed alongside socialism. Many party members considered the NEP to be a betrayal of the principles of the October Revolution. However, the Kronstadt rebellion persuaded them that the party needed unity and they needed the NEP as a 'temporary measure' in order to maintain power. As Bukharin argued, 'We are making economic concessions to avoid political concessions'.

What were the results of the NEP?

By 1922, the NEP had already had a positive impact on the economy. Food was once more available in the markets, and cities became centres of trading again. Both agricultural and industrial production increased. Between 1920 and 1923, factory output rose by almost 200 per cent.

Results of the NEP				
	1921	1922	1923	1924
Urban worker's average monthly wage (roubles)	10.2	12.2	15.9	20.8
Grain harvest (million tons)	37.6	50.3	56.6	51.4
Electricity (million kilowatt hours)	520	775	1,146	1,562
Value of factory output (millions of roubles)	2,004	2,619	4,005	4,660

One group of people who emerged as a result of the NEP were the 'Nepmen'; they were private traders who bought up goods from farmers and small businesses and sold them in the markets in the cities. By 1923 Nepmen handled as much as three-quarters of the retail trade and had become wealthy as a result. The peasants also did well as a result of the NEP due to the extra money that they could now make through selling goods and crafts.

There were problems as well as successes. Industry did not keep up with the growth in agriculture and while the Nepmen benefited, industrial workers faced high unemployment. By 1923 what Trotsky called '*the scissors crisis*' had emerged, which was caused by the large quantity of food pushing prices down while industrial goods remained expensive due to their scarcity.

The worry in this situation was that the peasants would now stop selling their produce as they would be unable to afford industrial goods. However, the government took action to bring industrial prices down and started to take peasant tax in cash rather than goods to encourage them to sell their food for money.

Political repression 1921–24

The easing of centralized control on the economy during the NEP did not mean an easing of political repression:
• Censorship became more systematic.
• Attacks on other political parties increased.
• Show trials (see the next chapter, on Stalin) appeared for the first time, in which Socialist Revolutionaries accused old colleagues of terrible crimes against the state.
• Peasants who had participated in revolts against the state were brutally dealt with and whole villages destroyed.
• Attacks on the Church were stepped up.
• The Cheka was renamed the GPU in 1922 and grew in importance during the NEP. Citizens were still subjected to arbitrary arrest and execution.

In addition, the process of centralization within the Bolshevik Party did not end following the civil war. At the Tenth Party Congress of 1921, the 'Ban on Factions' was passed. This was a response to pressure groups within the party. One of these, named 'The Workers' Opposition', had called for more worker involvement in the running of factories and a greater role for independent trade unions. Another group, the 'Democratic Centralists', also called for greater involvement in policymaking for ordinary party members. To Lenin, such groups were a distraction given the enormity of the problems facing Russia in 1921, and he called for unity. The resulting 'Ban on Factions' meant that party policy could not be challenged; in fact the death penalty could be used against those breaking this rule.

Activity 8 — ATL Thinking skills

Read the following extract:

> By 1924 the Communist party had established a system of strong, central rule. This was an authoritarian state, justified by the Bolsheviks in terms of the need to establish a Dictatorship of the Proletariat in the face of enormous difficulties. The party saw itself as the vanguard of the Revolution taking on the role of organising the workers and steering a path towards a socialist state. The Civil War had revealed the serious threat posed by counter-revolutionaries and weakened the proletariat. The mass movement of people from the towns to the countryside during the Civil War had decimated the proletariat and left the Bolsheviks exposed. Lenin realised that in this situation authoritarian rule by the party was needed and circumstances pushed the Bolsheviks into a more ruthless and authoritarian approach than they had envisaged. These circumstances can be said to have militarised the culture of the party. That the Bolsheviks continued to rely on the use of terror showed their continued insecurity, as did the growth of an inflexible and authoritarian bureaucracy. These were instruments that were starting to be used to maintain a dictatorship of the party rather than a Dictatorship of the Proletariat.

Philips, S (2000). *Lenin and the Russian Revolution*. Heinemann, p. 137.

1. According to the extract, what factors justified the growth of a strong, centralized state?
2. How did the civil war affect the character of the Bolshevik Party?
3. What is meant by the last sentence of this extract?
4. Do you think that these developments made the establishment of a dictatorship under Stalin inevitable?

▶▶▶ Historians' perspectives

Lenin's legacy

Historians disagree as to the extent that Lenin laid the foundations for Stalinism. Many of the features of Stalin's regime: labour camps, the Great Terror, and show trials were established after 1918, and it is argued by historians such as Richard Pipes that Stalin's dictatorship was a logical continuation of the one established by Lenin. However other historians have highlighted the fact that there were fundamental differences between Lenin's regime and that of Stalin, in the nature and extent of the totalitarianism and terror that occurred. Thus, although Lenin did indeed lay the foundations for many aspects of Stalinism, the transition from Leninism to the worse horrors of Stalinism was not inevitable.

To what extent did the Bolsheviks change society?

Poster by Alexander Rodchenko encouraging workers to attend education classes following the revolution.

Restructuring society

The Bolsheviks wanted to change society. One of their promises had been that they would firstly change society by ending all privilege and setting up a state of equals. After the revolution, they attempted to achieve this aim by attacking the rich and the middle classes; as the lives of the poor failed to improve despite this utopian vision, the Bolshevik regime still aimed to get approval of the workers through their attacks on the wealthy. Members of the propertied class, or bourgeoisie, lost all titles and property and became known as 'former people'; everyone was now called 'comrade' to imply equality. Acts of intimidation and violence including looting of property were encouraged.

One of the humiliations 'former people' were forced to suffer was sharing their living space. The wealthy could end up giving their best rooms over to their former servants, who were delighted to have their revenge. The 'former people' were also put to work on such tasks as clearing the streets of snow, the main aim being to humiliate them. As Trotsky wrote: 'We must make life so uncomfortable for them that they will lose the desire to remain bourgeois'.

Changing society, however, involved more than destroying the bourgeoisie. It also meant attempting to change attitudes and practices connected with roles of women and the family, eradicating the position of religion in society, expanding educational opportunities for workers, and using education to indoctrinate the young.

Women and the family

The Bolsheviks wanted to change the position of women in society; this meant freeing them from the drudgery of housework and the constraints of marriage, which were regarded as 'bourgeois' institutions. One Soviet poster proclaimed, *'Women of Russia, Throw Away Your Pots and Pans!'* Laws were passed immediately to make divorce easier and, in 1920, abortion was made available on demand. It was hoped that this would liberate women from the tyranny of their husbands. Crèches were encouraged in the workplace and there were also some attempts to remould family life by encouraging communal spaces in housing blocks, in the hope that this would break down the traditional family unit.

There was some success with these measures. Within urban populations there was a rise in divorce and the numbers of abortions; indeed by the mid-1920s Russia's divorce rate was the highest in Europe. However, positive change in the lives of women as a result of these developments was limited; those who divorced but had children, for example, received little in financial support from fathers. Meanwhile, the government found that the idea of providing enough crèches or public canteens to free women from childcare and housework was too costly. In addition, after the civil war there was a reversal of some of the measures – particularly with regard to abortion, which once again became restricted by law.

Within the workplace, the numbers of women employed actually declined during the Bolshevik years. During the First World War, the percentage of women in the urban workforce doubled but at the end of the civil war, many of their jobs were given back to the returning men. During the NEP many women were forced from skilled to unskilled work, mainly in the textile and domestic service areas. Many also drifted into prostitution and crime.

Alexandra Kollontai was a leading feminist of the Bolshevik era who argued for greater emancipation for women in all areas of life. Research her beliefs regarding marriage, the family, work and children, along with her role and influence in the Bolshevik Revolution and government.

197

Within politics, women also saw little improvement. Despite proclaiming equality for women, only 12.8 per cent of the party membership were women by 1928 (as opposed to 10 per cent in 1917). Indeed, change was limited by the traditional Russian attitudes of men regarding the role of women, which excluded them from party activities.

Religion

The Russian Orthodox Church was fully entrenched in people's lives and an important part of Russian national identity. However, Karl Marx had claimed that religion was '*the opium of the masses*', in other words that it had been designed by rulers to keep the ordinary people quiet and in their place (and certainly it had been used by the tsars as an instrument of social control). As Marxists, Lenin and the leading Bolsheviks were atheists and they were determined that people should believe only in communism. Thus, immediately after the revolution, a series of measures were introduced to severely limit the power and influence of religion:

- The Decree on the Separation of Church and State, January 1918, declared that the Church could not own property, Church schools were to be taken over and church buildings destroyed or used for other purposes.
- Priests and clerics were declared '*servants of the bourgeoisie*' which meant that they could not vote or receive ration cards; many priests were arrested by the Cheka.
- A massive propaganda campaign set out to prove to the Russian people that God did not exist; various methods were used to prove that Christian miracles were in fact myths. This went to the extent of taking peasants for rides in aeroplanes so that they could see for themselves that there were no angels in the sky. The Society of the Godless (also known as the League of Militant Atheists) was established with the specific aim of turning people against religion and promoting atheism.
- Religious holidays were replaced with secular holidays such as May Day and Revolution Day.
- Traditional religious ceremonies were 'Bolshevized' so that, for example, couples took a marriage vow in front of a portrait of Lenin instead of the altar, and children were said to be 'Octobered' instead of baptised.

After 1921, the Church was attacked more directly. The shooting of priests began and local soviets were told to remove valuables from churches to pay for famine relief. There was bitter resistance to this, resulting in violent clashes between Bolshevik soldiers and ordinary peasants. Although many in the Politburo felt that the anti-Church campaign had gone too far and should be ended, Lenin adamantly refused claiming, '*I have come to the unequivocal conclusion that we must now wage the most decisive and merciless war against the Black Hundred Clergy*'. It is estimated that throughout 1922–23 as many as 700 clergy were killed in clashes with soldiers and that 8,000 people were executed.

Nevertheless, although the influence of the Orthodox Church as an organization was broken, surveys of the peasantry in the mid-1920s indicate that over half of all peasantry were still Christian and that they still continued with religious practices, keeping their priests by paying them with voluntary donations.

Education

Education was seen as vital for changing society, and efforts were made to transform education for children as well as bring it to the workers. Institutes or workers faculties were set up to help workers prepare themselves for higher education, while soldiers in the Red Army who were illiterate were given reading and writing classes as part of their training.

The aim with regard to children was to combine education with Bolshevik propaganda. In 1919, the Party Programme defined schools as '*an instrument for the Communist transformation of society*'. However, the man in charge of education, Lunacharsky, was also interested in progressive educational ideas. He wanted the children of workers to have a wide general education but also to '*learn by doing*'. Thus he planned a vocational and academic curriculum that was to be followed by children of all social classes; this allowed working-class people to have a knowledge of culture as well as of industrial skills. Progressive ideas were also introduced into teaching methods: he believed it was important to focus on the development of a child's personality, thus there was to be relaxed discipline and project work instead of examinations.

The drive for literacy had notable successes: between 1920 and 1926 approximately 5 million people in European Russia took education courses. By 1926, 51 per cent of the population were considered literate compared to 43 per cent in 1917. Within schools however, few teachers understood the progressive methods proposed by Lunacharsky and eventually the more liberal methods were abandoned. Lack of resources also prevented the dream of providing free universal education to all children up to the age of 17. In fact, during the NEP, many children left school.

Culture

The era from 1917 to 1929 saw a period of experimentation and new freedoms in culture in which 'avant-garde' artists such as Marc Chagall and Wassily Kandinsky rejected bourgeois art and ways of life, and produced more abstract work. This was encouraged by Lenin, at least at the beginning.

One group of artists aimed to create a socialist style of art known as 'constructivism'. Constructivism tried to bring contemporary art into everyday life by designing clothes and furniture for use in the factory; the idea was that art was to help alter everything – from the way people dressed to how they lived and how they travelled.

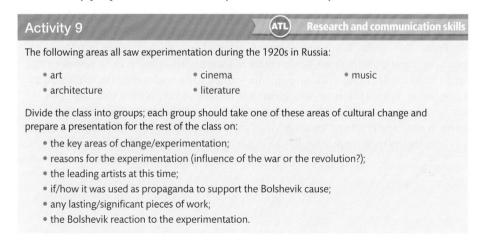

Activity 9 (ATL) **Research and communication skills**

The following areas all saw experimentation during the 1920s in Russia:

- art
- architecture
- cinema
- literature
- music

Divide the class into groups; each group should take one of these areas of cultural change and prepare a presentation for the rest of the class on:

- the key areas of change/experimentation;
- reasons for the experimentation (influence of the war or the revolution?);
- the leading artists at this time;
- if/how it was used as propaganda to support the Bolshevik cause;
- any lasting/significant pieces of work;
- the Bolshevik reaction to the experimentation.

Discuss the impact of the First World War on one European country (other than Germany, Italy or Spain) in the 1920s.

Command term: Discuss

Topic: Impact of the First World War on Russia in the 1920s.

Concept: Consequence

As the command word here is 'discuss' you will only need to focus on the impact of the First World War on Russia – you will not have to look at other factors affecting the country in this period.

Introduction

As this essay is allowing you to choose the case study, you need to make it clear that you have chosen Russia. You need to give some context – the fact that the 1920s were dominated by Lenin and the Bolsheviks attempting to secure and consolidate power, but that their very existence and the circumstances in which they had to operate, especially in the early 1920s, were influenced by the impact of the First World War.

Paragraphs

Here are some examples of paragraphs that you could include:

The establishment of the Bolshevik government which came to dominate Russia in the 1920s was directly the result of the First World War.
- the overthrow of the Tsar;
- the impact of continuing the war on the fate of the provisional government.

The immediate problem of civil war which was faced by the Bolshevik government in the 1920s also partly stemmed from the impact of the First World War.
- opposition created by the Treaty of Brest-Litovsk;
- the invasion by foreign troops contributing to the White armies;
- the role of the Czech Legion in triggering the start of the war.

The First World War also had an impact on the economic crisis that faced Russia in the 1920s.
- economic situation created by the war;
- the impact of losing land in the Treaty of Brest-Litovsk.

Conclusion

Overall, how important was the First World War in affecting Russia?

For top markbands for Paper 3 essays:

Introduction and main body paragraphs

Responses are clearly focused.

The question is fully addressed and implications are considered.

The essay is well structured and the material effectively organized.

Supporting knowledge is detailed, accurate, relevant to the question and used to support arguments.

Arguments are clear, well developed and consistently supported with evidence.

There is evaluation of different perspectives.

Conclusion

The conclusion is clearly stated and it is consistent with the evidence presented.

The power struggle: 1924–28

Key concepts: *Significance*

From 1921 until his death in 1924, Lenin suffered a series of strokes. Although he kept on working, his increasing frailty and incapacitation meant that leading members of the Politburo – Stalin, Kamenev, Zinoviev – started putting themselves into favourable positions for succeeding him. Lenin was well aware of this rivalry. In December 1922, he dictated a letter to the Politburo that he wanted to be read out at the Twelfth Party Congress in April. This letter, which came to be seen as his political testament, set out his concerns regarding the structure of the Central Committee of the Communist Party. It also clearly set out his misgivings about the personal qualities of some of the key contenders for his position, in particular, those of Joseph Stalin.

Read through these extracts from Lenin's testament.

What criticisms does Lenin have of Stalin? What appears to have been the purpose of this testament?

Extracts from Lenin's testament, 25 December 1922:

> Comrade Stalin, having become General Secretary, has immeasurable power concentrated in his hands, and I am not sure that he always knows how to use that power with sufficient caution. Comrade Trotsky, on the other hand… is distinguished not only by his outstanding ability. He is personally perhaps the most capable man in the present Central Committee, but has displayed excessive self-assurance and excessive concern with the purely administrative side of the work. These two qualities of the two outstanding leaders of the present Central Committee can inadvertently lead to a split.
>
> I shall not give any further appraisals of the personal qualities of the members of the Central Committee, I shall just recall that the **October episode** with Zinoviev and Kamenev was, of course, no accident, but neither can blame be laid upon them personally… Speaking for the younger members… Bukharin is not only a most valuable and major theorist of the Party; he is also rightly considered the favourite of the whole Party.

(Postscript added 4 January 1923)

> Stalin is too rude, and this fault… becomes unacceptable in the office of General Secretary. Therefore, I propose to the comrades that a way be found to remove Stalin from that post and replace him with someone else who differs from Stalin in all respects, someone more patient, more loyal, more polite, more considerate.

The 'October episode'

This is a reference to October 1917, when Kamenev and Zinoviev had disagreed with Lenin regarding his determination to seize power; they felt that his plan was too risky and should be postponed.

Lenin's testament indicated that Stalin was not in a strong position to take over from him and, indeed, had Lenin lived longer, it seems that he would have taken stronger measures to ensure that Stalin was removed from a position of influence. However, as Robert Conquest writes, '*Stalin was saved, in fact, by luck*'. Lenin died on 21 January 1924. Following this, Stalin moved quickly to lead the mourners at Lenin's funeral and to give a speech, in which he was able to portray himself as a true disciple of Lenin and the one who would carry on Lenin's work.

Trotsky, a key contender for leadership, was not at the funeral and Trotsky later claimed that this was due to Stalin misinforming him about the actual date of the funeral. Trotsky was on his way to the Black Sea for a rest-holiday and apparently Stalin told him that he would not have time to get back to Moscow in time. This was a serious blow to Trotsky's bid for leadership; his absence made it look as though he could not be bothered to turn up.

Stalin still faced the hurdle of Lenin's 'testament', which would be severely damaging to his leadership chances. However, when the Central Committee was presented with the document in May 1924, they agreed not to have it read out to the Thirteenth Party Congress. This was probably because it contained damning comments on several members; certainly Zinoviev and Kamenev did not want congress's attention brought to their actions in October 1917. Trotsky also did nothing to insist that the document be read out. Furthermore, the other party members agreed that Stalin had '*improved*' his character as described by Lenin and they voted to put aside Lenin's recommendations regarding Stalin.

The chief contenders to Lenin's leadership

At the time of Lenin's death, there were several contenders. On the left of the party were Trotsky, Zinoviev and Kamenev; on the right of the party were Rykov and Bukharin. The majority of the party members lay somewhere in between. Stalin was part of this centre group, and it was by no means clear that he would emerge as the outright winner.

Leon Trotsky

Trotsky came from a Russian-Jewish family; he was well educated, intelligent and a key theorist within the party, as well as one its best orators. He had played a significant role in the 1905 revolution as chair of the Petrograd Soviet, which had been set up as part of this revolution, and was influential in the organization and timing of the Bolshevik takeover of power in October 1917. His organization, determination and energy had played a key role in the success of the Reds in the civil war. However, he was regarded by fellow Bolsheviks as aloof and superior in attitude, and indeed had an arrogance that meant that he was sometimes dismissive of other Bolsheviks. He was also regarded as an outsider by some, as he had only joined the Bolshevik Party in 1917, having been a member of the Menshevik Party prior to this. These factors worked against him, as did his frequent illnesses.

Joseph Stalin

Stalin had been born into a poor family in Georgia and entered politics after being expelled from a seminary school where he had been training as a priest. He joined the underground world of Marxist revolutionaries and spent time robbing banks and organizing strikes in support of the Bolsheviks. He was arrested and sent to Siberia frequently, from where he managed to escape on five occasions. He was invited on to the party Central Committee in 1912 and was one of the first Bolsheviks to arrive in Petrograd for the February Revolution. However, he does not seem to have played a key role in the October Revolution. He was appointed commissar for nationalities after the revolution and played a role in organizing food supplies in Tsaritsyn (later named Stalingrad) and defending it, coming into conflict with Trotsky several times. In 1919 he was made head of Rabkin, which was an organization set up to check on the work of those in the government service. This gave Stalin the power to inspect all government departments. He was the only Politburo member who was also a member of the Orgburo, which supervised party affairs. In 1922 he became the party's first General Secretary, a role that placed him in charge of general organization. These positions gave him control of party organization and membership; this power was to be key in the leadership contest. At the time, however, he was considered to be, as the diarist Sukhanov put it, '*a grey blur*', who had a reputation for '*industrious mediocrity*'.

Grigory Zinoviev

Zinoviev had been active in the party from 1903 and he was a passionate orator. He was in exile with Lenin before the revolution, and arrived back in Russia with him in April 1917. However, he opposed the timing of the October Revolution, and co-wrote with Kamenev an article in the press that expressed criticism of the planned coup. He also favoured a socialist coalition after the revolution and so was not given a post in the *Sovnarkom*. Nevertheless, he was Party Secretary in Leningrad, which allowed him to build up a strong power base. In 1919 he was made a member of the Comintern, an organization set up to spread revolution outside of Russia. He was not popular and was seen by others as being incompetent and cowardly. The historian EH Carr describes him as *'weak, vain, ambitious'*.

Lev Kamenev

Kamenev had been involved in the Bolshevik Party since 1905 and was in exile with Lenin before the First World War. He had urged cooperation with the provisional government after the February Revolution, he criticized Lenin's 'April Theses' and openly attacked the timing of the planned Bolshevik coup in the press, along with Zinoviev. He also wanted a broad socialist coalition after the success of the October Revolution and resigned his chairmanship of the Central Executive Committee of Soviets when Lenin refused to agree to this. However, he was made Party Secretary in Moscow, which brought him into the Politburo and so placed him in a position to make a challenge for the leadership. He was a moderate and was liked by other members of the party, although he lacked the strong character and vision necessary to become a leader.

Nikolai Bukharin

Bukharin was the youngest member of the Politburo. He had joined the Bolsheviks in 1906 as a teenager. He was an important theorist and wrote many articles in *Pravda*, the party newspaper, during 1917. He had opposed the Brest-Litovsk Treaty, believing that revolution would have spread if the war had continued. However, he had become an enthusiastic supporter of the NEP once he realized that international revolution was unlikely to take place immediately. Lenin called him the *'darling of the Party'* and *'the Party's best theoretician'*; he loved the arts and was very popular.

Alexei Rykov

Rykov had a reputation as a moderate and as a good administrator, though he also had a reputation for drinking. He acted as people's commissar of the interior 1917–18 and chairman of the Supreme Council of the National Economy in 1918–20 and 1923–24. He also succeeded Lenin as chairman of the *Sovnarkom*. He was a strong supporter of the NEP.

What were the key issues in the leadership contest?

The key issues that divided the contenders were: the style of leadership that should be adopted; the NEP and whether or not it should be continued; and the extent to which the USSR should start spreading revolution globally or just concentrate on developing it within Russia.

Dictatorship or collective leadership?

As you have read, the party had become highly centralized during the civil war and many party members were unhappy with this trend, fearing that a dictatorship could develop. Instead they wanted a collective leadership.

The person that they feared most in terms of establishing a dictatorship was Trotsky; along with the fact that he appeared arrogant, he potentially had the force of the Red Army behind him. In fact, Trotsky had no intention of becoming a dictator or of using the Red Army to secure his position, and he had argued for more openness in the party in the 1920s.

NEP or rapid industrialization?

By the mid-1920s, there was increasing concern with the NEP. Many party members were unhappy with the capitalist elements of it that emerged, such as the Nepmen, property dealing, and land speculation. Problems were also starting to emerge; many workers were unemployed and wages did not keep pace with the price of consumer goods. Food shortages also started to appear with peasants holding onto their produce and grain.

Although none of the contenders believed that the NEP was a permanent solution to the economy, there was still the question of how long it should be kept going for. Trotsky, Kamenev and Zinoviev, who were on the left of the party, wanted to end the NEP and go for rapid industrialization. This would involve central control of labour and forcing the peasants to hand over their produce to allow industrialization to take place. Bukharin and Rykov, however, believed that it would be very damaging to force a confrontation with the peasants; they wanted to continue with the NEP in order for the peasants to become more wealthy. This would encourage them to spend on consumer goods, which would in turn stimulate the growth of the manufacturing industry.

Socialism in one country or revolution abroad?

Trotsky believed that the communist revolution could not fully succeed until it had the support of workers in other countries, and argued, *'There is not enough proletarian yeast in our peasant dough'*. He thought the first priority should therefore to be to spread revolutionary ideas abroad in order to achieve *'permanent revolution'*.

Stalin, however, argued that a world revolution was unlikely and that Russia should concentrate on building up socialism within Russia. By focusing on *'socialism in one country'*, and achieving communism by its own efforts, Russia would be able to show the rest of the world the superiority of a socialist system.

Why did Stalin win the leadership race?

When Lenin died, Stalin's chances of succeeding him seemed remote; however, by 1929, Stalin had successfully eliminated the competition not only from Zinoviev and Kamenev but also Bukharin and Trotsky. How was this possible?

You have already read, on page 201, that Stalin moved quickly to establish himself as the true heir to Lenin at the funeral, and that he also managed to prevent Lenin's will being read out. At this point, the other contenders, in particular Zinoviev and Kamenev, regarded Trotsky as their main rival and the main threat to the stability of the party, so they collaborated with Stalin. This led to a power-sharing **triumvirate**. Stalin then played a clever tactical game to play off the other candidates against each other; this took place in three stages.

First stage: Defeat of Trotsky

Stalin was able to use Trotsky's unpopularity within much of the party to keep him isolated. At the Thirteenth Party Congress, Trotsky criticized the party for becoming bureaucratic and less democratic. This was clearly an attack on Stalin and his control of the Secretariat. However, despite brilliant speeches, he was easily defeated in the votes due to the control exercised over delegates by Stalin. Trotsky expanded his arguments in a series of essays. In the *Lessons of October*, he attacked Zinoviev and Kamenev for their actions in opposing Lenin in 1917. However, this led to vicious retaliations such as Kamenev's *Leninism or Trotskyism?* in which he highlighted Trotsky's previous membership of the Menshevik Party and differences in policy that had existed between Trotsky and Lenin.

Denouncing Trotsky became routine at party meetings. In January 1925, he was replaced as Commissar for War. Trotsky could have appealed to his supporters inside and outside of the party but, due to the 'Ban on Factions' (see page 195), this was now difficult. He also made no move to use his command of the Red Army to protect his position.

Second stage: Defeat of Zinoviev and Kamenev

With Trotsky now in retreat, thanks mainly to the work of Zinoviev and Kamenev, Stalin was able to move against his previous allies. In 1925, Kamenev and Zinoviev became uneasy about Stalin's influence in the party and also concerned about the USSR's economic backwardness. They now switched to Trotsky's policies and called for an end to the NEP and also for the spread of proletarian revolutions in other nations to help the Soviet Union achieve socialism. At the Fourteenth Party Congress in 1925 they attacked Stalin, calling for a vote of no confidence in him; however, his control over the party machinery was now so complete that this was unsuccessful.

In 1926, they joined forces with Trotsky to form the 'United Opposition'. However, this meant that they could be accused of factionalism. All three were expelled from the Politburo. Trotsky was then exiled in 1929.

Stage three: Defeat of the right

Stalin now turned against the NEP and began to associate '*socialism in one country*' with rapid industrialization and breaking the power of the peasantry. This of course was basically Trotsky's position, without the insistence on spreading revolution to the rest of Europe. This was opposed by Bukharin and others on the right, who launched a strong defence of the NEP. However at the congress of 1929, they were outvoted by Stalin's supporters. Stalin accused them of plotting against the party's agreed strategy and they were forced to resign from the Politburo and the positions that they held within the party. Thus, by 1929, Stalin had defeated all competition.

Activity 12 Thinking and social skills

1. In pairs, discuss the different factors that helped Stalin to succeed.
2. Read the views of historians below. How do these compare to your own conclusions?
3. Overall, what do you think was/were the most important factor/s in allowing Stalin to take control by 1929?

Source A

 Among Stalin's political advantages was his ability to manoeuvre between factions. He avoided permanent commitments and loyalties to any grouping. At the same time he always posed as a moderate, often a centrist, which increased his chance of being misjudged or underestimated by his opponents. Indeed opponents were unlikely to be aware that they were in any real danger until Stalin had emerged from his 'moderate' cover to launch a deadly offensive.

Lee, S (2008). *The European Dictatorships.* **Routledge, pp. 44–45.**

Source B

 In the last analysis, Stalin's victory over Trotsky was not a question of ability or principle. Stalin won because Trotsky lacked a power base. Trotsky's superiority as a speaker and writer, and his greater intellectual gifts, counted for little when set against Stalin's control of the Party machine. It is difficult to see how Trotsky could have ever mounted a serious challenge to his rival. Even had his own particular failings not inhibited him from action at vital moments, Trotsky never possessed sufficient understanding, let alone control, of the political system as it pertained in Soviet Russia.

Lynch, M (2001). *Stalin and Khrushchev: The USSR, 1924–64.* **Hodder, pp. 21–22.**

Source C

 Politburo opponents of Stalin had had little practical experience of politics before 1917… they were singularly ill-equipped to recognise a party climber when they saw one. They were all superior to Stalin, or so they thought, despite what Lenin had written in his Testament. Their fierce intellectual independence ill prepared them for caucus politics. Stalin was moderate and methodical, not to say pedestrian, but he was the only one skilled at building tactical alliances and this put him head and shoulders above the rest…

Politburo members also suffered from the old blight of the Russian intelligentsia, personal animosity… Zinoviev hated Trotsky, Trotsky hated Zinoviev, Bukharin hated Trotsky, Trotsky hated Stalin, Stalin hated Trotsky and Bukharin came to hate Stalin.

McCauley, M (1996). *The Soviet Union 1917–1991.* **Longman, pp. 75–76.**

Activity 13

 **ATL** Self-management skills

Before tackling the next essay question, copy out and complete this grid to summarize the key political and economic changes of 1917–21.

	Economic developments	Political developments
Oct 1917–18		
1918–21 (civil war)		
1921–24		
1924–29		

Essay planning

Examine political and economic developments in one European country (other than Germany, Italy or Spain) during the 1920s.

Command term: Examine.

Topic: Political and economic developments.

Concept: Change.

Introduction: Again, as this is a question allowing you to choose the country to write about, you need to make it clear that you have chosen Russia. The key political development of this period is the growing centralization of power and the growing strength of the Bolshevik Party culminating in Stalin's dictatorship by 1929. In this essay you need to show this consistent trend and why it took place. With regard to economics, this was quite complex in the 1920s and you will need to show the different phases in Lenin's control of the economy.

Paragraphs: Here is a suggestion for opening sentences to paragraphs, dealing first with the political developments and then with economic developments. Don't forget to give precise factual information, including dates, as evidence and to also bring in historians' views. Particularly important here is the extent to which Lenin laid the foundations for Stalinism (see Historians' perspectives box on page 196).

The 1920s saw the development of a one party state...

The 1920s saw the growing centralization of political power over the party's own structure and its members...

Another development of the 1920s was that the Communist Party became more powerful than the actual institutions of government...

From 1926 there was a leadership race to determine which direction Russia should head in politically...

The initial economic measures taken by the Bolsheviks were...

The impact of the civil war led the Bolsheviks to take drastic economic measures under War Communism...

However, the economic policies followed by the Bolsheviks changed direction in the mid-1920s...

Conclusion: Come back to the question and state the overall developments in politics and economics that took place in the 1920s in Russia.

Essay planning

In pairs, now plan the following essay:

To what extent was there economic and social change in one European country (other than Germany, Italy or Spain) in the 1920s?

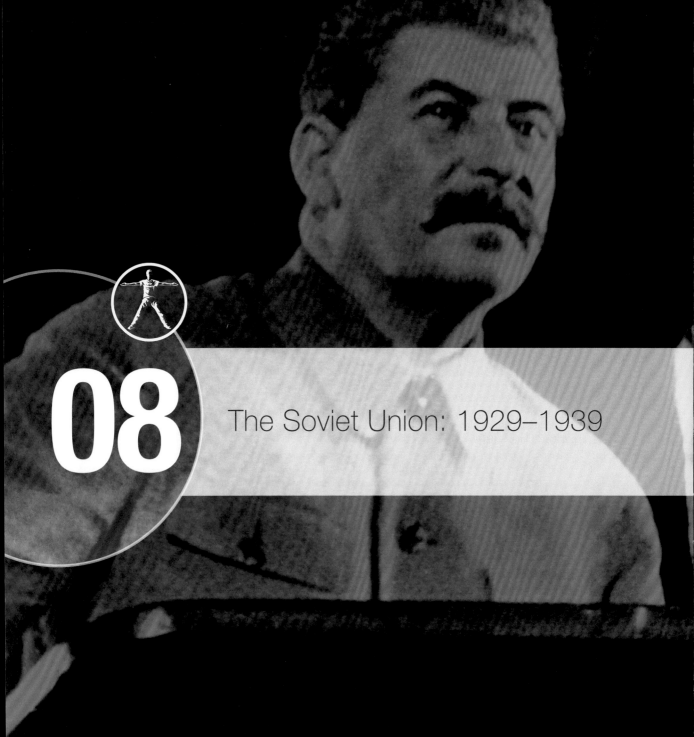

08

The Soviet Union: 1929–1939

> ❝ *Seldom perhaps in history has so monstrous a price been paid for so monumental an achievement.*
>
> **Carr, EH (1971). *Foundations of a Planned Economy, 1926–1929*. Penguin.**

КАПИТАН СТРАНЫ СОВЕТОВ ВЕДЕТ НАС ОТ ПОБЕДЫ К ПОБЕДЕ!

A poster from the 1930s showing Stalin as the helmsman of the Soviet Union.

The period 1928 to 1941 was one of tremendous change in the Soviet Union. The Five Year Plans and collectivization led to a radical transformation of the economy, causing severe hardship for the Soviet people in the process. At the same time the population was subjected to a Terror that indiscriminately targeted huge numbers of people. However, at the end of the 1930s Stalinism had transformed the Soviet Union from a backward state into an industrialized nation that would be capable of winning the war against Nazi Germany in the 1940s.

Essay questions:

- With reference to one European country (other than Italy, Germany or Spain), examine the success of economic policies in the 1930s.

- To what extent was there economic and social change in one European country (other than Germany, Italy or Spain) in the 1930s?

- Examine the political developments in one European country (other than Germany, Italy or Spain) in the 1930s.

Timeline of events – 1927–1939

1927		Stalin proposes Five Year Plan and collectivization
1929	Dec	Forced collectivization takes place
1930	Mar	Stalin pulls back from forced collectivization
1932–33		Famine in the Ukraine
1933		Second Five Year Plan
1934	Dec	Kirov murdered
1935	July	Moscow Metro officially opens
	Aug	Stakhanovite movement begins

1936	June	The Great Retreat
	Aug	Show trials of Kamanev and Zinoviev; both executed
	Dec	New Constitution adopted
1937	June	Purge of the military starts
		Third Five Year Plan starts
1938	Mar	Show trials of Bukharin and Rykov; both executed
1939	Mar	Stalin announces end of the Great Terror

How did Stalin transform the USSR economically?

The Great Turn

Key concepts: *Causation, change and consequence*

The Fifteenth Party Congress in December 1927 saw the introduction of the First Five Year Plan. This marked the end of the NEP and the move to rapid industrialization and collectivization in agriculture. Why was this?

By introducing radical economic changes that would take the country further towards socialism, Stalin sought to enhance his own status as a great revolutionary leader. However, there were also pragmatic reasons for his decision to achieve 'socialism in one country' through rapid industrialization. Although the NEP had brought about economic recovery and increased the grain supply, it was still inadequate to help Russia become an industrialized country. By 1926, pre-war levels of production had been achieved but figures were still well below the other economies of Western Europe. In agriculture, grain production was also inadequate; farming methods were still backward, with peasants using traditional methods on their smallholdings. Despite efforts by the government to get peasants to sell more grain on the market (see page 191) they were still unwilling to sell it for money when there were so few consumer goods to buy; at the end of 1927, grain production was three-quarters less than it had been in 1926. A bad harvest in 1928 meant that grain supplies to the cities fell sharply and rationing had to be introduced.

It was thus clear from the situation that existed in 1928 that the NEP was not allowing Russia to industrialize fast enough. However, there was also a strong ideological purpose behind introducing the Five Year Plans. For many Bolsheviks, the encouragement of private business and the development of the Nepmen meant that they were failing to produce a socialist society; industrialization would create many more members of the proletariat who would help secure the revolution. It would also bring the peasants into line; the Bolsheviks disliked the peasantry, particularly the wealthier peasants or 'kulaks', for having the power to hold back the grain that was so necessary for industrialization. In this sense, the Five Year Plans and collectivization can be seen as a class war against those who had benefited from the NEP and who were seen to be holding back the drive to socialism.

A further incentive for Stalin to speed up industrialization was the need to manufacture armaments. There was a war scare in the late 1920s when relations with France, Britain and Poland deteriorated. There were also concerns about Japanese intentions in the east; Japan took over Manchuria in 1931, which directly threatened Soviet railway interests and created a direct threat to the Soviet Union itself. Hence Stalin's justification for his policy in 1931: '*We are fifty or a hundred years behind the advanced countries. We must make good this distance in ten years. Either we do it, or we shall be crushed.*' Industrialization was seen as essential for the Soviet Union's ability to defend itself against attack from capitalist powers.

Activity 1	**ATL** Self-management skills

Create a mind map to show the reasons for the Great Turn under the headings: political reasons, economic reasons, and military reasons.

What was the significance of the Great Turn?

The momentous decision to move from the NEP to collectivization and industrialization was known as the 'Second Revolution'. It was also a 'revolution from above'. From now on, the Soviet state would centralize and control the country's economy. Although this had taken place to some extent under Lenin, Stalin's plans involved a much greater degree of planning, '*under Stalin, State control was to be comprehensive and all-embracing*' (Lynch). In the process, this revolution would also lead to great changes in the Communist Party and the relationship between the party and the people.

Collectivization

Industrial development was only possible if it was supported by agricultural productivity; the population in the growing industrial towns needed to be fed, and technology from abroad needed to be paid for by foreign exchange, which could only be gained by selling surplus grain. In addition, the increased number of workers needed in the cities was unachievable unless more peasants moved from the countryside to the cities – a situation that would only be possible once agriculture was more efficient.

In 1929, ***kolkhoz* (or collective farms)** were established to replace the peasants' individual farms. Local officials, supported by police and soldiers, went into the countryside to organize the setting up of collectives. They lectured the peasants on the advantages of forming a collective until enough of them had signed up as members; animals, grain supplies and buildings in the villages would then be taken over as property of the collective. The '*kulaks*' or rich peasants were considered to be '*class enemies*'. At the Party Congress in December 1929, Stalin demanded, '*We must break the resistance of the kulaks and deprive this class of its existence. We must eliminate the kulaks as a class.*' Thousands were arrested and sent to the *Gulag* in Siberia and the Urals; they were of course the most successful and enterprising of the peasants, a factor that was to contribute to the chaos that now developed. However, many ordinary peasants who resisted collectivization were also termed '*kulak*' and were deported.

The process of collectivization resulted in widespread opposition from the peasantry. As well as outright rebellion, which included the killing of officials who came to the villages, it also involved the peasants destroying and slaughtering anything that would be of use in the collective farm. '*Slaughter, you won't get meat in the Kolkhoz, crept the insidious rumours. And they slaughtered. They ate until they could eat no more. Young and old suffered from indigestion. At dinner time tables groaned under boiled and roasted meat*' (Sholokhov, M, *Virgin Soil Upturned*, p. 152; quoted in McCauley, 1996, p. 83). This resistance was met by brutal force.

The collective farms, and machine and tractor stations

The most common type of collective farm that was set up in the 1930s was the *kolkhoz*. This consisted of between 50 to 100 households. All land, tools and livestock were held in common, though each household could keep a private plot on which to grow vegetables and keep a cow, a pig and fowl. Payment to peasants was based on the productivity of the *kolkhoz*; it thus remained very low, and when there was no profit there was no payout.

Machines and tractor stations (MTS) were established to support the farms by hiring out machinery and giving farming advice. However, they also had a political purpose. They gave ideological lectures on the benefits of the collective farms and kept an eye out for troublemakers. They came to be despised by the peasantry as instruments of state control.

The *Gulag*

'The *Gulag*' is the term given to the labour camps that existed in the Soviet Union; it is an abbreviation for 'Main Prison Camp Administration'. The inmates of the *Gulag* included criminals and political prisoners alongside innocent peasants and others who were caught up in the Great Terror or who were there because of the need to meet 'quotas' of arrests. The camps were run first by the OGPU and then by the NKVD, and the inmates provided a major source of labour for large construction projects.

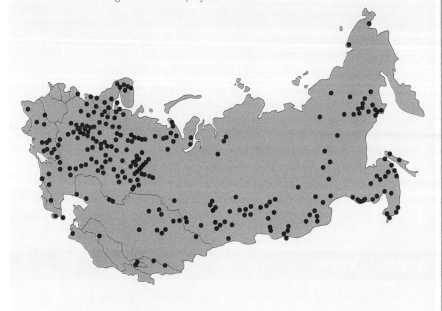

A map of the *Gulag* as drawn up by Memorial (an organization that works to ensure that the victims of Stalinism are not forgotten). Some of the *Gulag* operated only for a short amount of time.

Realizing, however, that further peasant resistance could lead to the total collapse of grain production, Stalin backed down. In an article for *Pravda* in March 1930, he said that officials had become overzealous and '*dizzy with success*'. Pressure on peasants to collectivize was thus reduced and official policy changed back to voluntary collectivization. Many peasants went back to farming for themselves. However, once the 1930 harvest had been collected in, collectivization continued just as brutally as before. Throughout 1931, peasants were forced back into the collectives. By 1932, 62 per cent of peasant households had been collectivized, rising to 93 per cent in 1937.

What were the short-term effects of collectivization?

During collectivization, the state continued to requisition grain for feeding the cities and for export to gain foreign currency to pay for essential industrial plants. This was disastrous for the peasantry, who were already facing a reduction in grain production due to the chaotic situation created by collectivization; the loss of the most productive peasants had robbed the countryside of its best farmers and the remaining peasants were unwilling to put the same effort into working on the *kolkhoz* as they had done on their own land. Some 19 million peasants also fled the countryside to work on industrial projects where they could escape the *kolkhoz* and gain higher wages. Production levels fell and livestock numbers halved. The overall result was the famine of 1932 to 1933. This was particularly devastating in Ukraine and it was the worst famine in Russia's history.

Activity 2

ATL Thinking skills

Study the tables carefully.

Table of statistics for grain production (millions of metric tons) and grain export 1929–33		
	Grain Production	Grain Export %
1929	71.7	0.18
1930	83.5	4.76
1931	69.5	5.06
1932	69.6	1.73
1933	68.4	1.69

Source: Alec Nove (1969). *An Economic History of the USSR*. Penguin; quoted in Norman Lowe (2002). *Mastering Twentieth Century Russian History*.

Table of statistics for numbers of farm animals 1929–34 (million head)						
	1929	1930	1931	1932	1933	1934
Cattle	67.1	52.3	47.9	40.1	38.4	42.4
Pigs	20.4	13.6	14.4	11.6	12.1	17.4
Sheep and Goats	147.0	108.8	77.7	52.1	50.2	51.9

Source: Alec Nove (1969). *An Economic History of the USSR*. Penguin; quoted in Chris Corin and Terry Fiehn (2002). *Communist Russia under Lenin and Stalin*.

1. What can you learn from these statistics about the impact of collectivization?
2. What is significant about the grain export figures in the first table?

Historians' perspectives

Can the Ukrainian famine be seen as genocide?

Robert Conquest has argued that Stalin was determined to break the resistance of the peasantry and so continued to take grain even though he knew it would lead to starvation; in this sense it was a man-made famine.

Some historians disagree. Robert Service argues that requisitioning quotas were cut three times during 1932 in response to the famine. He also points out that Stalin needed labour from the Ukraine and so it would not have made sense to carry out a deliberate policy of starvation.

Activity 3

ATL Thinking skills

What does the following source reveal about:

a) the process of collectivization
b) the results of collectivization.

 With the rest of my generation, I firmly believed that the ends justified the means. Our great goal was the universal triumph of Communism…

I saw what 'total collectivisation' meant – how they mercilessly stripped the peasants in the winter of 1932 – 33. I took part in it myself, scouring the countryside… testing the earth with an iron rod for loose spots that might lead to buried grain. With the others, I emptied out the old folks' storage chests stopping my ears to the children's crying and the women's wails, for I was convinced that I was accomplishing the great and necessary transformation of the countryside; that in the days to come the people who lived there would be better off…

In the terrible spring of 1933, I saw people dying of hunger, I saw women and children with distended bellies, turning blue, still breathing but with vacant lifeless eyes. And corpses – corpses in ragged sheepskin coats and cheap felt boots; corpses in peasant huts… I saw all this and did not go out of my mind or commit suicide… Nor did I lose my faith. As before, I believed because I wanted to believe.

L Kopelev, a Soviet activist, quoted in Conquest, R (1986). *The Harvest of Sorrow*, p. 233. (Taken from C Corin, and T Fiehn. 2002. *Communist Russia under Lenin and Stalin*, Hodder.)

How successful was collectivization in the long term?

The disruption caused by collectivization meant that it took until 1935 for grain harvests to produce the quantities of grain that had been procured in 1928, and this was still not back up to the level of grain produced in 1913. Meanwhile, livestock numbers did not recover until after the Second World War. Nevertheless, it could be argued that collectivization was an economic success for Stalin in that it had achieved its main aim of providing the resources for industrialization. Many peasants had moved to the new industrial centres, providing cheap industrial labour. As a result, the state was able to collect the grain that it needed to export in order to buy industrial machinery. Most importantly, it was now possible to feed the urban workers. The countryside could no longer hold the towns to ransom; if there was a shortage of grain due to bad harvests, it was now the countryside that would suffer and not the cities. The state's grain collections rose from 10.8 million tons in 1928–9 to 22.8 million tons in 1931–2. Collectivization also achieved Stalin's political aims as it enabled him to establish a firm control over the countryside.

Activity 4   (ATL) Thinking skills

Why could Stalin view collectivization as having 'favourable' results?

The Five Year Plans

Activity 5   (ATL) Thinking skills

A Soviet propaganda poster on the Five Year Plans.

The red book is titled 'Five Year Plan'. The capitalist on the top is saying: '*Fantasy, nonsense, utopia*'. Below the factories, flying banners say: '*Industrialization, Collectivization of Farms*'.

Пятилетний план и буржуазные злопыхатели
(Плакат художников Дени и Долгорукова, 1933 г.)

What is the message of this Soviet poster from 1928?

Stalin's industrialization programme was driven forward by the Five Year Plans; these were intended to transform the Soviet Union into an advanced, industrialized socialist state in ten years. The Soviet Union would then be less dependent on the West for industrial goods and could aim for autarky (self-sufficiency). The focus was on heavy industry as this is what had enabled countries such as Britain, Germany and the US to achieve their industrial supremacy. Heavy industries such as iron, coal and steel were also seen as essential for protecting the Soviet Union from invasion. This meant that consumer goods were given a low priority.

Key to the Five Year Plans were production targets set by the central planning body, Gosplan; each factory, works and mine was set quotas that had to be achieved over a five-year period. In actual fact, the plans were always declared complete a year ahead of schedule. This was to emphasize the superiority of the Soviet planning system over the capitalist economies of the West. It was also intended to act as a psychological boost to the workers in order to urge them on to achieve even more.

The creation of spectacular projects as part of the Five Year Plans were further intended to act as a propaganda showcase for Soviet achievement. These included the Dnieprostroi Dam in eastern Russia, which was the world's largest construction site for two years; the Moscow-Volga Canal; and the building of the Moscow metro. In addition, huge new industrial centres were built, the most significant being Magnitogorsk. The latter was held up as being a new 'socialist city' that would represent all the virtues of socialism.

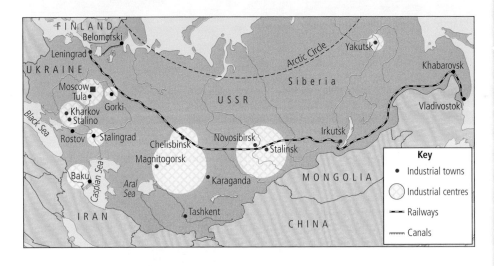

Expansion of Soviet industry and communications.

The First Five Year Plan, 1928 to 1932

The emphasis of the First Five Year Plan was on heavy industry – coal, iron, steel, oil and machine production – with the aim of increasing production by a massive 300 per cent! Light industry – chemicals, motor vehicles, synthetic rubber and artificial fibres – was also to double its output. Electricity was to increase by 600 per cent in order to ensure sufficient energy. The plan was introduced in 1928, but already by 1929 the five-year goal had been reduced to four.

Given the unrealistic targets that were established, it is not surprising that they were rarely reached. Nevertheless, the achievements were still impressive:

- electricity output trebled;
- coal and iron output doubled;
- steel production increased by one-third;
- engineering industry increased production;
- 1,500 new industrial plants were established;
- more than 100 new towns were built, such as Magnitogorsk;
- new tractor works were built to meet the needs of mechanized agriculture.

Workers at Magnitogorsk, 1932.

The Second Five Year Plan, January 1933 to December 1937

This generally set more realistic targets than the First Five Year plan and so was able to proceed more smoothly and build on the advances made in the first plan. Again, the emphasis was on heavy industry; consumer goods were low priority, although there was a greater importance placed on communication, especially railways to link cities and industrial centres. Steel, coal and electricity production rose substantially during the Second Five Year Plan. The chemical industry also made progress; oil production was the main disappointment because it fell below expectation (see table below for statistics). With the threat of Nazi Germany after 1933, more emphasis was placed on defence and between 1933 to 1938 the production of armaments trebled.

The Third Five Year Plan, January 1938 to June 1941

The third plan was heavily focused on defence, in the light of growing fears of war, and it was cut short by the German invasion of Russia in 1941.

How successful were the Five Year Plans?

Activity 6

In pairs, analyse the information on this table.

Soviet production between 1927 and 1937					
	1927 output	1932 target	1932 output	1937 target	1937 output
Steel (million tons)	4.0	10.4	5.9	17.0	17.7
Wool cloth (million metres)	97.0	270.0	93.3	226.6	108.3
Pig iron (million tons)	3.3	10.0	6.2	16.0	14.5
Coal (million tons)	35.4	75.0	64.3	152.5	128.0
Electricity (100m kwh)	5.0	22.0	13.4	38.0	36.2
Oil (million tons)	11.7	22.0	21.4	46.8	28.5

1. What can you learn about the planning and the achievements of the first two Five Year Plans?
2. What are the value and limitations of statistics such as these for the historian who is trying to find out about the impact of the Five Year Plans?

As a result of the Five Year Plans, Russia's gross national product grew by just under 12 per cent a year. By 1940, the Soviet Union had overtaken Britain in the production of iron and steel and was catching up with Germany.

Activity 7

Read Alan Bullock's conclusions regarding the First Five Year Plan. According to Bullock, in what ways can the plan be seen as a success?

> After the grey compromises of the NEP, the Plan revived the flagging faith of the party. Here at last was the chance to pour their enthusiasm into building the New Jerusalem they had been promised. The boldness of the targets, the sacrifices demanded and the vision of what 'backward' Russia might achieve provided an inspiring contrast with an 'advanced' West with millions unemployed and resources left to wanted because of the Slump. None of Stalin's targets might be achieved, but in every case output was raised: 6 million tons of steel was little more than half the 10 million allowed for, but 50 per cent up on the starting figure.
>
> **Bullock, A (1991). *Hitler and Stalin: Parallel Lives*. Harper Collins, pp. 295–96.**

What was the impact of the Five Year Plans on the workers?

Many workers entered enthusiastically into the challenge to modernize the Soviet Union. The government talked of '*a socialist offensive*' and '*of mobilizing forces on all fronts*', and many were inspired by the challenge of creating a new society that would be superior to those of capitalist countries. Thousands of young people volunteered to work on distant projects and were prepared to put up with terrible conditions in order to be part of this great socialist enterprise. John Scott, an American who was in the

Soviet Union at the time, wrote:

> *The hard life and sacrifices of industrialisation were consciously and enthusiastically accepted by the majority of workers. They had their noses to the grindstone but they knew that it was for themselves, for a future with dignity and freedom for all workers. Strange as it may appear, the forced labour was a source not only of privation but also of heroism. Soviet youth found heroism in working in factories and on construction sites…*
> **Scott, J (1942). *Behind the Urals: An American Worker in Russia's City of Steel*. Houghton Mifflin.**

The hard life and sacrifices that are referred to here by Scott were extreme indeed for workers. Wages remained low and, in the pressure to meet the targets set by the Five Year Plans, safety was neglected and working conditions were often appalling. For many peasants who had been forced off the land by collectivization or had volunteered to move to the cities, this was an alien world; many of these unskilled workers found it hard to adapt to the rules and monotony of factory life and disliked industrial work. This led to what Moshe Lewin has called '*the quicksand society*', with many moving from job to job in the hope of finding better work and conditions. Even skilled workers moved regularly as factory owners, desperate to meet targets, tried to attract them with higher wages or benefits.

In order to deal with these labour problems the Communist Party took several measures:

- A massive training programme was introduced, though this was often inadequate because it was rushed and was taught by poor trainers.
- Tough measures, including being sent to the *Gulag*, were brought in to deal with absenteeism, causing damage or leaving a job without permission.
- Internal passports were introduced to make it harder to move from one job to another.
- Incentives were given to those workers who stayed put or who were outstanding. These could include not just more money but also better living conditions or more rations.
- A huge propaganda campaign was launched. Special 'shock brigades' were created to attempt to achieve high production targets and to set examples for the other workers to follow. Workers were urged to be like the hero Stakhanov, a coalminer from the Donbass region who, in just one shift, mined 15 times the average amount of coal.
- Where there were shortages of labour, slave labour from the *Gulag* were used; these workers were sent to the harshest regions and faced appalling conditions. The 227-km Belomor Canal was built by the slave labour of 170,000 prisoners, of whom around 25,000 died in a year and a half. Despite such human loss, the canal turned out to be too shallow for the Soviet Navy's warships.

However, good workers, and even managers, risked being accused of industrial espionage. When targets were not met, scapegoats had to be found. Specialists could be found guilty of hindering production and put on trial; factory managers who failed to meet quotas could be arrested and sent to the *Gulag* or shot. This of course led to managers using a variety of methods to falsify their statistics or taking other drastic actions such as stealing resources that were meant for other factories, or bribing officials. Quality was also sacrificed for quantity.

What was the impact of the Five Year Plans on society?

The Five Year Plans led to a 38 per cent increase in the industrial proletariat between 1926 and 1933; this strengthened the position of socialism, which was supposed to be based on an urban society. However, it also meant that conditions in towns worsened; overcrowding was intense in poorly built accommodation with limited sanitation. Violence and crime flourished. The emphasis of the Five Year Plans on heavy industry also meant that consumer goods were in very short supply. There were perpetual shortages in the state shops for food and consumer goods, and people spent hours in endless queues. Rising prices contributed to the hardships. Alec Nove describes the years 1928–33 as experiencing '*the most precipitous decline in living standards known in recorded history*'. Although wages and consumer good production improved after 1933, real wages in 1937 were not much more than 85 per cent of the 1928 level.

The Five Year Plans also led to a rapid increase in the state's power over society, as all aspect of life, including housing, food and education, were controlled by the planned economy.

Activity 8  ATL Thinking skills

Copy out and complete the following grid on the Five Year Plans.

	Characteristics (or features)	Successes	Failures/ problems
First Five Year Plan 1928–32 Aims:			
Second Five Year Plan 1933–37 Aims:			
Third Five Year Plan 1938–41 Aims:			

Activity 9 ATL Thinking skills

Now consider the *impact* of the Five Year Plans under the following headings: economic, social and political. Draw up another table or a mind map to show the results using these themes.

Activity 10 ATL Thinking skills

Refer back to EH Carr's quote at the start of this chapter: '*Seldom perhaps in history has so monstrous a price been paid for so monumental an achievement.*'

How far would you agree with his assessment of Stalin's policies?

Essay planning

With reference to one European country (other than Italy, Germany and Spain), examine the success of economic policies in the 1930s.

Command term: Examine.

Topic: Success of economic policies in the 1930s.

Concept: Consequence.

There is a lot to write about in this answer, as you will need to cover both collectivization and the Five Year Plans, and consider the extent of success in each area; you may also want to consider the impact on Soviet citizens when evaluating the success. In any essay focusing on economic policy, statistics will be vital for providing evidence for your arguments; also, make sure you include historians' perspectives.

Introduction: In your introduction don't forget to make it clear that the case study you have chosen is Stalin's Soviet Union and to set out the areas of 'economic policy' that you will be examining. In order to measure 'success' you also need to set out what Stalin's objectives were in carrying out the Five Year Plans and collectivization.

Paragraphs: Here are some possible opening sentences to paragraphs in the main body of your answer:

The Five Year Plans were undoubtedly a success in transforming the USSR industrially. This is because...

Statistics for the transformation of industry between 1928 and 1939 are key here. Also, look at the impact that it had on strengthening socialism and the power of government.

Collectivization can also be regarded as a success because...

Refer back to Stalin's aims and also the extent of collectivization by 1939. Statistics on the number of farms collectivized and the amount of grain being produced by 1939 are key.

Also, note Robert Service's comments here.

However, the Five Year Plans faced certain problems...

In 'examining' the success you need to highlight the problems that limited that success.

In addition, collectivization was only achieved by...

Here you may want to highlight the impact of the downturn in grain production and destruction of livestock.

Conclusion

You may want to draw attention to the human cost of industrialization – but don't forget to come back to the extent of 'success' based on the evidence in your essay.

How did Stalin maintain political control?

The Great Terror

Causation and consequence

 One death is a tragedy; a million is a statistic.
Stalin.

As well as transforming the economy Stalin also sought to revolutionize the Communist Party and consolidate his power through a series of purges and show trials.

The machinery of terror had, as you have already read in the previous chapter, been established under Lenin. This was continued by Stalin; the Cheka was renamed the OGPU until 1934 and thereafter was known as the NKVD. Terror had been unleashed against the peasantry in 1932–33 in the process of collectivization, and against so-called 'wreckers' in industry; by 1933 there were already 1 million Soviet citizens in the forced labour camps of the *Gulag*. However, after 1934, the Great Terror escalated dramatically into what became known as the Great Purges.

The event that triggered the Great Purges was the murder in 1934 of Sergei Kirov, the Communist Party boss in Leningrad, by a man called Leonid Nikolayev. Kirov was popular within the party and had opposed Stalin over the pace of industrialization and the treatment of the peasantry. There was support within the party for him to replace Stalin and at the Seventeenth Party Congress more people voted for him than Stalin in elections to the Central Committee. These factors, along with the actual circumstances of the murder (see box below), suggest that Stalin was implicated in some way.

Significant individual: Sergei Kirov (1886–1934)

Sergei Kirov was the Communist Party leader in Leningrad. He was a popular politician who seemed to be a rising star in the party in the early 1930s before he was assassinated outside his headquarters in 1934. Although there is no evidence linking Stalin to Kirov's death, many factors surrounding the assassination are suspicious: the ease with which Nicolayev managed to evade Kirov's bodyguard; the fact that he was shot without a trial; and the fact that Kirov's bodyguard was killed in a traffic accident while being taken for questioning.

However, the official explanation was that this was evidence of a widespread conspiracy against the Soviet state and its leaders, and that it thus provided Stalin with an excuse to remove anyone from the party that he distrusted. Directly after the murder, Stalin passed the 'Law of 1 December 1934', which gave the NKVD special powers to execute without trial those accused of acting against the state. A purge of the Leningrad party was launched and thousands of Kirov's supporters were sent to the *Gulag*, accused of involvement in his death. This was followed by a nationwide purge of the party. By the time it ended, 1,108 out of a total of 1,966 delegates of the Seventeenth Party Congress had been arrested.

Key among the victims were Kamenev and Zinoviev – the 'old Bolsheviks' – now accused of being in league with Trotsky and stirring up discontent. They were put on trial in what became known as 'show trials'. These were elaborately staged events designed to create the feeling that there were enemies and spies everywhere and that nobody could be trusted. Both Kamenev and Zinoviev were found guilty by the notorious state prosecutor, Vyshinsky, and shot. A second show trial took place in January 1937, in which Karl Radeck, the industry chief, and Pyatakov, arrested because of his so-called involvement in explosions in Siberian mines, were accused of being Trotskyists. Vyshinsky accused them of being *'liars, and clowns, insignificant pigmies'*. They confessed and were found guilty.

The third show trial in March 1938 involved Bukharin alongside another old Bolshevik, Rykov, as well as Yagoda, who was the former head of the secret police. They were accused, among other things, of plotting to kill Lenin and being involved in a conspiracy with the Germans and the Japanese to partition the Soviet Union and reintroduce capitalism. Bukharin attempted to defend himself, but in the end 'confessed'. The three men were shot.

Why did these men confess, given that the crimes they were accused of were often ludicrous and clearly fabricated? Fear of what might happen to their families was a factor, as was the fact that they had been worn down by torture and interrogation. It is also possible that they believed that their sacrifice was in the best interest of the Soviet Union. WG Krivitsky, who worked for military intelligence and for the NKVD, wrote in his autobiography, *I Was Stalin's Agent*, that confessions were made *'in the sincere conviction that this was their sole remaining service to the Party and the Revolution'*.

The *Yezhovshchina*, 1937–38

Nicolai Yezhov took over from Yagoda as head of the NKVD and it was under Yezhov that the Great Terror reached its height during 1937–38. Purges within the party were widened beyond members of the party. 'The *Yezhovshchina*', as it was known, affected all areas of society – scientists, musicians, writers, artists, managers, administrators, historians, as well as 'ordinary' workers. Reasons for arrest were arbitrary. As historian Stephen Cohen puts it, *'No one was guilty, so no one was safe. Everyone was innocent, so everyone was vulnerable'* (Thames Television documentary, 1990). Denunciations were common as people settled old scores or sought to gain the assets of those they had denounced; they were encouraged by a media campaign that urged people to seek out and uncover *'hidden enemies'*. The NKVD would usually carry out arrests in the middle of the night, driving black vehicles known as the 'ravens'.

Quota systems applied to geographical areas and public bodies also meant that thousands of innocent people were arrested and sent to camps or shot. Melanie Ilic also points out:

> … *many of the executions that took place in these years were of people who belonged to socially marginal groups, which no longer conformed to the new Soviet way of life. These included former and serving religious personnel and independent peasants, who had continued to survive into the later 1930s outside the collective farm system.*
>
> **Ilic, M (2006). 'The Great Terror Reassessed',** *20th Century History Review,* **April (published by Philip Allan).**

A key group that was targeted during this period was the military. Believing that he could not trust the army to carry out his policies, Stalin had Marshal Tukachevsky, Soviet war hero and deputy commissar for defence, tried alongside many other top military leaders. Following their execution for 'treason', the purge of the forces was extended with devastating results: all 11 deputy commissars of defence and 75 of the 80 members of the Supreme Military Council were executed. All eight admirals were shot and half of the officer corps (about 35,000) were killed or imprisoned.

What was the impact of the Great Terror?

It is very difficult for historians to know exactly how many people were killed in the Great Terror, given the absence of reliable statistics from the time. It is also difficult to separate those killed as part of the purges from the liquidation of the *kulaks* and the deaths from famine. Before the opening of the Soviet archives in 1990, historians put estimates between 5 million and 18 million. However, the opening of the archives has given a different picture. Timothy Snyder writes:

> The total figure [for deaths in the Gulag] for the entire Stalinist period is likely between two million and three million. The Great Terror and other shooting actions killed no more than a million people, probably a bit fewer. The largest human catastrophe of Stalinism was the famine of 1930–1933, in which more than five million people died.
>
> **Snyder, T (2011). *Hitler vs Stalin: Who Killed More?* New York Review of Books, 10 March: http://www.nybooks.com/articles/2011/03/10/hitler-vs-stalin-who-killed-more/**

Nevertheless, even the lower casualty figures indicate that huge damage was done to the USSR by the Great Terror. Large numbers of government and party officials died which meant that administrative systems at both local and national levels suffered disruption; the loss of factory and businesses managers, along with skilled workers, had a negative impact on industrial production and in both management and the workforce, initiative of any kind was stifled. The purge of academics and teachers affected the quality of education. The purge of the army left it weak and demoralised and this was particularly harmful to the Soviet Union, given the growing international tension by 1939. For Stalin, however, the purges secured his position with the party.

The murder of Trotsky

In 1940, Trotsky – the greatest enemy of Stalin – was also murdered. He had escaped trial and was living in Mexico from where he continued to attack Stalin and to warn the world of his character. After several attempts at assassination, Stalin's agents were finally successful; one of them managed to get a job as Trotsky's bodyguard and on 21 August he struck Trotsky over the head with an ice pick, shattering his skull.

All opposition had been removed and old Russian revolutionaries had been replaced by a younger generation of officials loyal to Stalin.

> *Politically, it silenced dissent for good and cleared the way to an autocratic form of rule. It did this by wiping out what was left of the original Bolshevik Party, in which memories were still alive of the 1917 revolution and Civil War, no more than twenty years away, of Lenin's style of leadership and inner-party democracy, and of Marxism-Leninism as the ideology which gave the party its identity and bound its members tighter in a common faith… The delegates to the Eighteenth Congress… had known no other leader than Stalin, no other world as adults than the Soviet regime, and their knowledge of its earlier history and its Marxist-Leninist ideology would now be derived entirely from Stalin's version of both.*
>
> **Bullock, A (1991). *Hitler and Stalin: Parallel Lives*. Harper Collins, pp. 570–571.**

▶▶▶ Historians' perspectives

Who was responsible for the purges?

Totalitarian or intentionalist historians (see page 55) believe that, given Stalin's enormous power, he must have been responsible for ordering the purges. Robert Conquest in the *Great Terror: A Reassessment* (1990), follows this line arguing that *'the revolution of the purges still remains… above all Stalin's achievement'*. This view is supported by others such as Roy Medvedev and Isaac Deutscher. They argue that Stalin had much personal control over arrests and executions with the NKVD only the instrument of his orders. In carrying out the purges, Stalin was motivated by his need to establish control over the party by eliminating the old Bolsheviks and his wish to control the population by terrorizing them. Stalin's personality and his paranoia has also been cited as a factor.

This view has been challenged by revisionist historians. They argue that there was a 'bottom-up' dimension with leaders of the NKVD, such as Yezhov, acting on their own initiative and ordinary people playing a key role in the denunciations. Stalin had little idea what was going on in some areas; the Soviet state was in chaos in the mid-1930s and the NKVD was riven with internal divisions allowing the purges to spiral out of control and gain a momentum of their own. J Arch Getty is a key proponent of this view; although he now acknowledges that *'the fingerprints of Stalin'* are all over the purges, he nevertheless argues in *The Road to Terror* (1999), written with Oleg Naumov, that the Great Terror was not *'the culmination of a well-prepared and long-standing master design'*. Arch Getty is supported in this view by other historians such as Sheila Fitzpatrick, Graeme Gill and Roberta Manning.

Activity 11 **(ATL)** **Thinking and social skills**

1. What were the key features of the Great Terror after 1934?

2. What were the key features of the Great Terror (*Yezhovshchina*), during 1937–38?

3. In pairs, consider the following as possible reasons for the purges; what evidence is there to support each of these factors? What other factors could be added to the list?

    - Stalin's paranoia;
    - Stalin's tactics as a politician – willing to use violence to achieve ends;
    - Stalin's desire to get rid of political opponents;
    - the need for slave labour;
    - deflecting blame for economic problems;
    - chaos and hostility caused by the economic changes;
    - threat of war;
    - purges achieved a momentum of their own;
    - NKVD was able to enhance its importance via the purges.

4. Having considered the reasons for the Great Terror, which viewpoint regarding its causes do you think is more convincing – the intentionalist or the revisionist?

5. Why do you think it so hard for historians to reach a consensus about the Great Terror?

The cult of personality

The economic and political instability of the 1930s helped to foster a cult of personality that further helped Stalin to maintain power. With the ending of traditional patterns of work and society creating chaos and hardship, and with the uncertainties of the Great Terror and the realization that even former heroes of the Bolshevik revolution were traitors, there was a need to believe in the fact that Stalin was a strong leader who could steer the nation through difficult times. By the 1930s all art forms, alongside news documentaries and history books, were dedicated to proving that Stalin was an all-powerful, omnipresent leader. The media referred to him as 'universal genius' and 'shining sun of humanity'.

As the cult developed, history was rewritten to glorify his role in the revolution of 1917 and in the civil war. He was portrayed as Lenin's closest friend, while the other old Bolsheviks were given little credit and were removed from key photographs (see photo on page 226).

Such was the intensity of the propaganda promoting this image that even those affected by the purges continued to see Stalin as a wise, all-knowing genius.

The constitution of 1936

Stalin introduced a new constitution in 1936, which gave the Soviet Union the appearance of a democracy and again strengthened Stalin's position. Stalin called it 'the only truly democratic constitution in the world'. According to the constitution, everyone over 18 could vote and elections were to be held every four years by secret ballot. The problem was, however, that only Communist candidates could stand, as the Communist Party was the only political party allowed to exist. Everyone was expected to vote and this was why the turnout was always around 98 to 99 per cent, with results sometimes being announced before polling had even taken place! Elections were in fact used to highlight the achievements of the Communist Party.

Despite the new constitution establishing the Supreme Soviet as the lawmaking body of the Soviet Union, it rarely met and had no real power. The Soviet Union remained effectively governed by the Presidium, which consisted of the top members of the Communist Party, with Stalin ultimately in control.

The constitution also set out civil rights including freedom of speech and freedom from arrest without trial; clearly these were rights that did not exist as the NKVD ensured that there was no open criticism of Stalin or his policies.

In the top photo are Kamenev, Lenin and Trotsky on the third anniversary of the revolution, 1920. In the bottom photo, Kamenev and Trotsky have been removed.

What was the impact of Stalinism on society?

 Key concepts: *Consequence*

Stalin's rule began with a 'cultural revolution' in society. This lasted until 1931 and it involved returning to the class warfare of the early 1920s that you read about in the last chapter; after 1931 there was a return to more traditional values in society as a whole and a switch to 'socialist realism' in culture.

The Cultural Revolution led to substantial and lasting changes in Soviet society. The compromises that had taken place during the NEP were ended; the bourgeoisie, as well as the Nepmen and the *kulaks*, were now to be purged. Non-Marxists in all walks of life – academia, education, the arts, architecture – were denounced and bourgeois values were attacked. A cultural revolution took place in an attempt to find a truly 'proletarian' approach to all aspects of life. This involved creating a vision of a perfect socialist world; visionaries drew up plans for new cities involving communal living in large apartments, and it was believed that it was possible to create a *'new socialist man'*, who would be an enthusiastic participant in this utopian world.

Getting rid of class enemies meant liquidating the *kulaks*. It also involved removing technical experts from industry. The Shakhty trial of 1928 involved accusing a group of engineers from the Shakhty region of economic sabotage, and it indicated the government's intention to remove technical experts from industry. The attacks on 'bourgeois experts' continued throughout the first Five Year Plan; Nepman were denounced and the intelligentsia also found itself increasingly under attack. The young were at the forefront of this cultural revolution. The youth organization called the *Komsomol* took a key role in finding and attacking class enemies.

Within the Communist Party itself, members of proletarian origin were now promoted; these included Khrushchev, Kosygin and Brezhnev, who were to be future leaders of the USSR. With urbanization and increased access to education, social mobility also took place in industry and some from peasant backgrounds rose up to high levels in the workplace.

Interestingly, those who were now promoted in the party and in other areas became the new middle class in the 1930s; they embraced aspects of the customs and lifestyle of the old bourgeoisie that had been so despised. This meant owning cars, staying in hotels, eating in restaurants and enjoying holidays. Thus, a new privileged group developed – party officials and bureaucrats, artists, ballet dancers, scientists, doctors – with access to comforts that remained completely out of reach for ordinary people. The position of this new hierarchy was reinforced by the reimposition of more traditional and conservative values by the government after 1932.

Religion

The Cultural Revolution meant a renewed attack on the churches. *Komsomol* groups carried out attacks on what was still left of religious life in the villages; priests were thrown out of villages, accused of supporting the *kulaks* during collectivization. Churches were raided and any congregations, along with their place of worship, now had to be registered with the government. Many peasants resisted but, by the end of 1930, 80 per cent of the country's village churches were closed.

Education

The Cultural Revolution disrupted education; traditional teaching and discipline came under attack and theories were put forward for new approaches to teaching. Shulgin, who headed an education research institute, argued for the *'withering away of the school'* and a more practical approach to education. Many older non-party teachers were now driven out and replaced by *'Red specialists'*.

However, the government realized that education needed to be a key tool in shaping society and that the disruption caused by the Cultural Revolution was unhelpful to this process. Thus, from the mid-1930s, it reimposed control over education. Textbooks were prescribed by the government and formal examinations were reintroduced. Uniforms were imposed, with pigtails for girls, and traditional academic subjects were put back into the curriculum. By 1936, the insistence on a proletarian background for higher education was removed and fees were introduced. Nevertheless, opportunities for students from working-class backgrounds were still better than at any time before; a literacy campaign was also launched to ensure that peasants had basic reading and writing skills.

Women and 'The Great Retreat'

A Soviet propaganda poster showing a woman on the collective farm. The wording says, 'Give first priority to gathering the Soviet harvest'.

Activity 12

ATL Thinking skills

What is the message of this propaganda poster regarding collective farms?

As you have read in the previous chapter, new laws on divorce and abortion gave women more freedoms and marriage was looked upon as a bourgeois institution that was intended to exploit and degrade women. The return to more traditional values that took place in education, however, also affected women. In what as became known as 'The Great Retreat', the family was once again the central unit of society under Stalin and 'the old-style liberated woman, assertively independent and ideologically committed on issues like abortion was no longer in favour' (Fitzpatrick, S (1994). *The Russian Revolution, 1917–1932*. OUP, p. 151.).

To encourage population growth, abortion was once again made illegal. Divorce was now also made harder and more expensive, and women were financially rewarded for having more children. These changes were enshrined in the Family Act of 1936. Around the same time, laws were passed against prostitution and homosexuality. Part of this drive to reinstate the importance of family life was because of the need to create some stability after the chaos that had been caused in society by collectivization and rapid industrialization.

Women remained essential, however, to the industrial and agricultural revolutions that were taking place. Although many still remained in traditional female occupations such as clerical work, teaching and nursing, many others worked with the men in the new factories, coalmines and industrial projects, such as the building of the Moscow metro. Most factories now created crèches to allow women to continue working after having children. Between 1928 and 1940, the number of working women rose from 3 million to 13 million. They did not, however, receive the same pay as men or the same promotion opportunities.

Health and sport

The government put a strong emphasis on health, and hospitals and clinics were built across the country. Physical exercise was also encouraged and large stadia were built in towns and cities to allow athletics, football, and ice hockey to take place. State support was given to those who excelled in sports.

Activity 13 — ATL Thinking and social skills

Who were the winners and losers in Stalin's Soviet Union?

> In one important respect, Stalin achieved the aims of the Bolshevik revolution, by greatly expanding the urban working class from 11 million in 1928 to over 38 million by 1933, and by increasing the urban population overall from 18 per cent in 1926 to 33 per cent in 1939. Educational facilities, especially technical ones, expanded greatly. Whereas in 1926 only 11.8 million students were enrolled in secondary higher schools, by 1938–9 the figure was 12 million. In particular, the regime trained large numbers of engineers and technical specialists. It thereby gave opportunities to many young Russians. It was possible to rise up the social ladder from unskilled worker to skilled worker to official or party functionary, and many took their opportunities. Industrialisation had many supporters in Russia. It did promote a social revolution of massive proportions which brought benefits to considerable numbers of Russian people.

Culpin, C and Henig, R (2002). *Modern Europe 1870–1945.* **Longman, p. 217.**

1. According to this source who benefited from Stalin's Social Revolution?
2. In pairs discuss further who benefited and who suffered under Stalinism and why; you will also need to refer back to the discussion on how economic change affected society along with the section on the Great Terror. Create a mind map or other infographic to show your findings.

How did culture change in the 1930s?

The 1920s had seen cultural creativity in all areas of the arts. However, the Cultural Revolution involved a full-scale attack on the intelligentsia and the cultural elites; only artists who were fully committed to socialism were now tolerated. The youth in *Komsomol* disrupted theatre productions by playwrights whose loyalty was considered doubtful and the organization called RAPP (Russian Association of Proletarian Writers) increasingly policed the work of authors to ensure that they promoted the values of socialism.

In the middle of 1931, Stalin proclaimed that the Cultural Revolution was at an end. All proletarian artistic and literary organizations (such as RAPP) were closed down and all artists were told that they had to come together in a single union. The main aim of all art was now to be to promote socialist realism. This meant showing an idealized picture of socialist life: supposedly the reality that the Soviet Union was moving towards. It showed men and women working together to build the perfect socialist future. As Robert Service puts it, '*Above all, the arts had to be optimistic*' (2003. *A History of Modern Russia*. Penguin).

Activity 14 — ATL Thinking skills

What is the message of the painting below?

Sergei Gerasimov's 'Collective Farm Harvest Festival' (1937), painted in the style of socialist realism.

Activity 15

 Research and communication skills

Continue your research on Soviet culture. Divide the class into groups with each group taking one area of culture: art, architecture, music, literature, film (it can be the same one that you researched in the last chapter). Research your area considering the following questions and prepare a presentation for the rest of the class.

1. What examples can you find of socialist realism?
2. How were artists in your area of research controlled and monitored by the government?
3. Which artists gained particular status during this period?
4. Which artists were vilified and had their careers affected adversely?

Essay planning

In pairs, plan the following two essays using the Soviet Union as your example. Include:

- an introduction in full;
- opening sentences for each paragraph;
- bullet points evidence for each paragraph;
- reference to historical perspectives.

1. **To what extent was there economic and social change in one European country (other than Germany, Italy or Spain) in the 1930s?**
2. **Examine the political developments in one European country (other than Germany, Italy or Spain) in the 1930s.**

 Refer back to the chapter on Lenin, page 196, for the historical controversy over whether Stalinism was a natural progression of Leninism or was a completely different phenomenon.

The Extended Essay in History

As you are doing History at Higher level, you may well choose to do your Extended Essay in History. This will give you the opportunity to independently study an area of history in depth and give you the experience of writing a formal, university-style essay.

What can you expect when you choose to write an Extended Essay in History?

- You will need to write between 3,000 and 4,000 words.
- You are expected to spend about 40 hours on the essay.
- The essay should be based on a narrow, focused topic and framed around a question, which will allow you to be analytical in your response.
- You should use a range of primary and secondary sources.
- You will have a supervisor who will give you guidance throughout the process; you will have three 'formal' sessions to discuss the progress of your essay as well as other more informal sessions. The last of the 'formal' sessions will take place after you have finished your essay and will be a viva voce (an interview about your essay).
- The essay will be marked according to clear criteria (see below).
- You should use a consistent style of referencing throughout.
- You will be expected to reflect on your experiences of writing the essay by using a researcher's reflection space (RRS); this will form the basis of discussion at your formal sessions with your supervisor. These discussions will be recorded on the Reflections on Planning and Progress Form (RPPF).

Note that you cannot choose a topic from the last ten years or one that you have already covered in your Internal Assessment.

How do the Extended Essay criteria apply to a History essay?

These are the criteria against which your essay will be marked:

A: Focus and method	B: Knowledge and understanding	C: Critical thinking	D: Formal presentation	E: Engagement
• Topic • Research • Methodology	• Context • Subject specific terminology and concepts	• Research • Analysis • Discussion and evaluation	• Structure • Layout	• Process • Research focus
Marks	Marks	Marks	Marks	Marks
6	6	12	4	6

For an Extended Essay in History you need to consider the following questions for each of the criteria:

A: Focus and method

- Is your choice of topic appropriate and not in the last ten years?
- Have you a focused research question which can be answered within 4,000 words?
- Have you given the historical context for your topic and explained why it is worth investigating?
- Do you have an appropriate range of relevant sources, both primary and secondary, which will provide enough material to allow you to answer the question?

B: Knowledge and understanding

- Have you placed your research question in the broader historical context?
- Have you accurately and confidently used historical concepts and terms relevant to your topic?
- Have you used your sources effectively to help you analyse and answer your question?

C: Critical thinking

- Have you developed an argument that will answer your research question?
- Are your points supported with evidence from your sources?
- Are all of your points and evidence relevant to the question?
- Is your conclusion consistent with the evidence that you have presented and does it answer the question?
- Have you evaluated the sources that you have used to show an awareness of their value and limitations?

D: Formal presentation

- Are your sub-headings clear and relevant to the essay?
- Have you used a consistent method of referencing and acknowledged all information from other sources?
- Do you have a bibliography correctly presented in alphabetical order?
- Do you have a title page, table of contents and page numbering?
- Is the essay within the limit of 4,000 words?

E: Engagement

Assessment of this criterion will be based on what you have written in the RPPF. After your third formal session, which is the viva voce, your supervisor will also make a comment on this form as to your engagement with the whole research and writing process.

Make sure you consider the following in your reflections:

- *Are your reflections on your decision-making and planning evaluative (i.e. not just descriptive)?*
- *Do your reflections communicate a high degree of intellectual and personal engagement with the research process?*
- *Have you indicated where you faced challenges and how you overcame these challenges?*
- *Have you indicated where your conceptual understanding has developed or changed?*
- *Have you indicated what you might do differently if you did this task again or what questions you still have unanswered?*

Tips for choosing your topic and formulating your question
- Once you have chosen a subject area, decide on specific topics that interest you.
- Discuss these topics with your supervisor and narrow them down to one topic area.
- Begin to read around the topic so that you can identify possible research questions; check any recent research on this area and any areas of controversy that could be a focus for your question.
- Continue to discuss and refine possible questions with your supervisor as you find out more about your topic; you may end up changing your question several times.

These are examples of topics and questions that have led to effective investigations. Note the narrow and clearly defined focus of each question:

Topic: The Danish Resistance Movement in the Second World War

Question: To what extent was the Danish Resistance Movement successful in disrupting the Nazi occupation of Denmark (1940–45)?

Topic: The Falklands/Malvinas War

Question: How significant was the role of Galtieri in determining the outcome of the Malvinas War?

Topic: The fight for women's suffrage in Britain

Question: *'Women gained the right to vote in Britain in 1918 due to the skilled and dangerous war work they undertook.'* To what extent is this statement valid?

Topic: The Nazi-Soviet Pact

Question: To what extent did Joseph Stalin sign the Nazi-Soviet Pact in 1939 due to the impact of the military purges in the USSR?

Topic: Failure of the Khartoum Campaign

Question: To what extent did Major General Charles Gordon's leadership result in the fall of Khartoum in 1885?

Topic: The Thirty Years War (1618–48)

Question: To what extent was King Gustavus II's intervention in the Thirty Years War territorially motivated?

Topic: French Revolution

Question: To what extent was Robespierre's motivation for the Terror rooted in Rousseau's Social Contract?

Some tips for effective research
- Consult your school librarian for help with tracking down useful books and articles on your topic.
- Check online libraries and make use of the wide range of databases that are now accessible online.
- Check online bookshops to identify the most recent publications on your topic.
- Look at the references of an article or book that you have read, as this may lead you to other useful sources.
- Keep a record of all sources that you use and particularly of any quotes/detail that you will need to reference: you do not want to have to go back and find these later.

Glossary

Allies: The Allies in the First World War were predominantrly Great Britain, France, USA (as of 1917) and Russia (up to 1917).

anarchists: People who believe that government and law should be abolished.

appeasement: Achieving peace by giving concessions or by satisfying demands. It was the policy followed by the British government in the 1930s towards Nazi Germany.

armistice: An agreement to end fighting so that peace negotiations can begin.

arms race: Competition between states regarding numbers and/or types of weapons.

Assault Guard: Special police units that deal with urban violence.

authoritarian: A style of government in which there is complete obedience or subjection to authority as opposed to individual freedom.

bourgeoisie: Relating to the middle classes. It is usually used in a negative way in the context of Marxist writings, where the bourgeoisie are contrasted with the proletariat, or working classes.

capitalism: An economic system where a great deal of trade and industry is privately owned and runs to make a profit.

Comintern: The abbreviation for the Communist International. This organization was set up in Moscow in March 1919 and its task was to coordinate communist parties all over the world, helping the spread of global communism.

conscription: Compulsory enlistment in the armed forces.

coup: Violent or illegal seizure of power by a small group or clique.

diktat: A 'dictated' agreement in which there has been no discussion or mutual agreement.

fascism: A political ideology that favours limited freedom of people, nationalism, use of violence to achieve ends, and an aggressive foreign policy.

imperialism: The act of building an empire; the acquisition of colonies.

isolationism: A policy that involves not getting involved with other countries or international problems.

League of Nations: An international organization set up after the First World War, intended to maintain peace and encourage disarmament.

manifesto: A public declaration of a political party's or candidate's policy and aims, most likely to be issued before an election.

martial law: An extreme measure to control society during war or periods of civil unrest. Certain civil liberties are suspended and government military personnel have the authority to make and enforce civil and criminal laws.

Marxism: A political ideology based on the works of Karl Marx and Friedrich Engels, the main belief of which is that the workers rise up against the middle and upper classes to create a society where all resources are shared.

NATO: (North Atlantic Treaty Organization) A military alliance founded in 1949 by European and North American states for the defence of Europe and the North Atlantic against the perceived threat of Soviet aggression.

passive resistance: Opposition to a government or occupying force by refusing to comply with orders.

plebiscite: A process in which voters are given the opportunity to express their support of or opposition to a single issue.

proletariat : Meaning the working class, they are wage earners who must earn their living by working.

***pronunciamiento*:** A type of military coup specific to Spain, Portugal and Latin America, especially in the 19th century.

putsch: A sudden or violent takeover of a government.

self-determination: The process that enables a country to determine its own statehood and form its own government.

socialism: A political theory of social organization stressing shared or state ownership of production, industry, land, etc.

suffrage: The right to vote.

total war : A term used to describe a war in which all the resources of the state are put at the disposal of the government to achieve victory. This will often entail the taking over of vital industries for the duration of the war; the rationing of food and other necessities; the conscription of men (and women in some cases) into the army or into factories; restrictions on access to information, on travel, and so on.

Treaty of St Germain: Peace treaty concluded in 1919 between the Allies and the Austrian Republic which ended the Austro-Hungarian Empire, distributed parts of its territory, and forbade Austria to unite with Germany.

triumvirate: A group of three men holding power (usually referring to Ancient Rome).

***Untermenschen*:** People considered racially or socially inferior.

Index

Headings in bold are History concepts e.g. causation. Italic page numbers indicate an illustration, be it a picture, table or map. Bold page numbers indicate information on a significant individual.

Index

Index

Index